Weber · Greiner

Short-Story-Theorien
(1573 – 1973)

Athenäum Taschenbücher
Literaturwissenschaft

Alfred Weber · Walter F. Greiner

Short-Story-Theorien (1573 – 1973)

Eine Sammlung und Bibliographie englischer und amerikanischer Quellen

Athenäum Verlag
1977

CIP-Kurztitelaufnahme der Deutschen Bibliothek

Short-Story-Theorien: 1573 – 1973;
e. Sammlung und Bibliogr. Engl. u.
amerikan. Quellen / Alfred Weber;
Walter F. Greiner (Hrsg.). –
1. Aufl. – Kronberg : Athenäum Verlag, 1977.
(Athenäum-Taschenbücher; 2074: Literaturwiss.)
ISBN 3–7610–2074–0

NE: Weber, Alfred [Hrsg.]

Gesamtherstellung Friedrich Pustet, Regensburg
Printed in Germany
ISBN 3-7610-

Inhaltsverzeichnis

EINFÜHRUNG

Die Herausgeber wollen mit dieser Quellensammlung und Bibliographie zur englischen und amerikanischen Theoriegeschichte der Short Story ein Arbeitsbuch vorlegen, das auf die unterschiedlichen Bedürfnisse der Universität, der Pädagogischen Hochschule, des Gymnasiums und auch eines breiteren, an englischer und amerikanischer Literatur interessierten Publikums ausgerichtet ist. Damit wendet es sich nicht nur an Fachwissenschaftler, sondern vor allem auch an Lehrer und Studenten sowie alle diejenigen, die auf die so häufig gestellte Frage nach dem Wesen oder den besonderen Merkmalen der "Short Story" kompetente Antworten gesucht und sich in ihrer Lektüre mit den unterschiedlichen Formen und Intentionen des kurzen Erzählens auseinandergesetzt haben. Es verfolgt das Ziel, der theoretischen und historischen Untersuchung der anglo-amerikanischen Short Story eine bisher vernachlässigte Perspektive zu eröffnen und in diesem Bereich zu weiteren Fragestellungen anzuregen. Es ist aber zugleich als ein Textbuch für Seminare und Arbeitsgemeinschaften gedacht, die sich mit theoriegeschichtlichen oder gattungshistorischen, autorenbezogenen oder textanalytischen Studien zur englischen und amerikanischen Kurzgeschichte befassen. Es ist ein Band zum Nachschlagen und zum eigenen kritischen Arbeiten.

Mit dieser Konzeption und durch die Breite der Dokumentation schließt er offensichtlich eine Lücke auf dem anglistisch-amerikanistischen Buchmarkt. Die beiden bereits vorliegenden Quellensammlungen *What Is the Short Story?* von Eugene Current-García und Walton R. Patrick (1961 zum ersten Mal und 1974 in einer zweiten, leicht revidierten Auflage erschienen) und *Short Story Theories* von Charles E. May (1976) sind durch ihre einseitige Ausrichtung auf die Ansprüche des amerikanischen College-Unterrichts in ihrer Nützlichkeit stark eingeschränkt. Ihre knappe, beliebige und fast ausschließlich auf amerikanische Quellen beschränkte Textauswahl mindert ihren Wert für forschungsbezogene Arbeitsvorhaben erheblich.

Die hier vorgelegte, einen Zeitraum von vier Jahrhunderten ausmessende Quellensammlung von 103 Texten und die kommentierte Bibliographie von 212 weiteren Publikationen sind das Ergebnis einer langjährigen gemeinsamen Arbeit der Herausgeber, die beide am Seminar für Englische Philologie der Universität Tübingen tätig sind. Für den englischen Bestandteil des Buches zeichnet Walter F. Greiner, für den amerikanischen Alfred

Weber verantwortlich. Sie werden dieses Arbeitsbuch durch zwei Studien ergänzen, die im Frühjahr 1978 unter dem Titel *Theorien der Short Story in England und Amerika* im gleichen Verlag erscheinen werden und in denen ausführlich auf die methodologischen Überlegungen und theoriegeschichtlichen Konzepte eingegangen wird, die ihre Arbeit leiteten. Sie werden auch Interpretationen wichtiger Theorietexte dieser Sammlung bieten und einige bedeutsame Entwicklungen aufzeigen, die sich seit dem Ende des 16. Jahrhunderts in England und seit dem späteren 18. Jahrhundert in Amerika feststellen lassen.

Die Quellensammlung, die Bibliographie und die damit verbundenen historischen Studien entstanden aus dem Bemühen, der seit langem geführten und immer noch bewegten Diskussion über das Wesen der Short Story im einzelnen nachzugehen. Dabei sollte versucht werden, rigide und normative Gattungsdefinitionen zu vermeiden, der Versuchung eines starren und zugleich bequemen Systematisierens zu entgehen und die Gattungsdiskussion historisch zu präzisieren. Bei diesen umfangreichen und weit in die Vergangenheit zurückführenden Quellenstudien mußten Entscheidungen gefällt werden, die für die Auswahl der Quellen, die Anlage der Sammlung und die Zielvorstellung der theoriegeschichtlichen Untersuchung von Bedeutung waren.

Es kann in einer theoriegeschichtlichen Dokumentation und Untersuchung nicht darum gehen, aus den theoretischen Äußerungen eine neue, überzeitliche Gattungsformel der Short Story zu destillieren, in der alle anderen enthalten sind. Dokumentiert und untersucht werden kann nur, wie sich im Laufe der Literaturgeschichte das Denken über das kurze Erzählen, die kurze Geschichte und die Kurzgeschichte entwickelte - und zwar vor allem bei denen, die selbst Kurzgeschichten schrieben und aktiv an der Entwicklung der Kurzgeschichtenpraxis teilnahmen. Eine Theoriegeschichte will nicht selbst Theorie bilden, sondern Einblick gewinnen in die verschiedenen Möglichkeiten und historischen Veränderungen der Theoriebildung.

Offensichtlich ist, daß die Short Story als erzählende Prosaliteratur zur großen Gattung des Epischen gehört. Sie ist in dichtungstheoretisch unwiderlegbarer Weise gattungsmäßig verwandt mit dem Roman. Geht man von der Kürze der Short Story, ihrem formspezifisch signifikanten Merkmal, aus, so ergibt sich ein *gradueller* Unterschied zur Langform des Romans.

Geht man dann einen "Theorie-Schritt" weiter, in dem die strukturellen und thematischen Konsequenzen der Kürze bedacht werden, lassen sich die *qualitativen* Unterschiede zwischen Short Story und Roman formulieren. Diese qualitativen Unterschiede, die sich zum Beispiel im Handlungsaufbau ("plot"), im Personalbestand, in der Charakterkonzeption und in der strengen Funktionalität der Teile nachweisen lassen, führen zu Theoriebildungen, in denen wesensmäßige Unterschiede zwischen Short Story und Roman postuliert werden. Die Schwierigkeiten für jede seriöse Gattungstheorie der Short Story liegen also darin, daß sie die qualitativen Spezifika der Short Story aus ihrer Verwandtschaft mit der Langform des Romans entwickeln muß. Symptomatisch für diese Schwierigkeiten sind Definitionen *ex negativo*: Die Short Story ist *nicht* mit dem Roman zu vergleichen. Diese Definitionen werden dann in der Regel ergänzt durch Versuche, die Wesensmerkmale der Short Story durch Übertragung spezifischer Qualitäten der Lyrik, des Dramas sowie des Films und anderer Künste zu bestimmen. Ziel der Quellensammlung und ihrer Analyse muß sein, die Komplexität dieser Theoriediskussion zur Anschauung zu bringen und analysierbar zu machen.

Dabei muß unterschieden werden zwischen Theorien, die von Short-Story-Autoren aus der Reflexion ihrer eigenen Praxis gebildet wurden - und solchen, die von Kritikern und Literaturwissenschaftlern formuliert wurden. Zwischen beiden Theoriekonzeptionen bestehen wichtige perspektivische und qualitative Unterschiede. Die vorliegende Quellensammlung (Nr. 1-103) erfaßt nur Texte von Autoren, die selbst Short Stories geschrieben haben, ergänzt durch anonyme Publikationen, bei denen anzunehmen ist, daß sie ebenfalls von Short-Story-Autoren verfaßt wurden. In der weiterführenden Bibliographie (Nr. 104-315) sind ab 1884 zusätzlich Texte erfaßt, die von Literaturkritikern und, einige Zeit später, auch von Literaturwissenschaftlern stammen. Der Akzent dieser Sammlung und der mit ihr verbundenen historischen Untersuchung liegt auf der praxisbezogenen Autoren-Theorie und nicht auf der Kritiker-Theorie. Diese perspektivische Differenzierung ist auch für die weiteren Erwägungen bedeutsam.

Als "Short-Story-Theorien" wurden Äußerungen der verschiedensten Art in die Sammlung aufgenommen. Sie erschienen in Essays, Vorworten, Rezensionen und Briefen. Sie erschienen sogar in Form von Gedichten sowie in Erzählwerken, in denen Geschichtenerzähler oder Kurzgeschichtenautoren als Protagonisten auftreten und in denen poetologische Probleme des Erzählens thematisiert sind (ein Quellenbereich der erzähltheoretischen Reflexionen, der hier nur exemplarisch berücksichtigt werden konnte). Es handelt sich hier also nicht nur um Versuche einer systematischen Darlegung detaillierter Short-Story-Theorien, sondern auch um gelegentliche Aussagen über begrenzte Aspekte, die in der anglo-amerikanischen Theoriediskussion von Bedeutung sind. Um welche Aspekte es hier geht und wie sie in der thematischen Spannweite der Theorieaussagen anzusiedeln sind, wird in der Einführung zum Schlagwortverzeichnis (S. 261-262) erläutert. Das heißt: Die Herausgeber der vorliegenden Quellensammlung und Bibliographie operieren hier mit keinem strengen, sondern einem offenen Theoriebegriff. Sie bezeichnen als Theorie nicht nur die systematischen, umfassenden und schlüssigen Explikationen des Phänomens Short Story, sondern schon viel bescheidenere Versuche einer begrifflichen Verallgemeinerung der Schreiberfahrungen und schöpferischen Prozesse, der Intentionen und künstlerischen Ideale einzelner Kurzgeschichtenautoren - d.h. alle Äußerungen, in denen von einem Autor eine verallgemeinernde oder ins Allgemeine zielende begriffliche Aussage über das Phänomen Short Story gemacht wird.

Für diese Sammlung mußte schließlich auch von einem Short-Story-Konzept ausgegangen werden, das mit keiner spezifischen und zeitbedingten Gattungs-, Form- oder Strukturvorstellung verbunden ist. Die Gattungsvorstellung der "modern short story", wie sie sich seit dem späteren 19. Jahrhundert etabliert und verhärtet hat, ist nicht geeignet für eine historische Dokumentation und Untersuchung, die weit über diese Zeit hinaus literarische Erscheinungen erfassen will. In diesem Zusammenhang erschien es auch als notwendig, den Gegenstandsbereich theoretischer Äußerungen auch auf die mündliche Erzählung auszudehnen: Kurze mündliche Erzählungen gab es schon, bevor es Schrift und Druck gab - die Tradition des mündlichen, geselligen Erzählens war von großem Einfluß auf die Entwicklung der Erzählliteratur - und die Short-Story-Autoren verweisen in ihren Theorietexten oft genug selbst auf die Bedeutung des mündlichen Erzählens.

Das primäre Interesse der Herausgeber an den Möglichkeiten und historischen Veränderungen literarischer Theoriebildung, ihr offenes und perspektivisch differenziertes Theoriekonzept sowie die Erweiterung des Short-Story-Begriffs ermöglichten das Zurückgehen der Quellensammlung bis zum Jahr 1573, in dem die erste aufgefundene englische Quelle die Bedeutung der mündlichen Erzähltradition belegt - das Ausgreifen in die englische Theoriediskussion des 17. Jahrhunderts, die bereits in einer

Lexikondefinition einen frühen Beleg für den Terminus "Short Story" liefert - und das Eingehen auf die englische und amerikanische Essayistik des 18. Jahrhunderts, in der "short stories" als moralisch-didaktische Exempla und Bestandteile der "polite conversation" erscheinen. Hier zeigt sich, daß das Denken über kurze Geschichten und kurzes Erzählen lange vor Poe begann. Trotz aller individuellen und zeitbedingten Unterschiede lassen sich in den Theorien, von der frühesten Zeit bis zur Gegenwart, durchgehende Aspekte feststellen, deren Kenntnis das Verständnis jeder einzelnen Quelle vertiefen und zu einer Präzisierung des gattungstheoretischen Denkens führen kann.

Die Anordnung der Texte in der QUELLENSAMMLUNG (S. 1-217) ist durchgehend chronologisch. Jedem Text sind als erste Zeile die laufende Nummer, der Name des Autors, das Jahr der Erstpublikation und, soweit ermittelt werden konnte, in kursiver Schrift das Entstehungsjahr vorangestellt. Die Namen aller amerikanischen Autoren werden hier - wie auch im Inhaltsverzeichnis, in der Bibligoraphie weiterer Beiträge zur Theorie der Short Story (S. 221-243) und im Gesamtverzeichnis der Autoren (S. 280-284) - durch kursive Schrift kenntlich gemacht. Dadurch läßt sich die theoriegeschichtliche Entwicklung in England und in den Vereinigten Staaten auch getrennt und im Vergleich miteinander studieren.

Dieser ersten Zeile folgen die bibliographischen Daten der hier benutzten Textvorlage und, soweit feststellbar und nützlich, die Publikationsgeschichte der Quelle. Abgedruckt werden nur Auszüge oder gekürzte Texte. Sie sind so ausgewählt oder gekürzt worden, daß sie - zusammen mit den bibliographischen Angaben - Art und Argumentationskontext der theoretischen Äußerungen des Autors deutlich erkennen lassen. Auslassungen im Text werden durch Pünktchen kenntlich gemacht.

Der Entschluß, sich auf gekürzte Texte und Auszüge zu beschränken und keine vollständigen Essays, Aufsätze und Vorworte abzudrucken, erklärt sich aus dem Bemühen, in handlicher und übersichtlicher Form eine große historische Entwicklungsspanne und eine größtmögliche Vielfalt der theoretischen Äußerungen zu dokumentieren. Für die Quellensammlung wurden die Texte ausgewählt, die inhaltlich am ergiebigsten sind und die Besonderheit des Autors in seiner Zeit am besten zur Darstellung bringen. Nicht aufgenommen wurden Äußerungen über besondere Formen des kurzen Erzählens, wie "detective story", Fabel, Anekdote oder Märchen, bis auf wenige Beispiele in der Bibliographie.

Die BIBLIOGRAPHIE weiterer englischer und amerikanischer Beiträge zur Theorie der Short Story (S. 221-243) erfaßt alle über die Quellensammlung hinausgehenden Texte, die von den Herausgebern ermittelt wurden und die für eine größere theoriegeschichtliche Untersuchung von Bedeutung sind. Auch dieser Teil ist in sich chronologisch geordnet, und die in der Quellensammlung begonnene Numerierung der Texte (von 1 bis 103) wird hier (von 104 bis 315) fortgesetzt. Wie die einzelnen bibliographischen Teile - auch die Liste der Symposien und Textsammlungen und das Verzeichnis der Sekundärliteratur - angelegt und zu nutzen sind, wird in kurzen Einführungen (S. 221, 244 und 247) dargelegt.

Das Neue an diesem Arbeitsbuch ist nicht die Verbindung von Quellensammlung und Bibliographie, sondern der INDEX (S. 251-284), der die abgedruckten Texte für weiterführende Untersuchungen erschließt. Vor allem das "Schlagwortverzeichnis" ist von Bedeutung: Es bietet einen Aspekt- und Begriffsraster, der für vielfältige vergleichende Inhaltsanalysen genutzt werden kann. Näheres darüber wird in der kurzen Einführung gesagt (S. 261-2).

Ein wissenschaftliches Projekt dieser Art ist auf konstruktive Kritik angewiesen. Die Herausgeber bitten daher die Benutzer dieses Bandes, sie auf übersehene Autoren und Texte hinzuweisen.

Sie danken den englischen und amerikanischen Verlagen, die hier nicht im einzelnen aufgeführt werden können, für die Erteilung der Abdruck-Lizenzen und der Deutschen Forschungsgemeinschaft für ihre Unterstützung bei der Quellenbeschaffung. Sie danken den Tübinger Studenten, die im Laufe der vergangenen Jahre durch ihre Anregungen und Beiträge das Zustandekommen dieses Buches gefördert haben, besonders Herrn Fritz Kemmler, Herrn Wolfgang Schäfer, Fräulein Helga M. Schultz und Herrn Klaus Walter Vowe für die tatkräftige und zuverlässige Mitarbeit bei der Herstellung des Manuskripts. Frau Renate Schneider und Frau Marie-Annick Hartmann sorgten für die Erstellung des reproduktionsfertigen Typoskripts.

Tübingen, im Juni 1977

Alfred Weber
Walter F. Greiner

Short-Story-Theorien
(1573 – 1973)

Eine Sammlung und Bibliographie
englischer und amerikanischer Quellen

1. GEORGE GASCOIGNE —— 1573

aus *A Hundreth Sundrie Flowres* (London, [1573]). - Hier zitiert nach der Edition von C. T. Prouty, University of Missouri Studies, XVII, 2 (Columbia, Missouri, 1942), 96 und 195.

They passed over their supper all in quiet, and sone after Mistresse *Fraunces*, being desirous to requite Dame *Pergoes* quippes, requested that they might continue the pastime which Dame *Pergo* had begon over night: whereunto they all consented, and the lot fell unto Dame *Fraunces* to propounde the second question, who adressing hir speeche unto *F. J.* sayde in this wyse. Noble governor, I will reherse unto you a straunge historie, not fayned, neither borowed out of any olde aucthorritie, but a thing done in deede of late daies, and not farre distant from this place where wee nowe remayne. It chaunced that a gentleman our neighbor being maried to a very fayre gentlewoman, lived with hir by the space of fower or five yeares in great contentation, trusting hir no lesse than he loved hir, and yet loving hir as much as any man coulde love a woman. ...

The Reporter

To tell a tale without authoritye,
Or fayne a Fable by invention,
That one proceedes of quicke capacitye,
That other proves but small discretion,
Yet have both one and other oft bene done.
And if I were a Poet as some be,
You might perhappes heare some such tale of me.

But for I fynde my feeble skyll to faynte,
To faine in figures as the learned can,
And yet my tongue is tyed by due constrainte,
To tell nothing but truth of every man:
I will assaye even as I fyrst began,
To tell you now a tale and that of truth,
Which I my selfe sawe proved in my youth.

I neede not seeke so farre in coastes abrode,
As some men do, which wryte strange historyes,
For whyles at home I made my chiefe abode
And sawe our lovers playe their Tragedyes,
I founde enowe which seemed to suffice,
To set on worke farre finer wits than mine,
In painting out the pangs which make them pine.

aus "The Preface" zum Kapitel XLIII von *Scarron's Comical Romance* (London, 1676), 227 f. - Dieses Kapitel der englischen Übersetzung des *Roman Comique* ist eine anonyme Fortsetzung. Es hat den Titel "The *Novel* of *Millamant*, or the *Rampant Lady*, as read by *Ragotin*".

To be able to draw a Natural Representation, and give in Words an easie and expressive Character of the Actions of Mankind, hath alwaies been thought a Master-piece of Eloquence. Thence it proceeds, in my opinion, that we have so few of them, and that in so many Ages, wherein the Language of Man hath been cultivated, and brought to a great deal of Perfection, we can scarce reckon above two or three Pieces of this nature. In the *Greek* Tongue, *Lucian*; in the *Latine, Petronius* and *Apuleius*; in the *Italian, Boccacio*; and in the *Spanish, Quevedo,* are, I think, the only Authors that have undertaken any thing of this nature, in the space of so many Ages.

The *French* Nation, though very laborious in enriching their Language, and very ingenious in their Inventions, have nevertheless in the greatest glory of their Tongue, under Cardinal *Richelieu*, seemed to employ themselves more in the vain descriptions of *Romantique* Idea's, and the mistaken Pomp and Loftiness of *Tragical* Poetry, than in the easie expressing of Nature, and making Copies whose Originals we might meet with somewhere. Without doubt, it was a happy Age for Authors whose Eloquence was confined to no other Theam than their own Imaginations; but certainly it was a very Childish one, which could be pleased with the Descriptions of Valour beyond Probability, Beauty without Defect, and Vertue enemy to both Nature and Fortune. Now therefore that we are past our Infancy, and that *Romances*, like our Nurses Tales, seem as ridiculous to us, as they seemed pleasant when we were little: Nothing but what is natural and probable will go down with us. The *French* themselves, our first *Romantique* Masters, are convinced of this truth, and have given over making of the World otherwise than it was; are now come to represent it to us as it is, and ever will be.

I know not whether I shall seem too bold, if to those famous Essaies of the Ancients, I dare adde this little Story of *Millamant*; for I think it comes as near them as any, except one we have had from the ingenious Marquiss *De Bussy Rabutin*, who may very justly challenge the honour of being the Knight that has delivered his Nation from the Charms of their Inchanted Castles. But that which he performed with so much Wit, could not it seems be done without some Malice, and that reflected its Venom upon the Author himself, who underwent a rude Prison, for having freed us from those of Romances.

Millamant is in that particular contrived with more cunning, and as pleasant a Genius; for veiling only the Persons, we described their Actions to the life, and left our selves the liberty of applying the Characters we meet with in this little History, to as many of our Acquaintance as we please. I hope, Reader, that in acknowledgment you will forgive him that writes it some little Liberties, and Like him as much in Private, as you will disown him in Publique.

3. WILLIAM CONGREVE —— *1691*, 1692

aus "The Preface to the Reader" in *Incognita: or, Love and Duty Reconcil'd* (London, 1692), o. S. - Auf dem Titelblatt wird auch die Lizenzerteilung vermerkt: "*Licens'd* Decemb. 22, 1691."

Reader,
Some Authors are so fond of a Preface, that they will write one tho' there be nothing more in it than an Apology for its self. But to show thee that I am not one of those, I will make no Apology for this, but do tell thee that I think it necessary to be prefix'd to this Trifle, to prevent thy overlooking some little pains which I have taken in the Composition of the following Story. Romances are generally composed of the Constant Loves and invincible Courages of Hero's, Heroins, Kings and Queens, Mortals of the first Rank, and so forth; where lofty Language, miraculous Contingencies and impossible Performances, elevate and surprize the Reader into a giddy Delight, which leaves him flat upon the Ground whenever he gives of, and vexes him to think how he has suffer'd himself to be pleased and transported, concern'd and afflicted at the several Passages which he has Read, *viz.* these Knights Success to their Damosels Misfortunes, and such like, when he is forced to be very well convinced that 'tis all a lye. Novels are of a more familiar nature; Come near us, and represent to us Intrigues in practice, delight us with Accidents and odd Events, but not such as are wholly unusual or unpresidented, such which not being so distant from our Belief bring also the pleasure nearer us. Romances give more of Wonder, Novels more Delight. And with reverence be it spoken, and the Parallel kept at due distance, there is something of equality in the Proportion which they bear in reference to one another, with that between Comedy and Tragedy; but the *Drama* is the long extracted from Romance and History: 'tis the Midwife to Industry, and brings forth alive the Conceptions of the Brain. *Minerva* walks upon the Stage before us, and we are more assured of the real presence of Wit when it is delivered *viva voce* -

Segnius irritant animos demissa per aurem,
Quam quae sunt oculis subjecta fidelibus, & quae
Ipse sibi tradit spectator. -

Horace.

Since all Traditions must indisputably give place to the *Drama*, and since there is no possibility of giving that life to the Writing or Repetition of a Story which it has in the Action, I resolved in another beauty to imitate *Dramatick* Writing, namely, in the Design, Contexture and Result of the Plot. I have not observed it before in a Novel. Some I have seen begin with an unexpected accident, which has been the only surprizing part of the Story, cause enough to make the Sequel look flat, tedious and insipid; for 'tis but reasonable the Reader should expect it not to rise, at least to keep upon a level in the entertainment; for so he may be kept on in hopes that at some time or other it may mend; but the 'tother is such a balk to a Man, 'tis carrying him up stairs to show him the Dining-Room, and after forcing him to make a Meal in the Kitchin. This I have not only endeavoured to avoid, but also have used a method for the contrary purpose. The design of the Novel is obvious, after the first meeting of *Aurelian* and *Hippolito* with *Incognita* and *Leonora*, and the difficulty is in bringing it to pass, maugre all apparent obstacles, within the compass of two days. How many probable Casualties intervene in opposition to the main Design, *viz.* of marrying two Couple so oddly engaged in an intricate Amour, I leave the Reader at his leisure to consider: As also whether every Obstacle does not in the progress of the Story act as subservient to that purpose, which at first it seems to oppose. In a Comedy this would be called the Unity of Action; here it may pretend to no more than an Unity of Contrivance. The Scene is continued in *Florence* from the commencement of the Amour; and the time from first to last is but three days. If there be any thing more in particular resembling the Copy which I imitate (as the Curious Reader will soon perceive) I leave it to show it self, being very well satisfy'd how much more proper it had been for him to have found out this himself, than for me to prepossess him with an Opinion of something extraordinary in an Essay began and finished in the idler hours of a fortnight's time: for I can only esteem it a laborious idleness, which is Parent to so inconsiderable a Birth. I have gratified the Bookseller in pretending an occasion for a Preface; the other two Persons concern'd are the Reader and my self, and if he be but pleased with what was produced for tha end, my satisfaction follows of course, since it will be proportion'd to his Approbation or Dislike.

aus "Preface" zu *The Secret History of Queen Zarah* (London, 1705), o. S.

The Romances in *France* have for a long Time been the Diversion and Amusement of the whole World; the People both in the City and at Court have given themselves over to this Vice, and all Sorts of People have read these Works with a most surprizing Greediness; but that Fury is very much abated, and they are all fallen off from this Distraction: The Little *Histories* of this Kind have taken Place of *Romances*, whose Prodigious Number of Volumes were sufficient to tire and satiate such whose Heads were most fill'd with those Notions.

These little Pieces which have banish'd *Romances* are much more agreeable to the Brisk and Impetuous Humour of the *English*, who have naturally no Taste for longwinded Performances, for they have no sooner begun a Book but they desire to see the end of it: The Prodigious Length of the Ancient *Romances*, the Mixture of so many Extraordinary Adventures, and the great Number of Actors that appear on the Stage, and the Likeness which is so little managed, all which has given a Distaste to Persons of good Sense, and has made Romances so much cry'd down, as we find 'em at present. The Authors of Historical Novels, who have found out this Fault, have run into the same Error, because they take for the Foundation of their History no more than one Principal Event, and don't overcharge it with *Episodes*, which wou'd extent it to an Excessive Length; but they are run into another Fault, which I cannot Pardon, that is, to please by Variety the Taste of the Reader, they mix particular Stories with the Principal *History*, which seems to me as if they reason'd Ill; in Effect the Curiosity of the Reader is deceiv'd by this Deviation from the Subject, which retards the Pleasure he wou'd have in seeing the End of an Event; it relishes of a Secret Displeasure in the Author, which makes him soon lose Sight of those Persons with whom he began to be in Love; besides the vast Number of Actors who have such different Interests, embarrasses his Memory, and causes some Confusion in his Brain, because 'tis necessary for the Imagination to labour to recal the several Interests and Characters of the Persons spoken of, and by which they have interrupted the *History*.

aus *The Spectator* No. 538 (Nov. 17, 1712). - Hier zitiert nach *The Spectator*, hrsg. von Donald F. Bond (Oxford, 1965), IV, 420-424.

... *ultra Finem tendere opus* Hor.

Surprize is so much the Life of Stories, that every one aims at it who endeavours to please by telling them. Smooth Delivery, an elegant Choice of Words, and a sweet Arrangement, are all beautifying *Graces*, but not the Particulars in this Point of Conversation which either long command the Attention, or strike with the Violence of a sudden Passion, or occasion the Burst of Laughter which accompanies Humour. I have sometimes fancy'd, that the Mind is in this Case like a Traveller who sees a fine Seat in Haste; he acknowledges the Delightfulness of a Walk set with Regularity, but wou'd be uneasy if he were oblig'd to pace it over, when the first View had let him into all its Beauties from one End to the other.

However, a Knowledge of the Success which Stories will have when they are attended with a Turn of Surprize, as it has happily made the Characters of some, so has it also been the Ruine of the Characters of others. There is a Sett of Men who outrage Truth, instead of affecting us with a Manner in telling it; who over-leap the Line of Probability, that they may be seen to move out of the common Road; and endeavour only to make their Hearers stare, by imposing upon them with a kind of Nonsense against the Philosophy of Nature, or such a Heap of Wonders told upon their own Knowledge, as it is not likely one Man shou'd ever have met with.

I have been led to this Observation by a Company into which I fell accidentally. The Subject of *Antipathies* was a proper Field wherein such false Surprizers might expatiate, and there were those present who appear'd very fond to shew it in its full Extent of traditional History. Some of them, in a learned Manner, offer'd to our Consideration the miraculous Powers which the Effluviums of Cheese have over Bodies whose Pores are dispos'd to receive them in a noxious Manner; others gave an Account of such who cou'd indeed bear the Sight of Cheese, but not the Taste; for which they brought a Reason from the Milk of their Nurses. Others again discours'd, without endeavouring at Reasons, concerning an unconquerable Aversion which some Stomachs have against a Joint of Meat when it is whole, and the eager Inclination they have for it when, by its being cut up, the Shape which had affected them is alter'd. From hence they pass'd to Eels, then to Parsnips, and so from one Aversion to another, till we had work'd up our selves to such a Pitch of Complaisance, that when the Dinner was to come in, we enquir'd the Name of every Dish, and hop'd it wou'd be no Offence to any in Company, before it was admitted. When we had sate down, this Civility amongst us turn'd the Discourse from Eatables to other Sorts of Aversions; and the eternal Cat, which plagues every Conversation of this Nature, began then to engross the Subject. One had sweated at the Sight of it, another had smell'd it out as it lay conceal'd in a very distant Cupboard, and he who crown'd the whole Set of these Stories, reckon'd up the Number of Times in which it had occasion'd him to swound away: At last, says he, that you may all be satisfy'd of my invincible Aversion to a Cat, I shall give an unanswerable Instance; As I was going through a Street of *London*, where I never had been till then, I felt a general Damp and a Faintness all over me, which I could not tell how to account for, till I chanced to cast my Eyes upwards, and found that I was passing under a Sign-post on which the Picture of a Cat was hung.

The Extravagance of this Turn in the way of Surprize, gave a Stop to the Talk we had been carrying on: Some were silent because they doubted, and others because they were conquer'd in their own Way; so that the Gentleman had Opportunity to press the Belief of it upon us, and let us see that he was rather exposing himself than ridiculing others.

I must freely own that I did not all this while disbelieve every thing that was said; but yet I thought some in the Company had been endeavouring who should pitch the Bar farthest; that it had for some Time been a measuring Cast, and at last my Friend of the Cat and Sign-post had thrown beyond them all.

I then consider'd the Manner in which this Story had been received, and the Possibility that it might have pass'd for a Jest upon others, if he had not labour'd against himself. From hence, thought I, there are two Ways which the well-bred World generally takes to correct such a Practice, when they do not think fit to contradict it flatly.

The first of these is a general Silence, which I would not advise any one to interpret in his own Behalf. It is often the Effect of Prudence in avoiding a Quarrel, when they see another drive so fast, that there is no stopping him without being run against, and but very seldom the Effect of Weakness in believing suddenly. The Generality of Mankind are not so grosly ignorant as some overbearing Spirits would perswade themselves; and if the Authority of a Character or a Caution against Danger make us suppress our Opinions, yet neither of these are of Force enough to suppress our Thoughts of them. If a Man who has endeavoured to amuse his Company with Improbabilities could but look into their Minds, he would find that they imagine he lightly esteems of their Sense when he thinks to impose upon them, and that he is less esteemed by them for his Attempt in doing so. His Endeavour to glory at their Expence becomes a Ground of Quarrel, and the Scorn and Indifference with which they entertain it begins the immediate Punishment: And indeed (if we should even go no further) Silence, or a negligent Indifference, has a deeper Way of Wounding than Opposition; because Opposition proceeds from an Anger that has a Sort of generous Sentiment for the Adversary mingling along with it, while it shews that there is some Esteem in your Mind for him; in short, that you think him worth while to contest with: But Silence, or a negligent Indifference, proceeds from Anger, mixed with a Scorn that shews another he is thought by you too contemptible to be regarded.

The other Method which the World has taken for correcting this Practice of false Surprize, is to over-shoot such Talkers in their own Bow, or to raise the Story with further Degrees of Impossibility, and set up for a Voucher to them in such a Manner as must let them see they stand detected. Thus I have heard a Discourse was once managed upon the Effects of Fear. One of the Company had given an Account how it had turned his Friend's Hair grey in a Night, while the Terrors of a Shipwreck encompass'd him. Another taking the Hint from hence, began, upon his own Knowledge, to enlarge his Instances of the like Nature to such a Number, that it was not probable he could ever have met with them; and as he still grounded these upon different Causes, for the sake of Variety, it might seem at last, from his Share of the Conversation, almost impossible that any one who can feel the Passion of Fear should all his Life escape so common an Effect of it. By this Time some of the Company grew negligent, or desirous to contradict him: But one rebuked the rest with an Appearance of Severity, and, with the known old Story in his Head, assured them they need not scruple to believe that the Fear of any thing can make a Man's Hair grey, since he knew one whose Perriwig had suffered so by it. Thus he stopp'd the Talk, and made them easy. Thus is the same Method taken to bring us to Shame which we fondly take to encrease our Character. It is indeed a kind of Mimickry by which another puts on our Air of Conversation to show us to our selves: He seems to look ridiculous before you, that you may remember how near a Resemblance you bear to him, or that you may know he will not lie under the Imputation of believing you. Then it is that you are struck dumb immediately with a conscientious Shame for what you have been saying: Then it is that you are inwardly grieved at the Sentiments which you cannot but perceive others entertain concerning you. In short, you are against your self; the Laugh of the Company runs against you; the censuring World is obliged to you for that Triumph which you have allow'd them at your own Expence; and Truth, which you have injured, has a near Way of being revenged on you, when by the bare Repetition of your Story you become a frequent Diversion for the Publick.

6. [ANONYMUS] ———————————————————————— 1713

aus *The Guardian* No. 42 (April 29, 1713). - Hier zitiert nach *The British Essayists: with Prefaces, Historical and Biographical by A. Chalmers* (Boston, 1866), XIII, 275-280.

Non missura cutem, nisi plena cruoris hirudo.

HOR. ARS POET. *ult.*

Sticking like leeches till they burst with blood.

ROSCOMMON.

Tom Lizard told us a story the other day of some persons which our family know very well, with so much humour and life that it caused a great deal of mirth at the tea-table. His brother Will, the Templar, was highly delighted with it, and the next day being with some of his inns-of-court acquaintance, resolved, whether out of the benevolence or the pride of his heart, I will not determine, to entertain them with what he called 'a pleasant humour enough.' I was in great pain for him when I heard him begin, and was not at all surprised to find the company very little moved by it. Will blushed, looked round the room, and with a forced laugh, 'Faith, gentlemen,' said he, 'I do not know what makes you look so grave; it was an admirable story when I heard it.'

When I came home, I fell into a profound contemplation upon story-telling, and as I have nothing so much at heart as the good of my country, I resolved to lay down some precautions upon this subject.

I have often thought that a story-teller is born as well as a poet. It is, I think, certain, that some men have such a peculiar cast of mind that they see things in another light, than men of grave dispositions. Men of a lively imagination and a mirthful temper, will represent things to their hearers in the same manner as they themselves were affected with them; and whereas serious spirits might perhaps have been disgusted at the sight of some odd occurrences in life; yet the very same occurrances shall please them in a well-told story, where the disagreeable parts of the images are concealed, and those only which are pleasing exhibited to the fancy. Story-telling is therefore not an art, but what we call a 'knack;' it doth not so much subsist upon wit as upon humour; and I will add, that it is not perfect without proper gesticulations of the body, which naturally attend such merry emotions of the mind. I know very well that a certain gravity of countenance sets some stories off to advantage, where the hearer is to be surprised in the end; but this is by no means a general rule, for it is frequently convenient to aid and assist by cheerful looks, and whimsical agitations. I will go yet further, and affirm that the success of a story very often depends upon the make of the body and formation of the features of him who relates it. I have been of this opinion ever since I criticized upon the chin of Dick Dewlap. I very often had the weakness to repine at the prosperity of his conceits, which made him pass for a wit with the widow at the coffee-house, and the ordinary mechanics that frequent it; nor could I myself forbear laughing at them most heartily, though upon examination I thought most of them very flat and insipid. I found after some time, that the merit of his wit was founded upon the shaking of a fat paunch, and the tossing up of a pair of rosy jowls. Poor Dick had a fit of sickness, which robbed him of his fat and his fame at once; and it was full three months before he regained his reputation, which rose in proportion to his floridity. He is now very jolly and ingenious, and hath a good constitution for wit.

Those who are thus adorned with the gifts of nature, are apt to show their parts with too much ostentation; I would, therefore, advise all the professors of this art never to tell stories but as they seem to grow out of the subject-matter of the conversation, or as they serve to illustrate or enliven it. Stories that are very common are generally irksome; but may be aptly introduced, provided they be only hinted at,and mentioned by way of allusion. Those, that are altogether new, should never be ushered in, without a short and pertinent character of the chief persons concerned; because, by that means, you make the company acquainted with them; and it is a certain rule that slight and trivial accounts of those who are familiar to us, administer more mirth than the brightest points of wit in unknown characters. A little circumstance in the complexion or dress of the man you are talking of, sets his image before the hearer, if he be chosen aptly for the story. Thus, I remember Tom Lizard, after having made his sisters merry with an account of a formal old man's way of complimenting, owned very frankly that his story would not have been worth one farthing, if he had made the hat of him whom he represented one inch narrower. Besides the marking distinct characters, and selecting pertinent circumstances, it is likewise necessary to leave off in time, and end smartly. So that there is a kind of drama in the forming of a story, and the manner of conducting and pointing it is the same as in an epigram. It is a miserable thing after one hath raised the expectation of the company by humorous characters and a pretty conceit, to pursue the matter too far. There is no retreating, and how poor is it for a story-teller to end his relation by saying, 'that's all!'

As the choosing of pertinent circumstances is the life of a story, and that wherein humour principally consists; so the collectors of impertinent particulars are the very bane and opiates of conversation. Old men are great transgressors this way. Poor Ned Poppy - he's gone - was a very honest man, but was so excessively tedious over his pipe, that he was not to be endured. He knew so exactly what they had for dinner, when such a thing happened, in what ditch his bay stone-horse had his sprain at that time, and how his man John - no! it was William - started a hare in the common field, that he never got to the end of his tale. Then, he was extremely particular in marriages and intermarriages, and cousins twice or thrice removed; and whether such a thing happened at the latter end of July, or the beginning of August. He had a marvellous tendency likewise to digressions; insomuch that if a considerable person was mentioned in his story, he would straightway launch out into an episode of him; and again, if in that person's story he had occasion to remember a third man, he broke off and gave us his history, and so on. He always put me in mind of what Sir William Temple informs us of the tale-tellers in the north of Ireland, who are hired to tell stories of giants and enchanters to lull people asleep. These historians are obliged by their bargain to go on without stopping; so that after the patient hath, by this benefit, enjoyed a long nap, he is sure to find the operator proceeding in his work. Ned procured the like effect in me the last time I was with him. As he was in the third hour of his story, and very thankful that his memory did not fail him, I fairly nodded in the elbow-chair. He was much affronted at this, till I told him, 'Old friend, you have your infirmity, and I have mine.'

But of all evils in story-telling, the humour of telling tales, one after another, in great numbers, is the least supportable. Sir Harry Pandolf and his son gave my Lady Lizard great offence in this particular. Sir Harry hath what they call a string of stories, which he tells over every Christmas. When our family visits there, we are constantly, after supper, entertained with the Glastonbury Thorn. When we have wondered at that a little, 'Ay, but, father,' saith the son, 'let us have the spirit in the wood.' After that hath been laughed at, 'Ay, but, father,' cries the booby again, 'tell us how you served the robber.' 'Alack-a-day,' saith Sir Harry, with a smile, and rubbing his forehead, 'I have almost forgot that; but it is a pleasant conceit, to be sure. 'Accordingly, he tells that and twenty more in the same independent order; and without the least variation at this day, as he hath done, to my knowledge, ever since the Revolution. I must not forget a very odd compliment that Sir Harry always makes my lady when he dines here. After dinner he strokes his belly, and says, with a feigned concern in his countenance, 'Madam, I have lost by you to-day.' 'How so, Sir Harry?' replies my lady. 'Madam,'says he, 'I have lost an excellent stomach.' At this, his son and heir laughs immoderately, and winks upon Mrs. Annabella. This is the thirty-third time that Sir Harry hath been thus arch, and I can bear it no longer.

As the telling of stories is a great help and life to conversation, I always encourage them, if they are pertinent and innocent, in opposition to those gloomy mortals who disdain every thing but matter of fact. Those grave fellows are my aversion, who sift every thing with the utmost nicety, and find the malignity of a lie in a piece of humour pushed a little beyond exact truth. I likewise have a poor opinion of those who have got a trick of keeping a steady countenance, that cock their hats and look glum when a pleasant thing is said, and ask, 'Well! and what then?' Men of wit and parts should treat one another with benevolence; and I will lay it down as a maxim, that if you seem to have a good opinion of another man's wit, he will allow you to have judgment.

7. CHARLES GILDON ——— 1719

aus "The Dedication" zu Sarah Butler, *Milesian Tales: or, Instructive Novels for the happy Conduct of Life* (London, 1719), ix-x.

The following Sheets, ...are allow'd by the Learned to be a useful sort of POETRY, tho' without the advantageous Harmony of Verse. For as all POETRY is an IMITATION, as ARISTOTLE justly observes, it is plain that all *Fables* are IMITATIONS of *Actions*, which is the essence of both the DRAMATIC and EPIC POESIE.

But this *Prosaic Poetry* is of as ancient a Date as the *Milesian Tales*, which so charm'd Antiquity it self. The Moderns since the Time of HELIODORUS, have often vary'd their Form; some Years ago they swell'd them into large Volumes, but of late the general Tast runs for such as are compriz'd in a much narrower Compass; from whence we derive so many Books of TALES, which have not yet fail'd of Success. These that follow, in my Opinion, fall not in the least short of the most excellent that have yet appear'd; there being a Pathetic Tenderness, that runs quite through them, supported by a Noble and Heroic Fortitude.

8. [*ANONYMUS*] —————————————————————————————— 1744

> aus "The Art of Story-Telling", *The American Magazine and Historical Chronicle*, I (July, 1744), 469-71. - Dieser Artikel wurde aus einer anderen Zeitschrift, *The Intelligencer*, übernommen.

There is one Kind of Conversation which every one aims at, and every one almost fails in; it is that of *Story-telling*. I know not any Thing which engages our Attention with more Delight, when a Person has a sufficient Stock of Talents necessary for it, such as *Good Sense, true Humour, a clear Head, a ready Command of Language,* and *a Variety of proper Gesture*, to give Life and Spirit to what he says. If any of these be wanting, the Listners, instead of being diverted, are disobliged; but if the Person be utterly void of them all, as is very often the Case, he becomes a Nuisance to the Company, and they are so long upon the Rack as he speaks. ...

I shall in a few Words, divide the *Story-tellers* into *the short, the long, the marvellous, the insipid,* and *the delightful*.

The *short Story-teller* is he, who tells a great deal in few Words, engages your Attention, pleases your Imagination, or quickly excites your Laughter. Of this Rank were *Xenophon, Plutarch, Macrobius,* among the Ancients. ...

The *Long Story-teller* is one who tells little or nothing in a great Number of Words; for this many among the Moderns are famous, particularly the *French*; and among our selves in this Kingdom, we have a vast Number of the better Sort. ...

The *Marvellous*, is he who is fond of telling such things as no Man alive, who has the least Use of his Reason, can believe. This Humour prevails very much in Travellers, and the vain-glorious, but very pardonable, because no Man's Faith is imposed upon, or if it should be so, ill Consequence attends Persons seriously extravagant, expecting another should give Credit to what he knows impossible for the greatest Dunce to swallow. ...

The *insipid,* who may not unfitly be called *Soporifick,* is one who goes plodding on in a heavy dull Relation of unimportant Facts: You shall have an Account from such a Person of ever minute Circumstance, which happened in the Company where he has been, what he did, and what they did, what they said, and what he said, with a Million of trite Phrases, with an *and so* beginning every Sentence; and *to make a long Story short*; and, *as I was saying,* with many more Expletives of equal Signification. It is a most dreadful Thing, when Men have neither the Talent of Speaking, nor the Discretion of holding their Tongues, and that of all People, such as are least qualified, are commonly the most earnest in this Way of Conversation.

The *Delightful Story-teller* is one, who speaks not a Word too much, or too little, who can, in a very careless Manner, give a great deal of Pleasure to others, and deserves rather to divert, than be applauded; who shews good Understanding, and a delicate Turn of Wit in every Thing which comes from him; who can entertain his Company better with the History of a Child and its *Hobby-Horse,* than one of the *Soporificks* can with an Account of *Alexander* and *Bucephalus*.

9. [ANONYMUS] —— 1751

Aus "Preface" zu *Constantia; or, A True Picture of Human Life ...after the Manner of Boccace* (London, 1751). - Text hier zitiert nach George L. Barnett (Ed.), *Eighteenth-Century British Novelists on the Novel* (New York, 1968), 92 f. und 95. In einer zeitgenössischen Rezension dieser 2-bändigen Novellen-Sammlung nach dem angeblichen Vorbild Boccaccios heißt es: "As these volumes are composed of a number of short stories, without any connection between them, the introductions are designed to give the history of the relaters...". Aus *The Monthly Review*, V (June, 1751), 10.

The famous Scarron ... introduced in his comical romance several short histories written on the Spanish model and which he pretended were translated from that language. ...

He was followed by many of his own nation, and some of them men of great talents, who shewed at least their inclination to, and high esteem for, this kind of writing by pursuing it after they had acquired a great reputation by works of another nature. Amongst these we may reckon Mr. Segrais, Bishop Huet, Abbé de St. Real, Voiture, and the famous Archbishop Fenelon, who besides his *Telemachus*, which is a book of a higher class, wrote several little histories that may well enough be styled novels. ...

Pieces of this nature serve to open the mind....We may take from books of this kind great advantages in impressing right principles, with respect to virtue, good sense and good manners....Young minds are more capable of discerning the connection between causes and events than is generally apprehended; neither are they at all unwilling to employ study and pains on such subjects, provided they are discreetly conducted, and their attention not too long taken up with the same object. For this reason, short stories are the most expedient, and it is to reach the same end that so many episodes are introduced in long works, which however do not answer the purpose so well, because they divide and distract the thoughts of an impatient reader, which are best contracted and settled by a relation that falls within a moderate compass.

10. JOHN HAWKESWORTH —— 1752

aus *The Adventurer* No. 4 (Nov. 18, 1752). - Hier zitiert nach *The British Essayists: with Prefaces, Historical and Biographical by A. Chalmers* (Boston, 1866), XIX, 66-70.

Ficta voluptatis causâ sint proxima veris.

HOR. ARS POET. 338.

Fictions, to please, should wear the face of truth.

ROSCOMMON.

No species of writing affords so general entertainment, as the relation of events; but all relations of events do not entertain in the same degree.

It is always necessary that facts should appear to be produced in a regular and connected series, that they should follow in a quick succession, and yet that they should be delivered with discriminating circumstances. If they have not a necessary and apparent connection, the ideas which they excite obliterate each other, and the mind is tantalized with an imperfect glimpse of innumerable objects that just appear and vanish; if they are too minutely related, they become tiresome; and if divested of all their circumstances, insipid; for who that reads, in a table of chronology or an index, that a city was swallowed up by an earthquake, or a kingdom depopulated by a pestilence, finds either his attention engaged or his curiosity gratified?

Those narratives are most pleasing, which not only excite and gratify curiosity, but engage the passions.

History is a relation of the most natural and important events; history, therefore, gratifies curiosity, but it does not often excite either terror or pity; the mind feels not that tenderness for a falling state, which it feels for an injured beauty; nor is it so much alarmed at the migration of barbarians who mark their way with desolation, and fill the world with violence and rapine, as at the fury of a husband, who, deceived into jealousy by false appearances, stabs a faithful and affectionate wife kneeling at his feet, and pleading to be heard. ...

Dramatic poetry, especially tragedy, seems to unite all that pleases in each of these species of writing, with a stronger resemblance of truth, and a closer imitation of nature; the characters are such as excite attention and solicitude; the action is important, its progress is intricate yet natural, and the catastrophe is sudden and striking; and as we are present to every transaction, the images are more strongly impressed, and the passions more forcibly moved.

From a dramatic poem to those short pieces, which may be contained in such a periodical paper as The Adventurer, is a bold transition. And yet such pieces, although formed upon a single incident, if that incident be sufficiently uncommon to gratify curiosity, and sufficiently interesting to engage the passions, may afford an entertainment, which, if it is not lasting, is yet of the highest kind. Of such, therefore, this paper will frequently consist; but it should be remembered that it is much more difficult and laborious to invent a story, however simple and however short, than to recollect topics of instruction, or to remark the scenes of life as they are shifted before us.

11. [ANONYMUS] —— 1787

aus "To the *Author* of the *Olla Podrida*", *Olla Podrida* No. 34 (Nov. 3, 1787), 199-204.

It is not my intention to trouble either you or your readers with remarks on any voluminous composition of eminent writers,or scrupulously to balance the nice discriminations of varying commentators. No Sir, mine is a virgin-theme, as yet untouched by the rude hand of criticism; and unrestrained by the galling shackles of prescriptive method. And, perhaps, my efforts may not be unattended with some advantage immediately to yourself, as the compositions to which I allude have commonly been diffused through periodical channels. These compositions are those narrations of blended fiction and sentiment, which, too inconsiderable from their size to swell into circulatory duodecimos, assume the general humble denomination of TALES, and are distinguished by the epithets tender, pathetic, sentimental, founded on fact, &c. &c.

As Aristotle deduced his Rules from the great Originals who preceded him, it shall be my province to follow so illustrious an example, and in this primary essay, to inculcate some general precepts, and not to point out in detail or extract individual excellences which are profusely scattered through the ample labours of writers of this description.

It is essential to a Tale that it should be tender, for who is there that would not desire for his Works the precious balm of a sigh or a tear, rather than that they should excite the applause of a smile or the boisterous acclamation of laughter.

It should not abound too much in incident, lest the curiosity be excited as much as the finer feelings.

The opening of a Tale should be abrupt, and the author should commonly profess that his knowledge of it had arisen from some unforeseen accident. This saves the trouble of a long introduction, and brings the author and reader fairly at once into the subject. A piece of butter on a torn leaf, the being benighted on a long journey, the traveller's horse losing a shoe, have been such hacknied expedients that I cannot possibly approve their repetition. The introduction of the mailcoach is however a new and fortunate epoch; and I doubt not of its being speedily adopted by several writers in every variation of fracture, until the whole stock of casualties be exhausted.

The principal incident should not be extravagant, but be some common occurence, that it may come home to the bosoms of a great Number. A tender fair-one seduced by her lover - a dutiful son turned out of doors by an unnatural Father - a marriage of love and inclination thwarted by unfeeling parents - and all common events of a similar nature are admirable topics.

So much for the plot or ground-work in which at intervals should be interspersed inferior circumstances, pathetic if possible, but the more minute they are, the greater will be their effect. A dog - a cow lowing for its calf - a weeping willow - a withered oak - an old woman - thin grey hairs on a human head - and the like, may certainly be introduced with great success.

The Diction may be allowed to be generally unequal, but should unquestionably be florid and elevated at those intervals of the narration, where such embellishments may be requisite. Horace's prohibition of the "purpurei panni," must be totally disregarded.

Exclamations should never be used without the most absolute necessity. They are a species of affront on the feelings of the reader, who throws down the book with indignation when he is *informed* at what passages he is to be affected. *Alas* has had its day, and must now submit in its turn to the common chance of wordly revolutions. Indeed it would be scarcely noticed were not the mark of interjection ! commonly annexed to it. - Dashes are more striking and pathetic, - and are besides a very neat addition of typographical ornament.

In respect to Epithets great caution is indispensable. The sun is ever golden, the moon ever silver: the sea is azure, and the meadow verdant: the foliage of the trees is commonly green, except in the sombre or dark-pathetic, when the autumnal tinge greatly enhances the pathos.

Mythology and Allegory must be introduced with circumspection. The *darts* of *Cupid*, the *fires* of *ambition*, the *warmth* of *love*, the *coldness* of *disdain*, from their general acceptation, may be used without danger. ...

Though at first sight it may appear inconsiderable, it is really material to assign, appropriate, and characteristic names and places; *Cassander, Cleora,* and all the list of Romantic or Historic appellations, have been long exploded, and invention is now freely permitted to create and to apply. The name of the Hero should therefore excite respect by a due arrangement of harmonious and sonorous letters; and that of the Heroine should melt into liquid softness. Titles of amiable personages should gently flow: such as are intended to create disgust, should hoarsely rumble.

Place is far from being an unimportant consideration in the texture of tales. - To introduce the reader to an amiable pair, sitting by a good coal fire, is a minute but unsentimental circumstance. I would always therefore recommend a bower, which though not common in real, is very convenient in fictitious gardens, - but lest it might be mistaken for one of the lath edifices so frequent under this denomination in the vicinity of London, it should likewise be covered with honeysuckle or jasmin, *whose truant sprigs the Heroine's gentleh and may be supposed to have conducted along the convex trellis*.

The Denouement of a Tale must be simple if the principal incident be so. Yet it will admit endless variations, and in all cases, where the author is in the least degree embarrassed, a Fragment is a never-failing expedient, - and here I cannot but commend the great convenience of those intervals which occur in periodical publications; for by them an author is enabled to drop his narrative all at once, and to leave his reader for a week in an agreeable state of suspense and expectation.

Morality, though not essential, is a pretty ornament to a Tale; yet it should be sparingly adopted. I have ever greatly admired the insinuation which authors of this description so delicately convey respecting the conjugal fidelity of their married heroines; for we are universally informed, that the boys are the very pictures of their fathers, and that the girls have all the graces of their mothers.

Such, Sir, are some of the opinions I have formed on this subject, which I have thrown together without order or connection; and if from them the rising generation of tale writers may cull any useful or improving hints, my ambition will be gratified: - If *you* imagine that they may contribute to the amusement of the publick, they are very much at your service.

A. M.

12. [*ANONYMUS*] —— 1793

aus "On Tediousness in Telling a Story", *The Lady's Magazine; and Repository of Entertaining Knowledge*, II (Feb., 1793), 130-134. - Dieser Beitrag ist gezeichnet mit den Initialen "A. B."

Among the various pleasantries which give hilarity to company, a story neatly and aptly related, is to be ranked as one of the principal. To give a story its due effect, to produce mirth without tiring, is a very happy talent. No little judgment is required to select such a story as may illustrate the subject of conversation if useful, or end it in a laugh if improper. He that wishes to succeed in a story ought to attend to three things. - First, That what he relates be truth; secondly, that it comes naturally, and is not forced into conversation; or interrupts the more important discussion of a useful subject - and thirdly, that he be so perfect in the circumstances as to give it full effect. And when he is master of these cautions, to prevent disappointment, let him reflect that some people have so little relish for anecdote, that music to the deaf, or painting to the blind is not more unprofitable.

Another rule may be added, which all writers on this subject have commended, that the story be short. To render a long story interesting is almost impossible; an ingenious artist has therefore, very properly, in a print called the long story, represented the greater part of the company asleep, while one of them is telling a long story of his adventures abroad. Self-love is a principle so general, that we discover it even in the relation of a story, where the man imagines that the petty adventures which he has encountered must be as pleasing to others to hear, as to himself to relate.

aus "Art. VI. [Review of:] *Popular Tales*. By Maria Edgeworth... London, 1804", *The Edinburgh Review*, IV (July, 1804). - Hier zitiert nach der sechsten Auflage dieser Zeitschrift (Edinburgh, 1816), 329-337.

The design of these tales is excellent, and their tendency so truly laudable, as to make amends for many faults of execution. There is nothing new, indeed, in the idea of conveying instruction in the form of an amusing narrative; for from the days of Homer downwards, almost all the writers of fictitious history have been thought to aim at the moral improvement of their readers. The means which they have employed for this purpose, however, have hitherto been but indifferently calculated to effect it. The truth is, that almost all moral tales which are not expressly accommodated to the taste and condition of *children*, seem to have been intended for the benefit of persons of high fashion and splendid accomplishments only; they seldom condescend to the incidents or the duties of ordinary characters or ordinary life, but are occupied entirely in adjusting the claims of nice honour and heroic affection, or in describing the delicate perplexities and fantastic distresses of those who set vulgar sorrows at defiance. Now, considering that there are in these kingdoms at least *eighty thousand* readers, it is obvious, that no great moral utility could result from the general perusal of those brilliant narratives; and that the lessons which they were calculated to teach, were quite inapplicable, to say the least of them, to that great multitude who are neither high-born nor high-bred. It is for this great and most important class of society that the volumes before us have been written; and their object is, to interest, amuse and instruct them by stories founded on the incidents of common life, and developed by the agency of ordinary characters; to withdraw their attention from those dazzling displays of fashionable manners, with which they have no natural connexion, and to fix it upon those scenes and occurrences which have an immediate application to their own way of life; and in this way to impress upon their minds the inestimable value and substantial dignity of industry, perseverance, prudence, good humour, and all that train of vulgar and homely virtues that have hitherto made the happiness of the world, without obtaining any great share of its admiration.

This is an attempt, we think, somewhat superior in genius, as well as utility, to the laudable exertions of Mr Thomas Paine to bring disaffection and infidelity within the comprehension of the common people, or the charitable endeavours of Messrs Wirdsworth & Co. to accommodate them with an appropriate vein of poetry. Both these were superfluities which they might have done very tolerably without; but Miss Edgeworth has undertaken to improve, as well as to amuse them, and to bring them back from an admiration of pernicious absurdities, to a relish for the images of those things which must make the happiness of their actual existence. In this view, she rather deserves to be compared to those patriotic worthies who first ventured, after the revival of letters, to write in their native language, and to interest their countrymen in stories of their home manufacture; who spoke of love without allusion to Ovid, - constructed dramas altogether independent of the Scriptures, - and published tales that were not to be found in the Book of Troy. It required almost the same courage to get rid of the jargon of fashionable life, and the swarms of peers, foundlings and seducers, that infested our modern fables, as it did in those days to sweep away the mythological personages of antiquity, and to introduce characters who spoke and acted like those who were to peruse their adventures.

The success of such an experiment depends, no doubt, in a great degree, on the skill with which it is conducted; nor are we sanguine enough to hope that it will be very suddenly completed. The millinery misses and aspiring apprentices of our country towns will long hanker, we are afraid, after the elegant adventures of counts, baronesses, or Adelines; and will think every story intolerably low which does not contain anecdotes of masquerades and gaming-houses, elegiac stanzas, duels, and descriptions of the Appenines. This class will certainly be the last to be converted. But in the great and respectable multitude of English tradesmen, yeomen, and manufacturers - in that most important part of our population which consists of the well-educated in the lower and middling orders of the people, we do believe that there is so much good sense and good principle, as to secure the favourable reception of a work which professes to interest them by a picture of their own condition, to make them proud of their independence, and cheerful in their submission, and to point out the happiness which is placed within the reach of all who are industrious and affectionate.

Notwithstanding the unqualified praise which we are disposed to bestow on the design of this work, we cannot help observing, that the execution is extremely unequal. Many of the incidents are childish, and several of the stories unmeaning and improbable; yet they all inculcate an unexceptionable and practical morality, and are written throughout in a strain of admirable good sense, liberality, and cheerfulness. There is nothing tawdry or sophisticated about them; no idle description or affected reflection: the story moves on with uninterrupted rapidity; and the writer never seems to pause to admire her own powers of composition, or to wait for the admiration of her readers. ...

We cannot take our leave of these volumes, without reminding the fastidious part of our readers, that they were not written to challenge the criticism of scholars, or to gratify the taste of persons of the highest accomplishments. They are not tried by a fair standard, unless the design of writing them be kept constantly in view; and this design appears to us to be so laudably conceived, and so ably pursued, as to entitle them to more consideration than is usually bestowed on works of this description.

14. *WASHINGTON IRVING* ———————————————————— 1824

aus "To the Reader" in *Tales of a Traveller* (1824). - Hier zitiert nach *Irving's Works*, Geoffrey Crayon Edition, (New York, 1865), IV, 13.

As I know this to be a story-telling and a story-reading age, and that the world is fond of being taught by apologue, I have digested the instruction I would convey into a number of tales. They may not possess the power of amusement, which the tales told by many of my contemporaries possess; but then I value myself on the sound moral which each of them contains. This may not be apparent at first, but the reader will be sure to find it out in the end. I am for curing the world by gentle alteratives, not by violent doses; ...

I am not, therefore, for those barefaced tales which carry their moral on the surface, staring one in the face; ... On the contrary, I have often hid my moral from sight, and disguised it as much as possible by sweets and spices, so that while the simple reader is listening with open mouth to a ghost or a love story, he may have a bolus of sound morality popped down his throat, and be never the wiser for the fraud.

15. *WASHINGTON IRVING* ———————————————————— 1824

aus einem Brief vom 11. Dezember 1824 in *Letters of Washington Irving to Henry Brevoort*, hrsg. von George S. Hellman (New York, 1918), 398-401.

I fancy much of what I value myself upon in writing, escapes the observation of the great mass of my readers: who are intent more upon the story than the way in which it is told. For my part I consider a story merely as a frame on which to stretch my materials. It is the play of thought, and sentiment and language; the weaving in of characters, lightly yet expressively delineated; the familiar and faithful exhibition of scenes in common life; and the half concealed vein of humour that is often playing through the whole - these are among what I aim at, and upon which I felicitate myself in proportion as I think I succeed. I have preferred adopting a mode of sketches & short tales rather than long works, because I chose to take a line of writing peculiar to myself; rather than fall into the manner or school of any other writer: and there is a constant activity of thought and a nicety of execution required in writings of the kind, more than the world appears to imagine. It is comparatively easy to swell a story to any size when you have once the scheme & the characters in your mind; the mere interest of the story too carries the reader on through pages & pages of careless writing and the author may often be dull for half a volume at a time, if he has some striking scene at the end of it, but in these shorter writings every page must have its merit. The author must be continually piquant - woe to him if he makes an awkward sentence or writes a stupid page: the critics are sure to pounce upon it. Yet if he succeed: the very variety & piquancy of his writings; nay their very brevity; makes them frequently recurred to - and when the mere interest of the story is exhausted, he begins to get credit for his touches of pathos or humour; his points of wit or turns of language. I give these as some of the reasons that have induced me to keep on thus far in the way I had opened for myself ... I believe the works I have written will be oftener re-read than any novel of the size that I could have written. It is true other writers have crowded into the same branch of literature, and I now begin to find myself elbowed by men who have followed my footsteps; but at any rate I have had the merit of adopting a line for myself instead of following others.

16. [*ANONYMUS*] ———————————————— 1825

aus [Rezension von:] "*National Tales. Vol. II.* New York. A. P. Houston, &c. &c. 1825", *New York Review and Atheneum Magazine*, II (1825), 32-38.

Those compositions which pass under the name of tales, as distinguished from novels, require talents of a peculiar kind to insure success. They are not, it is true, so great an effort on the whole, nor do they perhaps require powers of so great an order as the novel; - they do not admit of the same complete development of character - the same fulness and variety of description, nor in general of that large mixture of dialogue, which gives to modern novels such a dramatic air. They require, however, greater vivacity of narration, and more point and polish of style; a little occasional tediousness is not so readily forgiven, and some negligence and heaviness of manner, is not so easily overlooked. To construct the plot of a tale, is perhaps a matter of as much invention and difficulty, as to construct that of a novel, - the chief difference lies in the execution. One is the miniature, the other the full-length picture; it is the former, therefore, which requires the highest and most delicate finish. Accordingly, we shall find that the successful instances of this sort of writing in all languages, have been at the same time examples of the most perfect and graceful composition. The stories of Boccacio are the model of Italian prose; the gay and sprightly tales of the French, of which the *Nouvelles* of Florian, are a good sample, are among the most engaging and skilful productions of their literature; and the best specimens of this sort of writing to be found in the English language, among which are those of Mackenzie and Irving, are as much distinguished by the beauty of their composition, as for their other delightful qualities. In short, these things must be exceedingly well done, or they perish with the other trifles of the day; and we recommend to such of our countrymen as are disposed to adventure in this apparently easy, but really difficult walk of our literature, in the first place not to be sparing of the necessary intellectual effort, and in the second place, instead of copying the novel writers, to take for their model the successful examples of that kind of composition, in which they propose to try their powers.

17. *NATHANIEL HAWTHORNE* ——— 1834

aus "The Story Teller, No. I", *The New England Magazine* (Nov., 1834), dem Beginn einer zyklischen Rahmenerzählung. - Abgedruckt unter dem Titel "Passages from a Relinquished Work" in *The Works of Nathaniel Hawthorne*, Standard Library Edition, hrsg. von G. P. Lathrop (Boston & New York, 1891), II, 455-475.

I do not over-estimate my notoriety when I take it for granted that many of my readers must have heard of me in the wild way of life which I adopted. The idea of becoming a wandering story teller had been suggested, a year or two before, by an encounter with several merry vagabonds in a showman's wagon, where they and I had sheltered ourselves during a summer shower. The project was not more extravagant than most which a young man forms. Stranger ones are executed every day; and, not to mention my prototypes in the East, and the wandering orators and poets whom my own ears have heard, I had the example of one illustrious itinerant in the other hemisphere, - of Goldsmith, who planned and performed his travels through France and Italy on a less promising scheme than mine. I took credit to myself for various qualifications, mental and personal, suited to the undertaking. Besides, my mind had latterly tormented me for employment, keeping up an irregular activity even in sleep, and making me conscious that I must toil, if it were but in catching butterflies. But my chief motives were, discontent with home and a bitter grudge against Parson Thumpcushion, who would rather have laid me in my father's tomb than seen me either a novelist or an actor, two characters which I thus hit upon a method of uniting. After all it was not half so foolish as if I had written romances instead of reciting them.

The following pages will contain a picture of my vagrant life, intermixed with specimens, generally brief and slight, of that great mass of fiction to which I gave existence, and which has vanished like cloud shapes. Besides the occasions when I sought a pecuniary reward, I was accustomed to exercise my narrative faculty wherever chance had collected a little audience idle enough to listen. These rehearsals were useful in testing the strong points of my stories; and, indeed, the flow of fancy soon came upon me so abundantly that its indulgence was its own reward, though the hope of praise also became a powerful incitement. Since I shall never feel the warm gush of new thought as I did then, let me beseech the reader to believe that my tales were not always so cold as he may find them now. With each specimen will be given a sketch of the circumstances in which the story was told. Thus my airdrawn pictures will be set in frames perhaps more valuable than the pictures themselves, since they will be embossed with groups of characteristic figures, amid the lake and mountain scenery, the villages and fertile fields, of our native land. ...

Hitherto I had immensely underrated the difficulties of my idle trade; now I recognized that it demanded nothing short of my whole powers, cultivated to the utmost, and exerted with the same prodigality as if I were speaking for a great party or for the nation at large on the floor of the Capitol. No talent or attainment could come amiss; everything, indeed, was requisite - wide observation, varied knowledge, deep thoughts, and sparkling ones; pathos and levity, and a mixture of both, like sunshine in a raindrop; lofty imagination, veiling itself in the garb of common life; and the practised art which alone could render these gifts, and more than these, available. Not that I ever hoped to be thus qualified. But my despair was no ignoble one, for knowing the impossibility of satisfying myself, even should the world be satisfied, I did my best to overcome it; investigated the causes of every defect; and strove, with patient stubbornness, to remove them in the next attempt. It is one of my few sources of pride, that, ridiculous as the object was, I followed it up with the firmness and energy of a man.

I manufactured a great variety of plots and skeletons of tales, and kept them ready for use, leaving the filling up to the inspiration of the moment; though I cannot remember ever to have told a tale which did not vary considerably from my preconceived idea, and acquire a novelty of aspect as often as I repeated it. Oddly enough, my success was generally in proportion to the difference between the conception and accomplishment. I provided two or more commencements and catastrophes to many of the tales, - a happy expedient, suggested by the double sets of sleeves and trimmings which diversified the suits in Sir Piercy Shafton's wardrobe. But my best efforts had a unity, a wholeness, and a separate character that did not admit of this sort of mechanism.

18. *JOHN NEAL* ——— 1835

aus "Story-Telling", *The New-England Magazine* (Jan., 1835). - Hier zitiert nach "Critical Essays and Stories by John Neal" hrsg. ... von Hans-Joachim Lang, *Jahrbuch für Amerikastudien*, VII (1962), 210-219.

What a difference between *story-telling* and *story-tellers*! ... Story-tellers are avoided - story-telling cultivated: the one as a nuisance - the other as an accomplishment; the former looked upon by the wise and thoughtful as no better than they should be, and all companionship with them as rather disreputable at the best; even children having it for a byword and a reproach, and saying of their bitterest foe, under the fiercest exasperation, that he is a *story-teller,* as the shortest possible way of insinuating that he is not to be associated with; while the latter - *story-telling* would appear to be the great business of life with a majority of mankind, the chief purpose of language almost everywhere, and the sole employment of multitudes who are perpetually breaking away from the dead level of their age - warring with the spirit of the Past, and storming the cloudy battlements of the Future ...

Whole races are addicted to story-telling. The very language of the East, that other world, out of whose glorious fragments and august ruins, our world has been slowly and gradually and most laboriously put together - what is it but a series of profound apothegms and significant allusions, each a story of itself and heavy with the fine gold of ancient wisdom, and bright with the half-smothered sunshine of Past Experience? ...

Story-telling, indeed! Why, there is hardly a distinguished man alive who does not owe the chief part of his reputation to story-telling - story-telling by himself or another, in person or by proxy. ...

And what should we know of Caesar but for his commentaries? or of Napoleon but for his? - of Miltiades and Themistocles, and Pyrrhus, and Epaminondas, with half a thousand more of these Gods and godlike men, but for that prince of story-tellers after Munchausen, captain Trollop and Pilpay, - Plutarch? What are the fables of Aesop, the traditions of the priesthood among every people, their tropes and metaphors, the parables, the maxims, the inscriptions and the allegories, the very alphabets indeed, of all nations, kindreds, and tongues, but so many different kinds of story-telling?

What is there at the very foundation of all which the upward-striving have most yearned after and battled for - they 'of the purple robe and diadem of gold', Warriors and Legislators, Philosophers and Statesmen, Orators and Poets, from the beginning of the world up to this day? What is the very ground-work of all history? What are the materials of biography, the very ore of poetry? What the imperishable, the inextinguishable elements of renown? - *Story-telling*. ...

[W]hat are the very arts and sciences and the most devoted followers thereof? All painters and sculptors, and poets and players, dancers and architects and musicians? Nothing but *story-tellers*. ... Go to the merchant, the lawyer, the politician, the day-laborer, even to the preacher of the gospel, who persuades himself, and would, if it were possible, persuade others that he is the ambassador of the Most High, and that he understands the awful nature of his relationship - and what find you after all but so many different story-tellers, each employed in a way of his own to effect a purpose of his own - and that a purpose moreover, nine times out of ten, that nobody need be ashamed of. ...

But then, though all men are story-tellers, and the greatest, by profession, what a difference in the same story told by different persons. With the glorious few, a story is never old - it may be repeated forever. With the many, it is never new - nobody listens to it with patience even for the first time. There are those, and among the most indefatigable and pertinacious story-tellers you ever meet with, who spoil everything they touch. You have the very words of the original, perhaps the very tone, with all the facts and embellishments, and yet you are tired to death; or you may have a trustworthy, minute and most particular copy of another's manner - a running accompaniment of oaths and laughter - and still you are tired to death, fretted and sore and exasperated. ...

But then there are others among story-tellers with such a knack at the business, that if you should help them to one of the oldest and commonest Joe Millers that ever underwent a regular series of newspaper transmutations, and they happen to take a fancy to it, why, lord you! you wouldn't know it again! They have but to strip off its rags, give it a good scouring with brickdust and soap-suds, and there's an end of all previous ownership. I have known a story repeated over and over again to the very face of the original author, and that too in the presence of others quite as familiar with it as he was, and nobody knew it. Nay more, I have known a little stray story, after it had been licked into shape over sea, reproduced here in the very neighborhood of its own father - who had to pay a dollar a night along with some ten or fifteen hundred more to have it repeated. There's our friend Jarvis now, the portrait painter by trade, the story-teller and humorist by profession. ... Did you ever hear his Kilkenny Cats? - You know the story - one of the oldest and most undoubted *Joes* - the whole pith whereof consists in their fighting till they had eaten one another up, or till there was nothing left but the tips of their tails, I forget which. Well, Jarvis would tell you that story, old as it is and foolish as it is, so that you wouldn't forget it to your dying day. I have known him to repeat it to the very same persons, in the very same way, year after year; and yet every man of them would go fifty miles to hear it again. ...

But people differ. They do indeed, strange as it may appear. With most, nothing but a new story will do. For others, a story cannot be too old - the older the better. If it smack of the pyramids, of the hoar of ages (or of Babylon) they could listen forever. Now, as for me, I care nothing about the age of a story - old or new, if it's a whapper, that's all I care for. With some stories, everything depends upon *how* they are told - the stories of Shakespeare for example. In such a case, if the *manner* is good, though not altogether new we are apt to be satisfied with our pennyworth, for the sake of the *matter*.

But of all the stories I meet with, none are so delightful to me as those I *over*-hear on board a steamboat or a stage-coach. Ten to one there's a decided character in them, whether true or false; and fifty to one you are a fool if you cannot see at a glance how much to believe. I remember two or three cases in point. I happened to be one of a hundred who were huddled together not long ago on board a large Ohio steamboat. The cholera had appeared and was raging far and wide along shore; the captain was running a race with another boat; and we were all getting ready for a blow-up. ...

On my way to my state room, I had to pass a group of female passengers in earnest conversation. Cholera was the subject, and I stopped and listened, and listened, till I had forgotten my errand below and scarcely thought of the danger about us. The stories were evidently true - they were a part of the actual history and experience of the narrators. Many of them were exceedingly affecting, and some terrible, so much so that I could not sleep afterwards for thinking of them. But what astonished me more than every thing else was the strange apathy - the absolute carelessness - the every day sort of manner that distinguished all the sufferers in relating their experience. Many were yet pale - very pale with watching and bereavement, or it might be from long and solitary illness, but none with fear. They spoke of Death and of his terrors with a frightful child-like familiarity. Many stories were told that I shall never forget, and all with the straightforward simplicity of truth. ...

One other brief specimen of 'stories from real life,' such as you may hear day after day on board the stage coaches and steam boats of our country - *live* stories, I should call them - and I have done. Where do you find an old traveler, especially from the Western country, who has not had many a narrow escape worth publishing? - And in his own language too if he would but tell the truth? You have but to step on board a steamboat or a stagecoach, to enter a bar-room or a barber's shop, especially as I have said before in the Western country, that wilderness of Empires, where human life, like every thing else of a home growth is thought nothing of - dog cheap in the estimation of the people themselves, and no great bargain at that in the estimation of others - and what a world of adventure, of trial, hardship and suffering is opened to your view! Books might be made of the stories you would hear in a single evening, and capital books too, I assure you; brimful of energy and vivacity and truth; and always told with a straightforwardness and simplicity which are irresistibly impressive. ...

[They] are things of daily occurrence in the great western country - that store house of kingdoms - and tough stories.

19. *EDGAR ALLAN POE* —— 1836

aus "[Review of:] Watkins, and Other Sketches ... By Boz..." in *The Complete Works of Edgar Allan Poe*, hrsg. von James A. Harrison, Virginia Edition (New York, 1902), IX, 45-48. - Ursprünglich erschienen in *The Southern Literary Messenger* (June, 1836).

We cannot bring ourselves to believe that less actual ability is required in the composition of a really good "brief article," than in a fashionable novel of the usual dimensions. The novel certainly requires what is denominated a sustained effort - but this is a matter of mere perseverance, and has but a collateral relation to talent. On the other hand - unity of effect, a quality not easily appreciated or indeed comprehended by an ordinary mind, and a *desideratum* difficult of attainment even by those who can conceive it - is indispensable in the "brief article," and not so in the common novel. The latter, if admired at all, is admired for its detached passages, without reference to the work as a whole - or without reference to any general design - which, if it even exist in some measure, will be found to have occupied but little of the writer's attention, and cannot, from the length of the narrative, be taken in at one view, by the reader.

20. *EDGAR ALLAN POE* —— 1841

aus "[Review of:] *Night and Morning: a Novel*. [By Bulver] ..." in *The Complete Works of Edgar Allan Poe*, hrsg. von James A. Harrison, Virginia Edition (New York, 1902), X, 114-133. - Ursprünglich erschienen in *Graham's Magazine* (April, 1841).

The word *plot*, as commonly accepted, conveys but an indefinite meaning. Most persons think of it as a simple *complexity*; and into this error even so fine a critic as Augustus William Schlegel has obviously fallen, when he confounds its idea with that of the mere *intrigue* in which the Spanish dramas of Cervantes and Calderon abound. But the greatest involution of incident will not result in plot; which, properly defined, is *that in which no part can be displaced without ruin to the whole*. It may be described as a building so dependently constructed, that to change the position of a single brick is to overthrow the entire fabric. In this definition and description, we of course refer only to that infinite perfection which the true artist bears ever in mind - that unattainable goal to which his eyes are always directed, but of the possibility of attaining which he still endeavours, if wise, to cheat himself into the belief. The reading world, however, is satisfied with a less rigid construction of the term. It is content to think that plot a good one, in which none of the *leading* incidents can be *removed* without *detriment* to the mass. ...

We have defined the word *plot* in a definition of our own to be sure, but in one which we do not the less consider substantially correct; ...

The interest of plot, referring, as it does, to cultivated thought in the reader, and appealing to considerations analogous with those which are the essence of sculptural taste, is by no means a popular interest; although it has the peculiarity of being appreciated in its atoms by all, while in its totality of beauty it is comprehended but by the few. ...

In the wire-drawn romances which have been so long fashionable (God only knows how or why) the pleasure we derive (if any) is a composite one, and made up of the respective sums of the various pleasurable sentiments experienced in perusal. Without excessive and fatiguing exertion, inconsistent with legitimate interest, the mind cannot comprehend at one time and in one survey the numerous individual items which go to establish the whole. Thus the high ideal sense of the *unique* is sure to be wanting; for, however absolute in itself be the unity of the novel, it must inevitably fail of appreciation. We speak now of that species of unity which is alone worth the attention of the critic - the unity or totality of *effect*.

But we could never bring ourselves to attach any idea of merit to mere *length* in the abstract. A long story does not appear to us necessarily twice as good as one only half so long. ... Now if [an] author ... *will* persist in writing long romances because long romances have been written before, - if, in short, he cannot be satisfied with the brief tale (a species of composition which admits of the highest development of artistical power in alliance with the wildest vigour of imagination), - he must then content himself, perforce, with a more simply and more rigidly narrative form.

aus "[Second Review of:] Twice-Told Tales. By Nathaniel Hawthorne ..." in *The Complete Works of Edgar Allan Poe,* hrsg. von James A. Harrison, Virginia Edition (New York, 1902), XI, 104-113. - Ursprünglich erschienen in *Graham's Magazine* (May, 1842); in einer veränderten Fassung noch einmal veröffentlicht in *Godey's Magazine and Lady's Book* (Nov., 1847).

The book [i.e. Hawthorne's *Twice-Told Tales*] professes to be a collection of *tales* ... These pieces ... are by no means *all* tales, either in the ordinary or in the legitimate understanding of the term. Many of them are pure essays ...

They are each and all beautiful, without being characterised by the polish and adaptation so visible in the tales proper. A painter would at once note their leading or predominant feature, and style it *repose*. There is no attempt at effect. All is quiet, thoughtful, subdued. Yet this repose may exist simultaneously with high originality of thought; and Mr. Hawthorne has demonstrated the fact. At every turn we meet with novel combinations; yet these combinations never surpass the limits of the quiet. We are soothed as we read; and withal is a calm astonishment that ideas so apparently obvious have never occurred or been presented to us before. Herein our author differs materially from Lamb or Hunt or Hazlitt - who, with vivid originality of manner and expression, have less of the true novelty of thought than is generally supposed, and whose originality, at best, has an uneasy and meretricious quaintness, replete with startling effects unfounded in nature, and inducing trains of reflection which lead to no satisfactory result. ... The Spectator, Mr. Irving, and Mr. Hawthorne have in common that tranquil and subdued manner which we have chosen to denominate *repose*; but, in the case of the two former, this repose is attained rather by the absence of novel combination, or of originality, than otherwise, and consists chiefly in the calm, quiet, unostentatious expression of commonplace thoughts ... In the essays before us the absence of effort is too obvious to be mistaken, and a strong under-current of *suggestion* runs continuously beneath the upper stream of the tranquil thesis. In short, these effusions of Mr. Hawthorne are the product of a truly imaginative intellect,...

But it is of his tales that we desire principally to speak. The tale proper, in our opinion, affords unquestionably the fairest field for the exercise of the loftiest talent, which can be afforded by the wide domains of mere prose. Were we bidden to say how the highest genius could be most advantageously employed for the best display of its own powers, we should answer, without hesitation - in the composition of a rhymed poem, not to exceed in length what might be perused in an hour. Within this limit alone can the highest order of true poetry exist. We need only here say, upon this topic, that, in almost all classes of composition, the unity of effect or impression is a point of the greatest importance. It is clear, moreover, that this unity cannot be thoroughly preserved in productions whose perusal cannot be completed at one sitting. We may continue the reading of a prose composition, from the very nature of prose itself, much longer than we can persevere, to any good purpose, in the perusal of a poem. This latter, if truly fulfilling the demands of the poetic sentiment, induces an exaltation of the soul which cannot be long sustained. All high excitements are necessarily transient. Thus a long poem is a paradox. And, without unity of impression, the deepest effects cannot be brought about. Epics were the offspring of an imperfect sense of Art, and their reign is no more. A poem *too* brief may produce a vivid, but never an intense or enduring impression. Without a certain continuity of effort - without a certain duration or repetition of purpose - the soul is never deeply moved. ... Extreme brevity will degenerate into epigrammatism; but the sin of extreme length is even more unpardonable. *In medio tutissimus ibis.*

Were we called upon, however, to designate that class of composition which, next to such a poem as we have suggested, should best fulfil the demands of high genius - should offer it the most advantageous field of exertion - we should unhesitatingly speak of the prose tale, as Mr. Hawthorne has here exemplified it. We allude to the short prose narrative, requiring from a half-hour to one or two hours in its perusal. The ordinary novel is objectionable, from its length, for reasons already stated in substance. As it cannot be read at one sitting, it deprives itself, of course, of the immense force derivable from *totality*. Worldly interests intervening during the pauses of perusal, modify, annul, or counteract, in a greater or less degree, the impressions of the book. But simple cessation in reading, would, of itself, be sufficient to destroy the true unity. In the brief tale, however, the author is enabled to carry out the fulness of his intention, be it what it may. During the hour of perusal the soul of the reader is at the writer's control. There are no external or extrinsic influences - resulting from weariness or interruption.

A skilful literary artist has constructed a tale. If wise, he has not fashioned his thoughts to accomodate his incidents; but having conceived, with deliberate care, a certain unique or single *effect* to be wrought out, he then invents such incidents - he then combines such events as may best aid him in establishing this preconceived effect. If his very initial sentence tend not to the outbringing of this effect, then he has failed in his first step. In the whole composition there should be no word written, of which the tendency, direct or indirect, is not to the one pre-established design. And by such means, with such care and skill, a picture is at length painted which leaves in the mind of him who contemplates it with a kindred art, a sense of the fullest satisfaction. The idea of the tale has been presented unblemished, because undisturbed; and this is an end unattainable by the novel. Undue brevity is just as exceptionable here as in the poem; but undue length is yet more to be avoided.

We have said that the tale has a point of superiority even over the poem. In fact, while the *rhythm* of this latter is an essential aid in the development of the poet's highest idea - the idea of the Beautiful - the artificialities of this rhythm are an inseparable bar to the development of all points of thought or expression which have their basis in *Truth*. But Truth is often, and in very great degree, the aim of the tale. Some of the finest tales are tales of ratiocination. Thus the field of this species of composition, if not in so elevated a region on the mountain of Mind, is a table-land of far vaster extent than the domain of the mere poem. Its products are never so rich, but infinitely more numerous, and more appreciable by the mass of mankind. The writer of the prose tale, in short, may bring to his theme a vast variety of modes or inflections of thought and expression - (the ratiocinative, for example, the sarcastic, or the humorous) which are not only antagonistical to the nature of the poem, but absolutely forbidden by one of its most peculiar and indispensable adjuncts; we allude, of course, to rhythm. It may be added here, *par parenthèse*, that the author who aims at the purely beautiful in a prose tale is laboring at great disadvantage. For Beauty can be better treated in the poem. Not so with terror, or passion, or horror, or a multitude of such other points. And here it will be seen how full of prejudice are the usual animadversions against those *tales of effect*, many fine examples of which were found in the earlier numbers of Blackwood. The impressions produced were wrought in a legitimate sphere of action, and constituted a legitimate although sometimes an exaggerated interest. ...

We have very few American tales of real merit - we may say, indeed, none, with the exception of "The Tales of a Traveller" of Washington Irving, and these "Twice-Told Tales"of Mr. Hawthorne.

22. *EDGAR ALLAN POE* 1846

aus "The Philosophy of Composition" in *The Complete Works of Edgar Allan Poe,* hrsg. von James A. Harrison, Virginia Edition (New York, 1902), XIV, 193-208. - Ursprünglich erschienen in *Graham's Magazine* (April, 1846).

Nothing is more clear than that every plot, worth the name, must be elaborated to its *dénouement* before anything be attempted with the pen. It is only with the *dénouement* constantly in view that we can give a plot its indispensable air of consequence, or causation, by making the incidents, and especially the tone at all points, tend to the development of the intention.

There is a radical error, I think, in the usual mode of constructing a story. Either history affords a thesis - or one is suggested by an incident of the day - or, at best, the author sets himself to work in the combination of striking events to form merely the basis of his narrative - designing, generally, to fill in with description, dialogue, or autorial comment, whatever crevices of fact, or action, may, from page to page, render themselves apparent.

I prefer commencing with the consideration of an *effect*. Keeping originality *always* in view - for he is false to himself who ventures to dispense with so obvious and so easily attainable a source of interest - I say to myself, in the first place, "Of the innumerable effects, or impressions, of which the heart, the intellect, or (more generally) the soul is susceptible, what one shall I, on the present occasion, select?" Having chosen a novel, first, and secondly a vivid effect, I consider whether it can be best wrought by incident or tone - whether by ordinary incidents and peculiar tone, or the converse, or by peculiarity both of incident and tone - afterward looking about me (or rather within) for such combinations of event, or tone, as shall best aid me in the construction of the effect.

23. *JAMES RUSSELL LOWELL* 1849

aus "Art. IX - [Review of:] *Kavanagh, a Tale*. By Henry Wadsworth Longfellow. Boston... 1849. ...", *North American Review,* LXIX (1849), 196-215.

The first question to be asked is, what was the author's intention? Then, how has he fulfilled it? "Kavanagh," one may say pretty confidently, is *not* a novel, nor a romance, nor a drama. ...

The word "Tale," upon the title-page, if it be not merely a formal suffix, like the "*Esq.*" in the address of all American letters, we consider a misnomer. We think a truer name for the book would be, a prose pastoral. It had been better to have called it "Kavanagh" simply, and left it to the reader to find out what it was. And it is not as reader, but as critic, that we make the complaint. For, if we look at it critically as assuming this specific character, we find it wanting in many particulars. Where the chief concern is completeness of narrative effect, there should be no loose ends. Every divergent thread and fibre must be taken up and twisted firmly into the compact strand of the leading design. If we hold "Kavanagh" strictly to its responsibilities as a "Tale," we shall be obliged to condemn in it a disproportion of parts to the whole, and an elaboration of particulars at the expense of unity. ...

We will now look at it in what we consider its truer character of pastoral. In this kind of composition, repose is the leading characteristic. A tender pensiveness of tone best fulfils here the requisites of art. It allows of humor and pathos, only both must be subdued, and neither grief nor merriment must be allowed so noisy a vent as would jar upon the ear soothed by a certain out-of-doors quiet and contentment. It is a story told to us, as it were, while we lie under a tree, and the ear is willing at the same time to take in other sounds. The gurgle of the brook, the rustle of the leaves, even noises of life and toil (if they be distant,) such as the rattle of the white-topped wagon and the regular pulse of the thresher's flail, reconcile themselves to the main theme, and reinforce it with a harmonious accompaniment. ... We were going to object to the episode of Sally Manchester, as having no necessary connection with the rest of the story, and as not tending in any way to advance the plot. But we remember that the design here does not make the several parts subservient to the main incident. This is not so much a narrative as a succession of scenes.

24. [ANONYMUS] —————————————————— 1856

aus "The Art of Story-Telling", *Fraser's Magazine*, LIII (June, 1856), 722-732.

That a story must be constructed upon a plan of some kind is plain without any help from the critics, who very often spoil more enjoyment than they promote, by setting up regulations where there is no need for them. It is obvious enough, for example, that a story should begin at the beginning, unless there is some peculiar reason for beginning at the end. In this respect it resembles a house, which is usually built up from the foundations, architects generally finding it inconvenient to build down from the roof. It should not be very long, because the essential attribute which distinguishes a story from other modes of fiction is its brevity. It should not aim at grand effects, because grand effects must inevitably become ridiculous on a small scale. It should have nothing superfluous, for the best of all possible reasons, that it cannot afford space for superfluities. It should not make a severe strain upon the mental faculties, because people are not supposed to take it up for study, but for recreation. It should not put forward any show of pedantry, or make excursions into far-off regions of knowledge, because such impediments to the flow of the narrative interrupt the pleasure of the reader, and have much the same sort of effect upon him as would be produced upon a voluptuary by finding every now and then a fragment of cork in his wine. These conditions are exacted involuntarily by all people who indulge in the luxury of reading stories; and any considerable deviation from them is quite certain to diminish the zest of the entertainment, although it is not given to everybody to penetrate the cause. The multitude have a keen relish for what is good in its kind; and it is dangerous to trust too much in their lack of critical discernment. If they cannot always tell you why they dislike a thing, their dislike is not the less stubborn on that account. Indeed, it generally happens that when people are most at a loss to assign reasons for their faith, they are most obstinate in its defence. The Dr. Fell argument is the last that yields to the assaults of logic.

It must not be supposed that in indicating these general conditions as being necessary to be observed in the structure of a story, we invest them with the attributes of absolute laws, from which there is no appeal. They should rather be considered as elementary principles, elastic in their application to all varieties of stories. A story is so pleasant a literary pastime, that it would be disagreeable to contemplate it under any kind of fetters or restrictions. But as even most delectable pleasures must be regulated by some checks, and some forethought of the fitness of means to ends, or they will inevitably run to waste - so a story, to produce its legitimate effect, must be carefully contrived with a due regard to unity of conception, proportion of parts, and suitableness of treatment and materials. We are charmed in a fine picture by the arrangement of light and colour, the distribution of prominent objects, the management of the perspective, and, to speak technically, the composition of the whole. Such results are not to be attained without keeping constantly in view those difficult canons of art which make all great works appear easy and simple to the uninitiated. It is much the same with that very rare production - a good story. The art may be invisible; but it is there, nevertheless. We see only the lighted stage, with its columns, and gardens, and lakes; but the ropes, pulleys, and shaded lamps, and grooves and rollers, are all the time doing duty out of sight.

Of all countries in the world, England ought to be the country in which stories should enjoy the widest range of popularity. In no other country is time of so much value. ...

This should be the country for stories which condense into a few pages the essence of volumes; which realize in fiction the great economical maxim, by packing the largest quantity into the smallest space; and which, as pabulum for minds in a great hurry, that must travel light, and cannot afford to carry much provision with them, may be compared to the pemmican supplied to Arctic voyagers, a single grain of which is equal to many pounds' weight of bread and meat. Yet, inconsistent as it may appear with our wants and habits, there is no country in which stories are held in such low estimation. The French and Germans, who have plenty of leisure, and hardly ever seem to be doing anything but amusing themselves, possess a literature of fiction which consists almost exclusively of short stories. The English, on the contrary, who can scarcely be said to have any leisure at all, will have nothing to do with a story unless it is in three volumes. ...

The circulating librarian alleges that the public will not read short stories; that nothing short of a 'regular' novel will satisfy them; and that when stories are collected into three volumes, with a single title, to make them look like a novel, - 'Lights and Shadows,' for example, or 'Aspects of Life,' or any other generic appellation that might include an indefinite variety of species, - the said public consider themselves 'taken in,' and send back all such books with indignant remonstrances. We believe this is quite true. The English have an instinctive repugnance to kickshaws; they like solid pudding. A story is no better than a fritter. They must have roast beef. But there is probably action and reaction in this matter, and there may be some doubt as to the extent to which the circulating people have themselves encouraged this craving after heavy dishes. The cook, in a greater or lesser degree, guides the culinary taste of the age. The lender-out of books has the control of the intellectual banquet. He is not only the purveyor, but the critic and adviser. He is constantly consulted upon the merits of books, the popularity of their authors, and the current opinions of readers. He can recommend or suppress any book he pleases. ...

The earliest stories of which we have any knowledge came from the East. We see plainly enough that a great, busy, hard-working, heavily-taxed, commercial western community takes no delight in them; and that occupation, instead of encouraging their production, has exactly the contrary effect. The same result has followed in other places. Wherever industry has advanced, drawing the population out of their old quiet ways, the zest in this kind of literature has gradually diminished. The delicate nurture of former times ceases to satisfy the appetite, and a more robust diet and stronger stimulants become necessary. The profession of the *raconteur* requires a people comparatively idle, luxurious in the negation of mental and physical labour, not very highly educated in art or science, and therefore easily astonished by the wonders of 'natural magic,' credulous, superstitious, and imaginative. These conditions are incompatible with the steam-engine and the electric telegraph. It would be impossible to preserve such elements of simplicity, such a happy faith in the marvellous, or such motionless indulgence, amongst a people into whose ears the remotest corners of civilization are perpetually whispering along the wires that clasp the world. ...

The slow novel suits us better than the rapid tale. It is more like our actual daily experience. There is more room in it to adjust the scale of proprieties, and balance accounts between nature and convention. Its imposing weight gives importance to the shallow and trivial, and its elaborate dulness is a sort of homage to respectability. If the domestic virtues were never made to appear so insipid, they were never treated with so much deference. The flatness of the characters is an evidence of the success of our repressive system; and the routine of the incidents, seldom disturbed by any daring innovations, is a daguerreotype taken from the surface of our society.

It would be irrational, however, to throw the whole responsibility of our failure as story-writers upon the dense manners of the country. A portion of the responsibility undoubtedly lies at the door of the writers themselves. There is no soil so utterly barren as not to yield some herbage. It may be scanty, or it may be bitter, or it may grow only in isolated patches; but even a bed of sand, in the course of time, will throw up some blades of wild grass. Wherever men are congregated together, there are human passions, hopes, desires. The inner life is much the same everywhere. It is the external life, modified by social, moral, and physical circumstances, that presents the most material differences. The story in which the former is taken as the basis of the interest, and the latter as the vehicle, must make itself felt if it be true to its design. English story-tellers have seldom grasped both. Very rarely have they thought it necessary to give any serious consideration to subject or execution. A plot and a locality seem to suffice for all purposes. But there are other elements quite as essential.

...

An English story that should be as true in its pictures of life, and as rapid and vivid in its treatment, would be as good in its kind as a French story. But we must get rid of our old lazy way of setting about these matters before we can achieve such a consummation. We must shuffle off the traditional descriptions, the oppressive reflections, the sleepy dialogue, the bits of scenery which have nothing to do with the action, and all other extraneous fineries which are inserted only to show off the literary accomplishments of the author; and we must go straight to the vital interest, and keep to it to the end. But the subject is a large one, and if we were to yield to its temptations, would carry us much farther than we originally intended. The few points we have hastily indicated are enough for the present.

25. *WILLIAM GILMORE SIMMS* —————————————————— 1866

aus [Letters to Evert A. Duyckinck, July 11, and Aug. 3, 1866] in *The Letters of William Gilmore Simms*, hrsg. von Mary C. Simms, Alfred Taylor Odell & Duncan Eaves (Columbia, S. C., 1952-1956), IV, 580, 589.

Mr. Church, by the way, spoke of *short* stories, not to be published as serials. I replied that such productions were the most difficult of all to write, as they depended upon incidents which did not depend on *character*, - while the development of character, was the chief source & secret for the discovery & development of incidents. ...

I have recieved communications which cut out a good deal of future work for me, but the writer does not mention the *compensation* - which, as you know, is the important item to the Contributor. He desires sketches of the War & of Warriors. He would also like short stories &c. The obtaining of materials for the one, and the tasking invention for the other, makes these classes of writing more *costly*, to an author, than any other. The latter especially, since, in a short story where no room is allowed you for the development of character, you have to rely chiefly on incident and this tasks invention to the uttermost.

26. [*ANONYMUS*] ——————————————————————————————— 1869

aus "Table Talk", *Appleton's Journal*, I (May 29, 1869), 281 f.

No doubt one of the most agreeable things in literature is a thoroughly good short story. At the same time it is one of the most difficult to obtain. We have few or no trained writers in this branch of composition. Our professional novelists rarely attempt the short story, and, when they do, are far from increasing their reputation thereby. Since the time of Poe there has been no one eminently successful in this branch - no one whose invention or art has been sufficient for great success. A good short story should have one fresh, central incident, two or three well-conceived and sharply-drawn characters, a certain symmetrical unity in construction, a deep significance in the catastrophe or climax - not necessarily a moral, as ordinarily understood, but, as nothing should be purposeless, the short story should illustrate some defect or virtue in human character, or portray some special experience whereby the imagination of the reader may be gratified, his sympathies awakened, or his knowledge of the world increased. It is not easy to fix the limitations to the short story. Its construction is an art, far more so than is generally believed; it has its laws, and bears very nearly the same relation to the novel that the song does to poetry, which always properly possesses one definite idea thrown into a compact, symmetrical form. Writers of short stories cannot hope to attain success unless they make this form of composition a profound study; they must have brevity of expression, conception of character, keen feeling for unity and symmetry in art, and very decided dramatic perceptions. All these qualifications are necessary, but many of them can be acquired by study. There is no reason why we should not have a corps of men and women especially trained in this branch of art, and capable of producing a regular supply of highly-enjoyable novels in miniature.

27. *FREDERICK B. PERKINS* ——————————————————————————— 1877

aus "A Chat By Way of Preface. (To Writers, Rather Than Readers)" in *Devil-Puzzlers, and Other Studies* (New York, 1877), xiii, xv-xix. - Dieses Vorwort trägt das Datum des 4. Juni 1877.

NOTE: The distinction between a "sketch" and a "story," in the magazinish language, is, that the latter should contain some course of action or narrative of events - a *peripeteia*, the learned have sometimes called - the substance of some occurrence or dramatic cycle of occurrences amongst human beings; while "sketch" may be applied to almost any account of persons or things or thoughts which has not that element of movement.

Naturally, I think highly of the art of writing short stories. At any rate, there are not many people who can write good ones. My idea is that a good short story possesses all the merits of a long one, and others of its own besides. A short story, in short, is to a long one what a diamond is to a mountain. Thus thinking, I remember to have been much surprised to learn that there never had been any great sale for the volumes of short stories by EDGAR A. POE, nor for those by NATHANIEL HAWTHORNE. And yet those two writers are the best, in that department, in the English language. The German HOFFMANN is the only writer that I know of, who can be placed above them; and even he, only for the exhaustless flow of his fantastic imaginings; not for power of conception nor for force and finish of execution. ...

The claims of this particular kind of literature to artistic dignity as a class or department, have not been appreciated. POE, whose critical observations are often worth careful consideration - though, indeed, they always require it - said that a poem, to be perfect, must be no longer than may be read at a single sitting, say of an hour. For, he reasoned, the impression produced by a poem, being very emotional, is necessarily transitory and indivisible. You cannot sustain such emotion for a long period. You cannot read in a poem until you reach a high pitch of feeling, then break off and transact an interlude of trade or other hard work, and then come back and finish your high emotion and your poem from the pitch and point where you dropped them, as one might go back to the cupboard and eat the other half of a pie.

This is partly true and partly not. POE begged the question, by assuming that the only poems are those where a single pang of high and passionate emotion is their efficient cause, as it is their object and effect - that is, that lyrics are the only poems. This was natural enough in POE, who was a lyric poet and no other. But there is abundance of poetry that is not intense, and whose soul is not any single impulse. Now the prose tale, or short story, is not the highest order of prose composition, any more than the lyric of poetical; but it is entitled, like the lyric, to a high rank. It compares with other prose compositions as the lyric does with the epic, or narrative, or dramatic poem; as a melody with an opera or a sonata. Like a lyric song or a single melody, a really fine short story (after the grade of POE, HAWTHORNE, or the other masters I have named) is the production of a faculty lofty, unique and rare. It is a thing of power or beauty or fantastic pleasure, as truly and as fully as an oration, a melody, a picture, a statue, an edifice. It is at least, as much as any of them, the visible, appreciable embodiment of the knowledge, wisdom, brightness and love which are in the writer's soul. It is intrinsically as valuable, and as much contains the seeds of usefulness and power, and has the signs and certificates of immortality and fame, as any other thing that is made. Will the pure, antique, tender beauty of the ancient Greek tale of *Cupid and Psyche* ever perish? It has lived seventeen hundred years. It will live as long as there is literature.

28. *BRANDER MATTHEWS* ——— 1885

aus "The Philosophy of the Short-Story" in *Pen and Ink* (London, 1888), 67-94. - Die erste Fassung dieses Essays erschien unter dem Titel "Short Stories" im Juli 1884 in der Londoner *Saturday Review*. Die hier zitierte Fassung - eine Erweiterung des ersten Essays - erschien zum ersten Mal in der Nummer für Oktober 1885 im *Lippincott's Magazine* und wurde in die im Herbst 1888 erschienene erste Auflage der Sammlung *Pen and Ink* aufgenommen. Unter demselben Titel, aber mit einigen neuen Zusätzen und Anmerkungen, erschien dann dieser Essay im Jahre 1901 in Buchform.

Of late, certain of the novelists of Great Britain and the United States have been discussing the principles and the practice of the art of writing stories. ... But, with all its extension, the discussion did not include one important branch of the art of fiction: it did not consider at all the minor art of the Short-story. ... although, of course, their general criticisms of the abstract principles of the art of fiction applied quite as well to the Short-story as to the Novel, yet all their concrete examples were full-length Novels, and the Short-story, as such, received no recognition at all.

The difference between a Novel and a Novelette is one of length only: a Novelette is a brief Novel. But the difference between a Novel and a Short-story is a difference of kind. A true Short-story is something other and something more than a mere story which is short. A true Short-story differs from the Novel chiefly in its essential unity of impression. In a far more exact and precise use of the word, a Short-story has unity as a Novel cannot have it. Often, it may be noted by the way, the Short-story fulfils the three false unities of the French classic drama: it shows one action in one place on one day. A Short-story deals with a single character, a single event, a single emotion, or the series of emotions called forth by a single situation. Poe's paradox that a poem cannot greatly exceed a hundred lines in length under penalty of ceasing to be one poem and breaking into a string of poems, may serve to suggest the precise difference between the Short-story and the Novel. The Short-story is the single effect, complete and self-contained, while the Novel is of necessity broken into a series of episodes. Thus the Short-story has, what the Novel cannot have, the effect of "totality," as Poe called it, the unity of impression. The Short-story is not only not a chapter out of a Novel, or an incident or an episode extracted from a longer tale, but at its best it impresses the reader with the belief that it would be spoiled if it were made larger or if it were incorporated into a more elaborate work. The difference in spirit and in form between the Lyric and the Epic is scarcely greater than the difference between the Short-story and the Novel...

Another great difference between the Short-story and the Novel lies in the fact that the Novel, nowadays at least, must be a love-tale, while the Short-story need not deal with love at all. ...

But other things are required of a writer of Short-stories which are not required of a writer of Novels. The novelist may take his time: he has abundant room to turn about. The writer of Short-stories must be concise, and compression, a vigorous compression, is essential. For him, more than for any one else, the half is more than the whole. Again, the novelist may be commonplace, he may bend his best energies to the photographic reproduction of the actual; if he show us a cross section of real life we are content; but the writer of Short-stories must have originality and ingenuity. If to compression, originality, and ingenuity he add also a touch of fantasy, so much the better. ...

I have written Short-story with a capital S and a hyphen because I wished to emphasize the distinction between the Short-story and the story which is merely short. The Short-story is a high and difficult department of fiction. The story which is short can be written by anybody who can write at all; and it may be good, bad, or indifferent; but at its best it is wholly unlike the Short-story. In 'An Editor's Tales' Trollope has given us excellent specimens of the story which is short; and the stories which make up this book are amusing enough and clever enough, but they are wanting in the individuality and in the completeness of the genuine Short-story. ...they are, for the most part, either merely amplified anecdotes or else incidents which might have been used in a Novel just as well as not. Now, the genuine Short-story abhors the idea of the Novel. It can be conceived neither as part of a Novel nor as elaborated and expanded so as to form a Novel. A good Short-story is no more the synopsis of a Novel than it is an episode from a Novel. A slight Novel, or a Novel cut down, is a Novelette: it is not a Short-story. ...

It may be remarked also that there is a certain likeness between *vers de société* and Short-stories: for one thing, both seem easy to write and are hard. And the typical qualifications of each may apply with almost equal force to the other: *vers de société* should reveal compression, ingenuity, and originality, and Short-stories should have brevity and brilliancy. In no class of writing are neatness of construction and polish of execution more needed than in the writing of *vers de société* and of Short-stories. The writer of Short-stories must have the sense of form, which Mr. Lathrop has called "the highest and last attribute of a creative writer." The construction must be logical, adequate, harmonious. ... An idea logically developed by one possessing the sense of form and the gift of style is what we look for in the Short-story.

But, although the sense of form and the gift of style are essential to the writing of a good Short-story, they are secondary to the idea, to the conception, to the subject. ...the Short-story, far more than the Novel even, demands a subject. The Short-story is nothing if there is no story to tell. ...M. Emile Zola declares that the novelist of the future will not concern himself with the artistic evolution of a plot: he will take *une histoire quelconque,* any kind of a story, and make it serve his purpose, - which is to give elaborate pictures of life in all its most minute details. The acceptance of these theories [Matthews had previously mentioned Henry James's statement that the novel "is, in its broadest definition, a personal impression of life"] is a negation of the Short-story. Important as are form and style, the subject of the Short-story is of more importance yet. What you have to tell is of greater interest than how you tell it. ... As a Short-story need not be a love-story, it is of no consequence at all whether they marry or die; but a Short-story in which nothing happens at all is an absolute impossibility.

Perhaps the difference between a Short-story and a Sketch can best be indicated by saying that, while a Sketch may be still-life, in a Short-story something always happens. A Sketch may be an outline of character, or even a picture of a mood of mind, but in a Short-story there must be something done, there must be an action. Yet the distinction, like that between the Novel and the Romance, is no longer of vital importance. ... The fact is, that the Short-story and the Sketch, the Novel and the Romance, melt and merge one into the other, and no man may mete the boundaries of each, though their extremes lie far apart. With the more complete understanding of the principle of development and evolution in literary art, as in physical nature, we see the futility of a strict and rigid classification into precisely defined genera and species. All that is needful for us to remark now is that the Short-story has limitless possibilities: it may be as realistic as the most prosaic novel, or as fantastic as the most ethereal romance.

As a touch of fantasy, however slight, is a welcome ingredient in a Short-story, and as the American takes more thought of things unseen than the Englishman, we may have here an incomplete explanation of the superiority of the American Short-story over the English. ...

In dramatic composition, the equivalent of the Short-story is the one-act play, be it drama or comedy or comedietta or farce. As the novelists have learned their trade by the writing of Short-stories, so the dramatists might learn their trade, far more difficult as it is and more complicated, by the writing of one-act plays. ...

When we read the roll of American novelists, we see that nearly all of them began as writers of Short-stories. ...

I believe I have suggested the real reason of the superiority of the American Short-stories over the English. It is not only that the eye of patriotism may detect more fantasy, more humor, a finer feeling for art, in these younger United States, but there is a more emphatic and material reason for the American proficiency. There is in the United States a demand for Short-stories which does not exist in Great Britain, or at any rate not in the same degree. The Short-story is of very great importance to the American magazine. But in the British magazine the serial Novel is the one thing of consequence... In England the writer of three-volume Novels is the best paid of literary laborers. ... The result of this temptation is seen in the fact that there is not a single English novelist whose reputation has been materially assisted by the Short-stories he has written. ...

Now, the English short story, as the machine makes it and as we see it in most English magazines, is only a little English Novel, or an incident or episode from an English Novel. It is thus the exact artistic opposite of the American Short-story, of which, as we have seen, the chief characteristics are originality, ingenuity, compression, and, not infrequently, a touch of fantasy. I do not say, of course, that the good and genuine Short-story is not written in England now and then, ... but this is merely an accidental growth, and not a staple of production.

aus "Editor's Study", *Harper's New Monthly Magazine*, LXXIV (Feb., 1887), 482-486. - Der zweite größere Absatz dieses Textes erschien 1891 in *Criticism and Fiction*, seinem literaturkritischen Hauptwerk, das sich auf die Reihe von kritischen Beiträgen stützt, die seit 1886 in dichter Folge in *Harper's New Monthly Magazine* unter dem Titel "Editor's Study" erschienen waren. Siehe *Criticism and Fiction and Other Essays*, hrsg. von Clara Marburg Kirk & Rudolf Kirk (New York, 1959), 63 f.

It is this occasional lavishness in the writers of short stories which gives one question whether a branch of the art of fiction tempting to such profusion ought to be encouraged. The motives which are both great and simple are not so many that the profession can afford to waste them in the narrow limits of a tale or sketch, and we conjure the writer of short stories to make sure that he has not one of these in hand before he casts his plot irrevocably in that miniature mould. We think a little question will usually enable him to decide whether he has hold of a short-story motive or a long-story motive. We believe the two are readily distinguishable, though not so easily definable. The short story should perhaps involve merely an episode, a phase; what is more, and especially what contains the germ of much conditioning or characterization, belongs to the novel.

Commonly, however, the matter will decide itself through the age of the writer. The novelette, like the poem or the romance, may come from youth and the first acquaintance with life, but the novel is of years and experience. There are, of course, exceptions, in which what is or seems a novel is the work of a youthful hand; and if any one were to think that women, by reason of their more restricted lives and necessarily narrower outlook into the world, were more successful with the novelette than the novel, he had better not say it, because it might displease a whole sex, and it might not be true. Better reserve such a thought, we should say, for further meditation in secret. What is certain is that almost all novelists who begin early begin by writing short stories or novelettes, and that some of the most brilliant achievements in that sort have been the work of women. ...

[We] are not sure, ... that the Americans have not brought the short story nearer perfection in the all-round sense than almost any other people, and for reasons very simple and near at hand. It might be argued from the national hurry and impatience that it was a literary form peculiarly adapted to the American temperament, but we suspect that its extraordinary development among us is owing much more to more tangible facts. The success of American magazines, which is nothing less than prodigious, is only commensurate with their excellence. ... This sort of success is not only from the courage to decide what ought to please, but from the knowledge of what does please; and it is probable that, aside from the pictures, it is the short stories which please the readers of our best magazines. The serial novels they must have, of course; but rather more of course they must have short stories, and by operation of the law of supply and demand, the short stories, abundant in quantity and excellent in quality, are forth-coming because they are wanted. By another operation of the same law, which political economists have more recently taken account of, the demand follows the supply, and short stories are sought for because there is a proven ability to furnish them, and people read them willingly because they are usually very good. The art of writing them is now so disciplined and diffused with us that there is no lack either for the magazines or for the newspaper "syndicates" which deal in them almost to the exclusion of the serials.

30. ROBERT LOUIS STEVENSON ——— 1891

aus *Vailima Letters: Being Correspondence Addressed by Robert Louis Stevenson to Sidney Colvin* (London, 1895), I, 146 f. - Der Brief wurde im September 1891 geschrieben. Brander Matthews zitiert aus diesem Brief in seiner *Philosophy of the Short-story* (New York, 1901), 15 f.

I have just interrupted my letter and read through the chapter of the *High Woods* that is written, a chapter and a bit, some sixteen pages, really very fetching, but what do you wish? the story is so wilful, so steep, so silly - it's a hallucination I have outlived, and yet I never did a better piece of work, horrid, and pleasing, and extraordinarily *true*; it's sixteen pages of the South Seas; their essence. What am I to do? Lose this little gem - for I'll be bold, and that's what I think it - or go on with the rest, which I don't believe in, and don't like, and which can never make aught but a silly yarn? Make another end to it? Ah, yes, but that's not the way I write; the whole tale is implied; I never use an effect when I can help it, unless it prepares the effects that are to follow; that's what a story consists in. To make another end, that is to make the beginning all wrong. The dénouement of a long story is nothing; it is just a "full close," which you may approach and accompany as you please - it is a coda, not an essential member in the rhythm; but the body and end of a short story is bone of the bone and blood of the blood of the beginning.

31. *THOMAS WENTWORTH HIGGINSON* —— 1892

aus "The Local Short Story", *The Independent*, XLIV (Nov. 3, 1892), 1544 f.

[In the short story] we have the conditions of perfect art; there is no subdivision of interest; the author can strike directly in, without preface, can move with determined step toward a conclusion, and can - O highest privilege! - stop when he is done. For the most perfect examples of the short story - those of De Maupassant, for instance - the reader feels, if he can pause to think, that they must have been done at a sitting, so complete is the grasp, the single grasp, upon the mind. This completeness secures the end; they need not be sensational, because there is no necessity of keeping up a series of exciting minor incidents; the main incident is enough. Around the very center of motion, as in a whirlwind, there may be a perfect quiet, a quiet which is formidable in its very repose. In de Maupassant's terrific story of Corsican vengeance, "*Una Vendetta*," in which the sole actor is a lonely old woman who trains a fierce dog so that he ultimately kills her enemy, the author simply tells us, at the end, that this quiet fiend of destruction went peacefully home and went to sleep. "*Elle dormit bien, cette nuit-là.*" The cyclone has spent itself, and the silence it has left behind it is more formidable than the cyclone.

32. *MARK TWAIN (S. L. CLEMENS)* —— 1895

aus "How to Tell a Story". - Hier zitiert nach *The Complete Essays of Mark Twain*, hrsg. von Charles Neider (Garden City, N.Y., 1963), 155-160. - Dieser Essay erschien zum ersten Mal im Jahre 1895.

I do not claim that I can tell a story as it ought to be told. I only claim to know how a story ought to be told, for I have been almost daily in the company of the most expert story-tellers for many years.

There are several kinds of stories, but only one difficult kind - the humorous. I will talk mainly about that one. The humorous story is American, the comic story is English, the witty story is French. The humorous story depends for its effect upon the *manner* of the telling; the comic story and the witty story upon the *matter*.

The humorous story may be spun out to great length, and may wander around as much as it pleases, and arrive nowhere in particular; but the comic and witty stories must be brief and end with a point. The humorous story bubbles gently along, the others burst.

The humorous story is strictly a work of art - high and delicate art - and only an artist can tell it; but no art is necessary in telling the comic and the witty story; anybody can do it. The art of telling a humorous story - understand, I mean by word of mouth, not print - was created in America, and has remained at home.

The humorous story is told gravely; the teller does his best to conceal the fact that he even dimly suspects that there is anything funny about it; but the teller of the comic story tells you beforehand that it is one of the funniest things he has ever heard, then tells it with eager delight, and is the first person to laugh when he gets through. And sometimes, if he has had good success, he is so glad and happy that he will repeat the "nub" of it and glance around from face to face, collecting applause, and then repeat it again. It is a pathetic thing to see.

Very often, of course, the rambling and disjointed humorous story finishes with a nub, point, snapper, or whatever you like to call it. Then the listener must be alert, for in many cases the teller will divert attention from that nub by dropping it in a carefully casual and indifferent way, with the pretense that he does not know it is a nub.

Artemus Ward used that trick a good deal; then when the belated audience presently caught the joke he would look up with innocent surprise, as if wondering what they had found to laugh at. Dan Setchell used it before him, Nye and Riley and others use it to-day.

But the teller of the comic story does not slur the nub; he shouts it at you - every time. And when he prints it, in England, France, Germany and Italy, he italicizes it, puts some whooping exclamation-points after it, and sometimes explains it in a parenthesis. All of which is very depressing, and makes one want to renounce joking and lead a better life.

Let me set down an instance of the comic method, using an anecdote which has been popular all over the world for twelve or fifteen hundred years. The teller tells it in this way:

THE WOUNDED SOLDIER.

In the course of a certain battle a soldier whose leg had been shot off appealed to another soldier who was hurrying by to carry him to the rear, informing him at the same time of the loss which he had sustained; whereupon the generous son of Mars, shouldering the unfortunate, proceeded to carry out his desire. The bullets and cannon-balls were flying in all directions, and presently one of the latter took the wounded man's head off - without, however, his deliverer being aware of it. In no long time he was hailed by an officer, who said:

"Where are you going with that carcass?"

"To the rear, sir - he's lost his leg!"

"His leg, forsooth?" responded the astonished officer, "you mean his head, you booby."

Whereupon the soldier dispossessed himself of his burden, and stood looking down upon it in great perplexity. At length he said:

"It is true, sir, just as you have said." Then after a pause he added, "*But he* TOLD *me* IT WAS HIS LEG!!!!!"

Here the narrator bursts into explosion after explosion of thunderous horse-laughter, repeating that nub from time to time through his gaspings and shriekings and suffocatings.

It takes only a minute and a half to tell that in its comic-story form; and isn't worth the telling, after all. Put into the humorous-story form it takes ten minutes, and is about the funniest thing I have ever listened to - as James Whitcomb Riley tells it.

He tells it in the character of a dull-witted old farmer who has just heard it for the first time, thinks it is unspeakably funny, and is trying to repeat it to a neighbor. But he can't remember it; so he gets all mixed up and wanders helplessly round and round, putting in tedious details that don't belong in the tale and only retard it; taking them out conscientiously and putting in others that are just as useless; making minor mistakes now and then and stopping to correct them and explain how he came to make them; remembering things which he forgot to put in in their proper place and going back to put them in there; stopping his narrative a good while in order to try to recall the name of the soldier that was hurt, and finally remembering that the soldier's name was not mentioned, and remarking placidly that the name is of no real importance, anyway - better, of course, if one knew it, but not essential, after all - and so on, and so on, and so on.

The teller is innocent and happy and pleased with himself, and has to stop every little while to hold himself in and keep from laughing outright; and does hold in, but his body quakes in a jelly-like way with interior chuckles; and at the end of the ten minutes the audience have laughed until they are exhausted, and the tears are running down their faces.

The simplicity and innocence and sincerity and unconsciousness of the old farmer are perfectly simulated, and the result is a performance which is thoroughly charming and delicious. This is art - and fine and beautiful, and only a master can compass it; but a machine could tell the other story.

To string incongruities and absurdities together in a wandering and sometimes purposeless way, and seem innocently unaware that they are absurdities, is the basis of the American art, if my position is correct. Another feature is the slurring of the point. A third is the dropping of a studied remark apparently without knowing it, as if one were thinking aloud. The fourth and last is the pause. ...

The pause is an exceedingly important feature in any kind of story, and a frequently recurring feature, too. It is a dainty thing, and delicate, and also uncertain and treacherous; for it must be exactly the right length - no more and no less - or it fails of its purpose and makes trouble. If the pause is too short the impressive point is passed, and the audience have had time to divine that a surprise is intended - and then you can't surprise them, of course.

On the platform I used to tell a negro ghost story that had a pause in front of the snapper on the end, and that pause was the most important thing in the whole story. If I got it the right length precisely, I could spring the finishing ejaculation with effect enough to make some impressible girl deliver a startled little yelp and jump out of her seat - and that was what I was after.

33. *FRANK NORRIS* —— 1896

aus "The Modern Short Story" in *The Literary Criticism of Frank Norris*, hrsg. von Donald Pizer (Austin, Texas, 1964), 48-50. - Ursprünglich erschienen in *Wave* (Dec. 26, 1896).

Originally the short story was but a miniature novel, having all the features of a novel - introduction, plot, complication, development of character and the like - every characteristic in fact but that of length. Balzac introduced this type - the type of the long short story, and it still survives in the present day in the form of the serial of two numbers that appears from time to time in *Harper's* or *Century*, or more especially in the "Novelette" of *Lippincott's*. Among the best examples of this type are Stevenson's "Dr. Jekyll and Mr. Hyde," Amélie Rives' "Quick or the Dead," and Mr. Hope's "Indiscretion of the Duchess." These stories may be read at a single sitting. They are hardly more than condensed novels. The introduction is entirely dispensed with, the action is generally simple, the movement rapid, the range very limited. But the writer, however, still retains the succession of incidents and episodes of the larger forms of fiction, and by means of these evolves a considerable amount of complication. But ever since the introduction of the short story as a form of fiction the tendency has been towards brevity. The short story has been getting shorter and shorter, not so much, I am confident, because of limited time on the part of the reading public as because of limited space on the part of the magazines. ... It has become shorter and shorter from year to year, until from being a shorter form of novel of incidents and episodes, it has been reduced in some cases to the relation of a single incident by itself, concise, pungent, direct as a blow. There have been successful stories written upon an incident so brief that the whole matter can be summed up in a single sentence. For instance, "An English officer's return to his regiment after years of imprisonment in Siberia." ...

It is true, however, that a really good short story is one of the rarest things an editor meets with. But the difficulty lies not so much in the actual writing, in the condensing and suggesting, etc., as it does in the invention or selection - call it what you like - of the original idea, the motive. Consider the nature of the thing required. The author must devise or discover a single scene, a bit, an episode so full of meaning, so dramatic, so tremendously significant that it suggests to the mind of the reader an entire volume of explanatory matter. The reader must not only read between the lines, but between the very words. And all this must be accomplished within the compass of, at the very most, thirty-five hundred words. I say at the very most. Some of Mr. Kipling's strongest effects have been attained by means of two thousand.

The writing of the short story, whether it be the "long" short story or the "short" short story, has developed in many authors a certain amount of trick work that it is very amusing to note. ...

One of the most fetching "tricks" of the short story writer is his handling of the very last paragraph or sentence of his story. By its very position the last sentence of a tale gathers the enormous emphasis it may possess. ... This is trickery of course, but it is very clever trickery, since it discloses the whole purport of the story in a single instant, and the reader receives the accumulated effect of the preceding pages with the suddenness and force of a mild electric shock. ...

What is to be the future of the short story it would be difficult to say. It cannot continue indefinitely to shorten in length. There must inevitably come a time when it will reach its limit, a limit of brevity which if over-passed would bring it into the province of the anecdote.

34. *FRANK NORRIS* — 1897

aus "Fiction is Selection" in *The Literary Criticism of Frank Norris*, hrsg. von Donald Pizer (Austin, Texas, 1964), 50-53. - Ursprünglich erschienen in *Wave* (Sept. 11, 1897).

[The] story writer must go to real life for his story. You can never think out, or invent or imagine a tale that will be half so good as the things that have "really happened." The complications of real life are infinitely better, stronger and more original than anything you can make up. The only difference is in the matter of selection of details. The story writer's position in regards to the life of the world is like that of a maker of mosaics in front of a vast pile of tiny many-colored blocks. He doesn't make the blocks nor color them - the story writer does not invent nor imagine the parts of his story. Writer and mosaicist alike select and combine. The maker of a mosaic has a design in his brain, or, better still, infinitely better, sees in the pile of little colored blocks in front of him a certain little group or tiny heap that, by merest accident, has tumbled into a design of its own. The design is rough, very crude, the blocks do not fit together, and here and there a green or blue or red block jars in the color scheme. But, for all that, there is a suggestion of design there, much more original than any design he could work out. Well, he takes this group of blocks in hand, picks out and throws away the red and blue and the green that jar and fight, trims off the edges of the blocks and makes them fit compactly together;perhaps a gap or two is left. The whole vast heap is at his command. Deftly he goes over it, picking out here and there the blocks that he needs, a circular one here, a triangular one there, now one of a bright vermillion, now one of a sombre grey. Little by little he pieces together that crude and rough design, gets everything to fit, everything to harmonize; possibly he combines the first design with another; possibly these two designs suggest a third still better; so he proceeds.

At last the final design is complete. A little polishing, a very little, for in roughness there is strength and in sharp contrast, vividness; and there you are, a rounded whole, a definite, compact and complete thing, taken out of and isolated from a formless heap and jumble of shape and colors. ...

Some one objects at this point: "What about imagination? What about fancy? What about invention?" There is no such thing as imagination. What we elect to call imagination is mere combination of things not heretofore combined. ... It is only observation, after all. ... Imagination! There is no such thing; you can't imagine anything that you have not already seen and observed.

Like the skilled mosaic maker, any one with an eye accustomed to looking for short stories can run his glance over the heap of things we have elected to call life and here and there see combinations of form and color that are original, telling and worth working up.

35. *AMBROSE BIERCE* ——— 1897

aus "The Short Story" in *The Collected Works of Ambrose Bierce*, X: *The Opinionator* (New York & Washington, 1911), 234-248. - Der Essay ist datiert: 1897.

"The short story is always distinctly a sketch.It can not express what is the one greatest thing in all literature - intercommunion of human characters, their juxtapositions, their contrasts. ... It is not a high form of art, and its present extreme popularity bespeaks decadence far more than advance."

So said Edgar Fawcett, an author of no small note and consequence in his day. ... Fawcett did not write short stories, but exceedingly long ones. So "the intercommunion of human characters," and so forth, stands. Nevertheless, one fairly great thing in all literature is the power to interest the reader. Perhaps the author having the other thing can afford to forego that one, but its presence is observable, somehow, in much of the work that is devoid of that polyonymous element noted by Messrs. Fawcett, Thomas, Richard and Henry. Having that fact in mind, and the added fact that in his own admirable sonnets (for example) the intercommunion is an absent factor, I am disposed to think that Edgar was facetious.

The short story, quoth'a, "is not a high form of art"; and inferably the long story - the novel - is. Let us see about that. As all the arts are essentially one, addressing the same sensibilities, quickening the same emotions and subject to the same law and limitations of human attention, it may be helpful to consider some of the arts other than literary and see what we can educe from the comparison. It will be admitted, I hope, that even in its exterior aspect St. Peter's Church is a work of high art. But is Rome a work of high art? Was it ever, or could it by rebuilding be made such? Certainly not, and the reason is that it can not all take attention at once. We may know that the several parts are coördinated and interrelated, but we do not discern and feel the coördination and interrelation. An opera, or an oratorio, that can be heard at a sitting may be artistic, but if in the manner of a Chinese play it were extended through the evenings of a week or a month what would it be? The only way to get unity of impression from a novel is to shut it up and look at the covers.

Not only is the novel, for the reason given, and for others, a faulty form of art, but because of its faultiness it has no permanent place in literature. In England it flourished less than a century and a half, beginning with Richardson and ending with Thackeray, since whose death no novels, probably, have been written that are worth attention; ... Novels are still produced in suspicious abundance and read with fatal acclaim but the novel of to-day has no art broader and better than that of its individual sentences - the art of style. That would serve if it had style.

Among the other reasons why the novel is both inartistic and impermanent is this - it is mere reporting. True, the reporter creates his plot, incidents and characters, but that itself is a fault, putting the work on a plane distinctly inferior to that of history. Attention is not long engaged by what could, but did not, occur to individuals; and it is a canon of the trade that nothing is to go into the novel that might not have occurred. "Probability" - which is but another name for the commonplace - is its keynote. When that is transgressed, as in the fiction of Scott and the greater fiction of Hugo, the work is romance, another and superior thing, addressed to higher faculties with a more imperious insistence. The singular inability to distinguish between the novel and the romance is one of criticism's capital ineptitudes. It is like that of a naturalist who should make a single species of the squirrels and the larks. Equally with the novel, the short story may drag at each remove a lengthening chain of probability, but there are fewer removes. The short story does not, at least, cloy attention, confuse with overlaid impressions and efface its own effect. ...

The master of this school of literature is Mr. Howells. Destitute of that supreme and almost sufficient literary endowment, imagination, he does, not what he would, but what he can - takes notes with his eyes and ears and "writes them up" as does any other reporter. He can tell nothing but something like what he has seen or heard, and in his personal progress through the rectangular streets and between the trim hedges of Philistia, with the lettered old maids of his acquaintance curtseying from the doorways, he has seen and heard nothing worth telling. ...

As certain editors of newspapers appear to think that a trivial incident has investiture of dignity and importance by being telegraphed across the continent, so these story-writers of the Reporter School hold that what is not interesting in life becomes interesting in letters - the acts, thoughts, feelings of commonplace people, the lives and loves of noodles, nobodies, ignoramuses and millionaires; of the village vulgarian, the rural maiden whose spiritual grace is not incompatible with the habit of falling over her own feet, the somnolent nigger, the clay-eating "Cracker" of the North Carolinian hills, the society person and the inhabitant of south-western Missouri. ...

It is to him of widest knowledge, of deepest feeling, of sharpest observation and insight, that life is most crowded with figures of heroic stature, with spirits of dream, with demons of the pit, with graves that yawn in pathways leading to the light, with existences not of earth, both malign and benign - ministers of grace and ministers of doom. ... In short, he to whom life is not picturesque, enchanting, astonishing, terrible, is denied the gift and faculty divine, and being no poet can write no prose. He can tell nothing because he knows nothing. ...

Probability? Nothing is so improbable as what is true. It is the unexpected that occurs; but that is not saying enough; it is also the unlikely - one might almost say the impossible. ...

Fiction has nothing to say to probability; the capable writer gives it not a moment's attention, except to make what is related *seem* probable in the reading - *seem* true. Suppose he relates the impossible; what then? Why, he has but passed over the line into the realm of romance, the kingdom of Scott, Defoe, Hawthorne, Beckford and the authors of the *Arabian Nights* - the land of the poets, the home of all that is good and lasting in the literature of the imagination.

aus "The Short Story", *The Nineteenth Century*, XLIII (March, 1898), 406-416. - Wiederabdruck in Wedmores Essayband *On Books and Arts* (London, 1899), 1-24. - Brander Matthews verweist - bei Betonung seines Originalitätsanspruchs - auf diesen Essay in seiner *Philosophy of the Short-story* (New York, 1901), 26.

I am presumably invited by the editor of this Review to hold forth on the short story because I am not a popular writer. ... Small as my personal claims might be, were they based only on my books - *Renunciations*, for example, or *Pastorals of France* - I may say my say as one who, with production somewhat scanty, has for twenty years been profoundly interested in the artistic treatment of the Short Story; who believes in the short story, not as a ready means of hitting the big public, but as a medium for the exercise of the finer art - as a medium, moreover, adapted peculiarly to that alert intelligence, on the part of the reader, which rebels sometimes at the *longueurs* of the conventional novel: the old three volumes or the new fat book. ...

In the first place, then, what is, and what is *not*, a short story? Many things a short story may be. It may be an episode, like Miss Ella Hepworth Dixon's or like Miss Bertha Thomas's; a fairy tale, like Miss Evelyn Sharp's; the presentation of a single character with the stage to himself (Mr. George Gissing); a tale of the uncanny (Mr. Rudyard Kipling); a dialogue of comedy (Mr. Pett Ridge); a panorama of selected landscape, a vision of the sordid street, a record of heroism, a remote tradition or an old belief vitalised by its bearing on our lives to-day, an analysis of an obscure calling, a glimpse at a forgotten quarter. A short story - I mean a short imaginative work in the difficult medium of prose; for plot, or story proper, is no essential part of it, though in work like Conan Doyles's or Rudyard Kipling's it may be a very delightful part - a short story may be any one of the things that have been named, or it may be something besides; but one thing it can never be - it can never be 'a novel in a nutshell.' That is a favourite definition, but not a definition that holds. It is a definition for the kind of public that asks for a convenient inexactness, and resents the subtlety which is inseparable from precise truth. Writers and serious readers know that a good short story cannot possibly be a *précis*, a synopsis, a *scenario*, as it were, of a novel. It is a separate thing - as separate, almost, as the Sonnet is from the Epic - it involves the exercise almost of a different art.

That, perhaps, is one reason why it is generally - in spite of temporary vogue as pleasant pastime - a little underrated as an intellectual performance. That is why great novelists succeed in it so seldom - or at all events fail in it sometimes - even great novelists like Mr. Hardy, the stretch of whose canvas has never led him into carelessness of detail. Yet with *him*, even, in his short stories, the inequality is greater than befits the work of such an artist, and greater than is to be accounted for wholly by mood; so that by the side of *The Three Strangers*, or, yet better, that delightful thing, the *Interlopers at the Knap*, you have short tales tossed off with momentary indifference - as you can imagine Sheridan, with his braced language of comedy, stooping once to a charade. And if a *master* nods sometimes - a master like Hardy - does it not almost follow that, by the public at least, the conditions of the short story are not understood, and so, in the estimate of the criticism of the dinner-table, and by the criticism of the academic, the tale is made to suffer by its brevity? But if it is well done, it has done this amazing thing: it has become quintessence; it has eliminated the superfluous; and it has taken *time* to be brief. Then - amongst readers whose judgments are perfunctory - who have not thought the thing out - it is rewarded by being spoken of as an 'agreeable sketch,' 'a promising little effort,' an 'earnest of better things.' ...

I have suggested briefly what the short story may be; we have seen briefly the one thing it *cannot* be - which is, a novel told within restricted space. Let us ask what methods it may adopt - what are some of the varieties of its form.

The Short Story admits of greater variety of form than does the long novel, and the number of these forms will be found to be increasing - and we must not reject conventionally (as we are terribly apt to do) the new form because we are unfamiliar with it. The forms that are open to the novel are open to the short imaginative piece, and, to boot, very many besides. Common to both, of course, is the most customary form of all - that in which the writer narrates as from outside the drama, yet with internal knowledge of it - what is called the 'narrative form,' which includes within its compass, in a single work, narrative proper and a moderate share of dialogue. Common again to both short and long stories, obviously, is a form which, in skilled hands, and used only for those subjects to which it is most appropriate, may give strange reality to the matter presented - the form, I mean, in which the story is told in the first person, as the experience and the sentiment of one character who runs throughout the whole. The short story, though it should use this form very charily, adopts it more conveniently than does the long novel; for the novel has many more characters than the short story, and for the impartial presentation of many characters this form is a fetter. It gives of a large group a prejudiced and a partial view. ...

I devote a few lines to but two or three of the forms which by common consent are for the short story only. One of them is simple dialogue. For our generation, that has had the fascination of an experiment - an experiment made perhaps with best success after all in the candid and brilliant fragments of that genuine humorist, Mr. Pett Ridge. The method in most hands has the appearance of a difficult feat. It *is* one often - and so is walking on the slackwire, and the back-spring in acrobatic dance. Of course a writer must enjoy grappling with difficulties. We understand that. But the more serious artist reflects, after a while, that the unnecessary difficulty is an inartistic encumbrance. 'Why,' he will ask, 'should the story-teller put on himself the fetters of the drama, to be denied the drama's opportunities?' Pure dialogue, we may be sure, is apt to be an inefficient means of telling a story; of presenting a character. There may be cited one great English Classic who has employed the method - the author of *Pericles and Aspasia*, of that little gem of conversation between Henry the Eighth and Anne Boleyn. But then, with Walter Savage Landor, austere and perfect, the character existed already, and there was no story to tell. Pure dialogue, under the conditions of the modern writer, leaves almost necessarily the problem unsolved, the work a fragment. ...

Then, again, possible, though not often desirable for the short story, is the diary form - extracts from a diary, rather. Applied to work on an extensive scale, your result - since you would necessarily lack concentrated theme - your result would be a chronicle, not a story. Applied to the shorter fiction, it must be used charily, and may then, I should suppose, be used well. But I, who used the form in 'The New Marienbad Elegy' in *English Episodes*, what right have I to say that the form, in the hands of a master, allows a subtle presentation of the character of the diarist - allows, in self-revelation, an irony, along with earnestness, a wayward and involved humour, not excluding sympathy? It is a form not easily received, not suffered gladly. It is for the industrious, who read a good thing twice, and for the enlightened, who read it three times. ...

The great way, from Virgil's to Browning's, is the way of pregnant brevity. And where dialogue *is* employed in the finer short story, every line of it is bound to be significant. The short story has no room for the reply that is only *near* to being appropriate, and it deserves no pardon for the word that would not have been certainly employed. It is believed generally, and one can well suppose that it is true, that the average dialogue of the diffuse novel is written quickly. That is in part because so little of it is really dramatic - is really at all the inevitable word. But the limited sentences in which, when the narrator must narrate no more, the persons who have been described in the short story express themselves on their restricted stage, need, if I dare assert it, to be written slowly, or, what is better, re-read a score of times, and pruned, and looked at from without, and surveyed on every side. ...

One of the difficulties of the short story, the short story shares with the acted drama, and that is the indispensableness of compression - the need that every sentence shall tell - the difference being, that in the acted drama it must tell for the moment, it must tell till it is found out, and in the short story it must tell for at least a *modest* eternity, and something more, if that be possible - for if a 'Fortnight is eternity' upon the Stock Exchange, a literary eternity is, perhaps, forty years.

Of course the short story, like all other fiction to be read, does not share the other difficulties of the acted drama - above all, the disadvantage which drags the acted drama down - the disadvantage of appealing to, at all events of having to give sops to, at one and the same moment, gallery and stalls: an audience so incongruous that it lies outside the power of Literature to weld it really together. ...

But again, contrasting his fortunes with those of his brother, the dramatist, the writer of short stories must, even at the best, know himself denied the dramatist's crowning advantage - which is the thrill of actual human presence. ...

Among the better writers, one tendency of the day is to devote a greater care to the art of expression - to an unbroken continuity of excellent and varied style. The short story, much more than the long one, makes this thing possible to men who may not claim to be geniuses, but who, if we are to respect them at all, must claim to be artists. And yet, in face of the indifference of so much of our public here, to anything we can call Style - in face, actually, of a strange insensibility to it - the attempt, wherever made, is a courageous one.

aus "The Story-Teller at Large: Mr. Henry Harland" in *The American Essay of Henry James*, hrsg. von Leon Edel (New York, 1956), 186-193. - Zuerst erschienen in *Fortnightly Review* (April, 1898).

Mr. Harland's method is that of the "short story," which has of late become an object of such almost extravagant dissertation. If it has awaked to consciousness, however, it has doubtless only done what most things are doing in an age of organized talk. It took itself, in the comparatively silent years, less seriously, and there was perhaps a more general feeling that you both wrote and read your short story best when you did so in peace and patience. To turn it out, at any rate, as well as possible, by private, and almost diffident, instinct and reflection, was a part of the general virtue of the individual, the kind of virtue that shunned the high light of the public square. ... It [the short story] is a form delightful and difficult, and with one of these qualities ... the direct reason of the other. It is an easy thing, no doubt, to do a little with, but the interest quickens at a high rate on an approximation to that liberal *more* of which we speedily learn it to be capable. ...

Are there not two quite distinct effects to be produced by this rigor of brevity - the two that best make up for the many left unachieved as requiring a larger canvas? The one with which we are most familiar is that of the detached incident, single and sharp, as clear as a pistol-shot; the other, of rarer performance, is that of the impression, comparatively generalized - simplified, foreshortened, reduced to a particular perspective - of a complexity or a continuity. The former is an adventure comparatively safe, in which you have, for the most part, but to put one foot after the other. It is just the risks of the latter, on the contrary, that make the best of the sport. These are naturally - given the general reduced scale - immense, for nothing is less intelligible than bad foreshortening, which, if it fails to mean everything intended, means less than nothing. It is to Mr. Harland's honor that he always "goes in" for the risks. *The Friend of Man*, for instance, is an attempt as far removed as possible from the snap of the pistol-shot; it is an excellent example of the large in a small dose, the smaller form put on its mettle and trying to do - by sharp selection, composition, presentation and the sacrifice of verbiage - what the longer alone is mostly supposed capable of. It is the picture of a particular figure-eccentric, comic, pathetic, tragic - disengaged from old remembrances, encounters, accidents, exhibitions, and exposures, and resolving these glimpses and patches into the unity of air and feeling that makes up a character. It is all a matter of odds and ends recovered and interpreted. The "story" is nothing, the subject everything, and the manner in which the whole thing becomes expressive strikes me as an excellent specimen of what can be done on the minor scale when art comes in. There are, of course, particular effects that insist on space, and the thing, above all, that the short story has come to renounce is the actual *pursuit* of character. Temperaments and mixtures, the development of a nature, are shown us perforce in a tale, as they are shown us in life, only by illustration more or less copious and frequent; and the drawback is that when the tale is short the figure, before we have had time to catch up with it, gets beyond and away, dips below the horizon made by the little square of space that we have accepted.

38. *BRET HARTE* —— 1899

aus "The Rise of the American Short Story" in *The Achievement of American Criticism,* hrsg. von Clarence Arthur Brown (New York, 1954), 485-490. - Ursprünglich erschienen in *Cornhill Magazine* (July, 1899).

The short story was familiar enough in form in America during the early half of the century; perhaps the proverbial haste of American life was some inducement to its brevity. It had been the medium through which some of the most characteristic work of the best American writers had won the approbation of the public. Poe - a master of the art, as yet unsurpassed - had written; Longfellow and Hawthorne had lent it the graces of the English classics. But it was not the American short story of to-day. It was not characteristic of American life, American habits nor American thought. It was not vital and instinct with the experience and observation of the average American; it made no attempt to follow his reasoning or to understand his peculiar form of expression - which it was apt to consider vulgar; it had no sympathy with those dramatic contrasts and surprises which are the wonders of American civilisation; it took no account of the modifications of environment and of geographical limitations; indeed, it knew little of American geography. Of all that was distinctly American it was evasive - when it was not apologetic. And even when graced by the style of the best masters, it was distinctly provincial. ...

But while the American literary imagination was still under the influence of English tradition, an unexpected factor was developing to diminish its power. It was *Humour* - of a quality as distinct and original as the country and civilisation in which it was developed. It was at first noticeable in the anecdote or 'story,' and, after the fashion of such beginnings, was orally transmitted. It was common in the bar-rooms, the gatherings in the 'country store,' and finally at public meetings in the mouths of 'stump orators.' Arguments were clinched, and political principles illustrated, by 'a funny story.' It invaded even the camp meeting and pulpit. It at last received the currency of the public press. But wherever met it was so distinctly original and novel, so individual and characteristic, that it was at once known and appreciated abroad as 'an American story.' Crude at first, it received a literary polish in the press, but its dominant quality remained. It was concise and condense, yet suggestive. It was delightfully extravagant - or a miracle of understatement. It voiced not only the dialect, but the habits of thought of a people or locality. It gave a new interest to slang. From a paragraph of a dozen lines it grew into a half column, but always retaining its conciseness and felicity of statement. It was a foe to prolixity of any kind, it admitted no fine writing nor affectation of style. It went directly to the point. It was burdened by no conscientiousness; it was often irreverent; it was devoid of all moral responsibility - but it was original! By degrees it developed character with its incident, often, in a few lines, gave a striking photograph of a community or a section, but always reached its conclusion without an unnecessary word. It became - and still exists - as an essential feature of newspaper literature. It was the parent of the American 'short story.' ...

It would seem evident, therefore, that the secret of the American short story was the treatment of characteristic American life, with absolute knowledge of its peculiarities and sympathy with its methods; with no fastidious ignoring of its habitual expression, or the inchoate poetry that may be found even hidden in its slang; with no moral determination except that which may be the legitimate outcome of the story itself; with no more elimination than may be necessary for the artistic conception, and never from the fear of the 'fetish' of conventionalism. Of such is the American short story of to-day - the germ of American literature to come.

39. *BRANDER MATTHEWS* — 1901

aus *The Philosophy of the Short Story* (New York, 1901), 73-77. - Der Text dieser Buchpublikation entspricht im wesentlichen - bis auf eine Reihe neu eingesetzter Anmerkungen und einiger Zusätze am Anfang und Schluß - dem 1885 in *Lippincott's Magazine* erschienenen und drei Jahre später in *Pen and Ink* nachgedruckten Essay. Die folgenden Absätze waren, neben anderen, in der früheren Fassung nicht enthalten.

The more carefully we study the history of fiction the more clearly we perceive that the Novel and the Short-story are essentially different - that the difference between them is not one of mere length only, but fundamental. The Short-story seeks one set of effects in its own way, and the Novel seeks a wholly distinct set of effects in a wholly distinct way. We are led also to the conclusion that the Short-story - in spite of the fact that in our language it has no name of its own - is one of the few sharply defined literary forms. It is a *genre*, as Mr. Brunetière terms it, a species, as a naturalist might call it, as individual as the Lyric itself and as various. It is as distinct an entity as the Epic, as Tragedy, as Comedy. Now the Novel is not a form of the same sharply defined individuality; it is - or at least it may be - anything. It is the child of the Epic and the heir of the Drama; but it is a hybrid. ...

P. S. So far as the author is aware, he had no predecessor in asserting that the Short-story differs from the Novel essentially, - and not merely in the matter of length. So far as he knows, it was in the present paper the suggestion was first made that the Short-story is in reality a *genre*, a separate kind, a genus by itself. But although this distinction may not have been made explicitly by any earlier critic, there is little doubt that Poe felt it, even if he did not formulate it in set terms. It seems to be implicit in more than one of his critical essays, more particularly in that on 'Hawthorne's Tales.'

40. [ANONYMUS] — 1901

aus "[Rezension von Brander Matthews Buch] *The Philosophy of the Short Story*", *The Academy*, LX (March 30, 1901), 287 f.

In a tiny volume, *The Philosophy of the Short-story* (note well the hyphen, for it has a significance), by Prof. Brander Matthews, D. C. L., of Columbia University, published by Messrs. Longmans, the whole question of the short story is critically and historically "raised". ... His aim appears to be threefold: to define the short story, to give an outline of its history, and to prove that it differs essentially from the novel. ...

With only one portion of this careless and absurd compilation is it possible to deal at all seriously. In his appendix the Professor writes with naive complacency: "So far as the author is aware, he had no predecessor in asserting that the Short-story differs from the Novel essentially - and not merely in the matter of length. So far as he knows, it was in the present paper the suggestion was first made that the Short-story is in reality a *genre,* a separate kind, a genus by itself." No doubt it was the obsession of this theory which caused him, after stating it briefly in an English weekly in 1884, to restate it at greater length in an American monthly in 1885, then to include that second statement in a volume of essays in 1888, and, finally, to issue it, revised and enlarged, as a separate brochure in 1901. The Professor says: "The difference between a Novel and a Novelet is one of length only: a Novelet is a brief novel; but the difference between a Novel and a Short-story is a difference of kind. A true Short-story is something other and something more than a mere story which is short. A true Short-story differs from the Novel chiefly in its unity of impression. In a far more exact and precise use of the word, a Short-story has unity as a Novel cannot have it." All this is wrong, a negligent utterance of negligent thought. How can a Short-story be "something other than" a short story? The answer is that it cannot. All that can be usefully asserted is that a *précis* of a long novel might make a bad short story. The whole difference between the Novel and the Short-story arises from the difference of length. It is because the short story is short that it usually deals with "a single episode," &c. But some short stories deal with many episodes; for instance, de Maupassant's *Odyssée d'une Fille*. If Prof. Matthews says that the *Odyssée d'une Fille* is not a Short-story, or is a bad Short-story, or is an inferior "mere" short story, or is a *précis* of a long novel, he is mistaken: that is all. It is an ancient game to fit facts into a theory by the device of arbitrarily limiting the significance of everyday words, but a very tiresome game; and no one will follow the Professor in his attempt to lay down a rule that short stories are not short stories unless they happen to be short stories of a particular sort. There is no difference whatever of *kind* between a Novel and a Short-story. The latter relates an episode, the former a succession of episodes: each is self-complete. "Of a truth," the Professor says again, "the Short-story is not only not a chapter out of a Novel ... but [*sic*] at its best it impresses the reader with the belief that it would be spoiled if it were made larger, or if it were incorporated into a more elaborate work." Here is a platitude: every art work should be alterable only at the cost of its perfection. Not even in technique is there a difference between the two forms; the methods of narrative are the same for one episode as for a chain of episodes. And touching that alleged more absolute "Unity of impression" of the Short-story, what the Professor ought to mean is that the impression made by the Short-story is less complex, simpler (he might have added, less powerful) than that made by the Novel. But complexity does not exclude unity, nor need simplicity include it. The truth is that the professor has excogitated this part of his theory from the well-known paradoxical essay in which Poe tries to demonstrate that there can be no such thing as a long poem, and that every so-called long poem is, in fact, a series of short ones. But perhaps the most astonishing of all the Professor's assertions is that "the difference *in spirit* and in form between the Lyric and the Epic is scarcely greater than the difference between the Short-story and the Novel."

For years past it has been a fashion among prattlers to prattle about "the art of the short story," as though it were something apart, high, and of unique difficulty. The short story is a smaller, simpler, easier, and less important form of the novel. Other things being equal, a short story can never have the force of a novel. As to the comparative difficulty of the two, ask any author who has written both fine novels and fine short stories.

41. *WILLIAM DEAN HOWELLS* — 1901

aus "Some Anomalies of the Short Story" in *Literature and Life: Studies* (New York & London, 1902, 1911), 110-124. - Ursprünglich erschienen in *North American Review* (Sept., 1901).

I am obliged to ask myself whether our literary development can be recognized separately from that of the whole English-speaking world. I think it can, though, as I am always saying American literature is merely a condition of English literature. In some sense every European literature is a condition of some other European literature, yet the impulse in each eventuates, if it does not originate indigenously. A younger literature will choose, by a sort of natural selection, some things for assimilation from an elder literature, for no more apparent reason than it will reject other things, and it will transform them in the process so that it will give them the effect of indigeneity. The short story among the Italians, who called it the novella, and supplied us with the name devoted solely among us to fiction of epical magnitude, refined indefinitely upon the Greek romance, if it derived from that; it retrenched itself in scope, and enlarged itself in the variety of its types. But still these remained types, and they remained types with the French imitators of the Italian novella. It was not till the Spaniards borrowed the form of the novella and transplanted it to their racier soil that it began to bear character, and to fruit in the richness of their picaresque fiction. When the English borrowed it they adapted it, in the metrical tales of Chaucer, to the genius of their nation, which was then both poetical and humorous. Here it was full of character, too, and more and more personality began to enlarge the bounds of the conventional types and to imbue fresh ones. But in so far as the novella was studied in the Italian sources, the French, Spanish, and English literatures were conditions of Italian literature as distinctly, though, of course, not so thoroughly, as American literature is a condition of English literature. Each borrower gave a national cast to the thing borrowed, and that is what has happened with us, in the full measure that our nationality has differenced itself from the English.

Whatever truth there is in all this, and I will confess that a good deal of it seems to me hardy conjecture, rather favors my position that we are in some such period of our literary development as those other peoples when the short story flourished among them. Or, if I restrict our claim, I may safely claim that they abundantly had the novella when they had not the novel at all, and we now abundantly have the novella, while we have the novel only subordinately and of at least no such quantitative importance as the English, French, Spanish, Norwegians, Russians, and some others of our esteemed contemporaries, not to name the Italians. ...

The abeyance, not to say the desuetude, that the novella fell into for several centuries is very curious, and fully as remarkable as the modern rise of the short story. It began to prevail in the dramatic form, for a play is a short story put on the stage; it may have satisfied in that form the early love of it, and it has continued to please in that form; but in its original shape it quite vanished, unless we consider the little studies and sketches and allegories of the *Spectator* and *Tatler* and *Idler* and *Rambler* and their imitations on the Continent as guises of the novella. The germ of the modern short story may have survived in these, or in the metrical form of the novella which appeared in Chaucer and never wholly disappeared. ... But it was not till our time that its great merit as a form was felt, for until our time so great work was never done with it.

I remind myself of Boccaccio, and of the *Arabian Nights*, without the wish to hedge from my bold stand. They are all elemental; compared with some finer modern work which deepens inward immeasurably, they are all of their superficial limits. They amuse, but they do not hold, the mind and stamp it with large and profound impressions.

An Occidental cannot judge the literary quality of the Eastern tales; but I will own my suspicion that the perfection of the Italian work is philological rather than artistic, while the web woven by Mr. James or Miss Jewett, by Kielland or Björnson, by Maupassant, by Palacio Valdés, by Giovanni Verga, by Tourguénief, in one of those little frames seems to me of an exquisite color and texture and of an entire literary preciousness, not only as regards the diction, but as regards those more intangible graces of form, those virtues of truth and reality, and those lasting significances which distinguish the masterpiece.

The novella has in fact been carried so far in the short story that it might be asked whether it had not left the novel behind, as to perfection of form; though one might not like to affirm this. Yet there have been but few modern fictions of the novel's dimensions which have the beauty of form many a novella embodies. Is this because it is easier to give form in the small than in the large, or only because it is easier to hide formlessness? It is easier to give form in the novella than in the novel, because the design of less scope can be more definite, and because the persons and facts are fewer, and each can be more carefully treated. But, on the other hand, the slightest error in execution shows more in the small than in the large, and a fault of conception is more evident. The novella must be clearly imagined, above all things, for there is no room in it for those felicities of characterization or comment by which the artist of faltering design saves himself in the novel.

The question as to where the short story distinguishes itself from the anecdote is of the same nature as that which concerns the bound set between it and the novel. In both cases the difference of the novella is in the motive, or the origination. The anecdote is too palpably simple and single to be regarded as a novella, though there is now and then a novella like *The Father*, by Björnson, which is of the actual brevity of the anecdote, but which, when released in the reader's consciousness, expands to dramatic dimensions impossible to the anecdote. ... The anecdote offers an illustration of character, or records a moment of action; the novella embodies a drama and develops a type.

It is not quite so clear as to when and where a piece of fiction ceases to be a novella and becomes a novel. The frontiers are so vague that one is obliged to recognize a middle species, or rather a middle magnitude, which paradoxically, but necessarily enough, we call the novelette. First we have the short story, or novella, then we have the long story, or novel, and between these we have the novelette, which is in name a smaller [piece] than the short story, though it is in point of fact two or three times longer than a short story. ... [In] the novelette are possibilities for fiction as yet scarcely divined.

The novelette can have almost as perfect [a] form as the novella. In fact, the novel has form in the measure that it approaches the novelette; and some of the most symmetrical modern novels are scarcely more than novelettes, like Tourguénief's *Dmitri Rudine,* or his *Smoke,* or *Spring Floods. The Vicar of Wakefield,* the father of the modern novel, is scarcely more than a novelette...

I should like to say as my last word for it here that I believe there are many novels which, if stripped of their padding, would turn out to have been all along merely novelettes in disguise.

It does not follow, however, that there are many novelle which, if they were duly padded, would be found novelettes. In that dim, subjective region where the aesthetic origins present themselves almost with the authority of inspirations there is nothing clearer than the difference between the short-story motive and the long-story motive. One, if one is in that line of work, feels instinctively just the size and carrying power of the given motive. Or, if the reader prefers a different figure, the mind which the seed has been dropped into from Somewhere is mystically aware whether the seed is going to grow up a bush or is going to grow up a tree, if left to itself. Of course, the mind to which the seed is intrusted may play it false, and wilfully dwarf the growth, or force it to unnatural dimensions; but the critical observer will easily detect the fact of such treasons. Almost in the first germinal impulse the inventive mind forefeels the ultimate difference and recognizes the essential simplicity or complexity of the motive. There will be a prophetic subdivision into a variety of motives and a multiplication of characters and incidents and situations; or the original motive will be divined indivisible, and there will be a small group of people immediately interested and controlled by a single, or predominant, fact. ...

The right novel is never a congeries of novelle, as might appear to the uninspired. If it indulges even in episodes, it loses in reality and vitality. It is one stock from which its various branches put out, and form it a living growth identical throughout. The right novella is never a novel cropped back from the size of a tree to a bush, or the branch of a tree stuck into the ground and made to serve for a bush. It is another species, destined by the agencies at work in the realm of unconsciousness to be brought into being of its own kind, and not of another.

This was always its case, but in the process of time the short story, while keeping the natural limits of the primal novella (if ever there was one), has shown almost limitless possibilities within them. It has shown itself capable of imparting the effect of every sort of intention, whether of humor or pathos, of tragedy or comedy or broad farce or delicate irony, of character or action. The thing that first made itself known as a little tale, usually salacious, dealing with conventionalized types and conventionalized incidents, has proved itself possibly the most flexible of all the literary forms in its adaptation to the needs of the mind that wishes to utter itself, inventively or constructively, upon some fresh occasion, or wishes briefly to criticise or represent some phase or fact of life. ...

We become of a perfect intimacy and a devoted friendship with the men and women in the short stories, but not apparently of a lasting acquaintance. It is a single meeting we have with them, and though we instantly love or hate them dearly, recurrence and repetition seem necessary to that familiar knowledge in which we hold the personages in a novel.

It is here that the novella, so much more perfect in form, shows its irremediable inferiority to the novel, and somehow to the play, to the very farce, which it may quantitatively excel. We can all recall by name many characters out of comedies and farces; but how many characters out of short stories can we recall? Most persons of the drama give themselves away by name for types, mere figments of allegory, ... but perhaps, also, the dramatic form has greater facilities for repetition, and so can stamp its persons more indelibly on the imagination than the narrative form in the same small space. The narrative must give to description what the drama trusts to representation; but this cannot account for the superior permanency of the dramatic types in so great measure as we might at first imagine, for they remain as much in mind from reading as from seeing the plays. It is possible that as the novella becomes more conscious, its persons will become more memorable...

The defect of the novella which we have been acknowledging seems an essential limitation; but perhaps it is not insuperable; and we may yet have short stories which shall supply the delighted imagination with creations of as much immortality as we can reasonably demand. The structural change would not be greater than the moral or material change which has been wrought in it since it began as a yarn, gross and palpable, which the narrator spun out of the coarsest and often the filthiest stuff, to snare the thick fancy or amuse the lewd leisure of listeners willing as children to have the same persons and the same things over and over again. Now it has not only varied the persons and things, but it has refined and verified them in the direction of the natural and the supernatural, until it is above all other literary forms the vehicle of reality and spirituality.

42. *HENRY JAMES* —— 1909

aus "Preface" zu *The Lesson of the Master*, New York Edition of *The Novels and Tales of Henry James*, XV (New York, 1909), vii-viii; xviii. - Abgedruckt in *The Art of the Novel: Critical Prefaces*, hrsg. von Richard P. Blackmur (New York & London, 1934), 217-231.

I was invited, and all urgently, to contribute to the first number [of "The Yellow Book"], and was regaled with the golden truth that my composition might absolutely assume, might shamelessly parade in, its own organic form. ... For any idea I might wish to express I might have space, in other words, elegantly to express it - an offered licence that, on the spot, opened up the millenium to the "short story." One had so often known this product to struggle, in one's hands, under the rude prescription of brevity at any cost, with the opposition so offered to its really becoming a story, that my friend's emphasised indifference to the arbitrary limit of length struck me, I remember, as the fruit of the finest artistic intelligence. We had been at one - that we already knew - on the truth that the forms of wrought things, in this order, *were*, all exquisitely and effectively, the things... Among forms, moreover, we had had, on the dimensional ground - for length and breadth - our ideal, the beautiful and blest *nouvelle*; the generous, the enlightened hour for which appeared thus at last to shine. It was under the star of the *nouvelle* that, in other languages, a hundred interesting and charming results, such studies on the minor scale as the best of Turgenieff's, of Balzac's, of Maupassant's, of Bourget's, and just lately, in our own tongue, of Kipling's, had been, all economically, arrived at - thanks to their authors', as "contributors," having been able to count, right and left, on a wise and liberal support. It had taken the blank misery of our Anglo-Saxon sense of such matters to organise, as might be said, the general indifference to this fine type of composition. In that dull view a "short story" was a "short story," and that was the end of it. Shades and differences, varieties and styles, the value above all of the idea happily *developed,* languished, to extinction, under the hard-and-fast rule of the "from six to eight thousand words" - when, for one's benefit, the rigour was a little relaxed. For myself, I delighted in the shapely *nouvelle* - as, for that matter, I had from time to time and here and there been almost encouraged to show. ...

A marked example of the possible scope, at once, and the possible neatness of the *nouvelle,* it [i.e. "The Coxon Fund"] takes its place for me in a series of which the main merit and sign is the effort to do the complicated thing with a strong brevity and lucidity - to arrive, on behalf of the multiplicity, at a certain science of control. Infinitely attractive - though I risk here again doubtless an effect of reiteration - the question of how to exert this control in accepted conditions and how yet to sacrifice no real value; problem ever dearest to any economic soul desirous to keep renewing, and with a frugal splendour, its ideal of economy.

43. *HENRY JAMES* ——— 1909

aus "Preface" zu *The Author of Beltraffio,* New York Edition of *The Novels and Tales of Henry James,* XVI (New York,1909), v-viii; xii. - Abgedruckt in *The Art of the Novel: Critical Prefaces,* hrsg. von Richard P. Blackmur, (New York & London, 1934), 232-240.

What I had lately and most particularly to say of "The Coxon Fund" is no less true of "The Middle Years," first published in *Scribner's Magazine* (1893) - that recollection mainly and most promptly associates with it the number of times I had to do it over to make sure of it. To get it right was to squeeze my subject into the five or six thousand words I had been invited to make it consist of - it consists, in fact, should the curious care to know, of some 5550 - and I scarce perhaps recall another case, with the exception I shall presently name, in which my struggle to keep compression rich, if not, better still, to keep accretions compressed, betrayed for me such community with the anxious effort of some warden of the insane engaged at a critical moment in making fast a victim's straitjacket. The form of "The Middle Years" is not that of the *nouvelle,* but that of the concise anecdote; whereas the subject treated would perhaps seem one comparatively demanding "developments" - if indeed, amid these mysteries, distinctions were so absolute. (There is of course neither close nor fixed measure of the reach of a development, which in some connexions seems almost superfluous and then in others to represent the whole sense of the matter; and we should doubtless speak more thoroughly by book had we some secret for exactly tracing deflexions and returns.) However this may be, it was as an anecdote, an anecdote only, that I was determined my little situation here should figure; to which end my effort was of course to follow it as much as possible from its outer edge in, rather than from its centre outward. That fond formula, I had alas already discovered, may set as many traps in the garden as its opposite may set in the wood; so that after boilings and reboilings of the contents of my small cauldron, after added pounds of salutary sugar, as numerous as those prescribed in the choicest recipe for the thickest jam, I well remember finding the whole process and act (which, to the exclusion of everything else, dragged itself out for a month) one of the most expensive of its sort in which I had ever engaged.

But I recall, by good luck, no less vividly how much finer a sweetness than any mere spooned-out saccharine dwelt in the fascination of the questions involved. Treating a theme that "gave" much in a form that, at the best, would give little, might indeed represent a peck of troubles; yet who, none the less, beforehand, was to pronounce with authority such and such an idea anecdotic and such and such another developmental? ... One had only to be reminded that for the effect of quick roundness the small smooth situation, though as intense as one will, is prudently indicated, and that for a fine complicated entangled air nothing will serve that doesn't naturally swell and bristle - one had only, I say, to be so warned off or warned on, to see forthwith no beauty for the simple thing that shouldn't, and even to perversity, enrich it, and none for the other, the comparatively intricate, that shouldn't press it out as a mosaic. After which fashion the careful craftsman would have prepared himself the special inviting treat of scarce being able to say, at his highest infatuation, before any series, which might be the light thing weighted and which the dense thing clarified. ...

["Greville Fane"] is exactly an illustrative case: the subject, in this little composition, is "developmental" enough, while the form has to make the anecdotic concession; and yet who shall say that for the right effect of a small harmony the fusion has failed? We desire doubtless a more detailed notation of the behaviour of the son and daughter, and yet had I believed the right effect missed "Greville Fane" wouldn't have figured here.

Nothing, by the same stroke, could well have been condemned to struggle more for that harmony than "The Abasement of the Northmores" and "The Tree of Knowledge": the idea in these examples (1900) being developmental with a vengeance and the need of an apparent ease and a general congruity having to enforce none the less - as on behalf of some victim of the income-tax who would minimise his "return" - an almost heroic dissimulation of capital. These things, especially the former, are novels intensely compressed, and with that character in them yet keeping at bay, under stress of their failing else to be good short stories, any air of mutilation. They had had to be good short stories in order to earn, however precariously, their possible wage and "appear" - so certain was it that there would be no appearance, and consequently no wage, for them as frank and brave *nouvelles*. They could but conceal the fact that they *were* "nouvelles"; they could but masquerade as little anecdotes. I include them here by reason of that successful, that achieved and consummate - as it strikes me - duplicity: which, however, I may add, was in the event to avail them little - since they were to find nowhere, the unfortunates, hospitality and the reward of their effort. It is to "The Tree of Knowledge" I referred just above, I may further mention, as the production that had cost me, for keeping it "down," even a greater number of full revolutions of the merciless screw than "The Middle Years." ...

The merit of ["Europe", i.e. another short story] ... is in the feat, once more, of the transfusion; the receptacle (of form) being so exiguous, the brevity imposed so great. I undertook the brevity, so often undertaken on a like scale before, and again arrived at it by the innumerable repeated chemical reductions and condensations that tend to make of the very short story, as I risk again noting, one of the costliest, even if, like the hard, shining sonnet, one of the most indestructible, forms of composition in general use. I accepted the rigour of its having, all sternly, in this case, to treat so many of its most appealing values as waste; and I now seek my comfort perforce in the mere exhibited result, the union of whatever fulness with whatever clearness.

44. *HENRY JAMES* ——— 1909

aus "Preface" zu *Daisy Miller*, New York Edition of *The Novels and Tales of Henry James*, XVIII (New York, 1909), vi; xv. - Abgedruckt in *The Art of the Novel: Critical Prefaces*, hrsg. von Richard P. Blackmur, (New York & London, 1934), 267-287.

["Daisy Miller" is] essentially and pre-eminently a *nouvelle*; a signal example in fact of that type, foredoomed at the best, in more cases than not, to editorial disfavour. ...

There was always the difficulty - I have in the course of these so numerous preliminary observations repeatedly referred to it, but the point is so interesting that it can scarce be made too often - that the simplest truth about a human entity, a situation, a relation, an aspect of life, however small, on behalf of which the claim to charmed attention is made, strains ever, under one's hand, more intensely, *most* intensely, to justify that claim; strains ever, as it were, toward the uttermost end or aim of one's meaning or of its own numerous connexions; struggles at each step, and in defiance of one's raised admonitory finger, fully and completely to express itself. Any real art of representation is, I make out, a controlled and guarded acceptance, in fact a perfect economic mastery, of that conflict: the general sense of the expansive, the explosive principle in one's material thoroughly noted, adroitly allowed to flush and colour and animate the disputed value, but with its other appetites and treacheries, its characteristic space-hunger and space-cunning, kept down.

45. ARTHUR RANSOME ——— 1909

aus *A History of Story-Telling* (London, 1909), 309-311.

The short story must be a single melody ending with itself; the *nouvelle* a piece of music, the motive of whose opening bars, recurring again and again throughout, is finally repeated with the increase in meaning that is given it by the whole performance.

The short story proper is in narrative prose what the short lyric is in poetry. It is an episode, an event, a scene, a sentence, whose importance is such that it allows nothing in the story that is not directly concerned with its realisation. This is true of many specimens of the *nouvelle*, but it is the essential rule of the short story. Look at the end of *La Petite Ficelle*, or of any other of the *Contes* of de Maupassant. 'Une 'tite ficelle ... une 'tite ficelle ... t'nez la, voila, m'sieu le Maire.' 'A little bit of string ... a little bit of string ... look, there it is, M. le Maire.' That sentence, repeated by the dying man in his delirium, needs for the full pathos of its effect every word of the story. From the first paragraph about an ordinary market day, the accident of the old man picking up a piece of string in a place where a purse had been lost, the false accusation, and his guilt-seeming protestation of innocence, every detail in the story is worked just so far as to make the reader's mind as ready and sensitive as possible for the final infliction of those few words. Keats once coated the inside of his mouth with cayenne pepper to feel as keenly as he could 'the delicious coolness of claret.' The art of the short story is just such a making ready for such a momentary sensation.

Just as Time, with the clearer consciousness of technique, has made the moulds of the art more markedly distinct, so it has given the artist an infinite choice of amalgams with which to fill them. Although some of the most delightful examples of narrative are still produced with the old and worthy object of telling a tale to pass the time, although there are still men who lay their mats upon the ground, squat down on them, and keep their audiences happy by stories that demand no more intellectual attention than the buzz of bees in the magnolia flowers; yet, if we consider only those artists who have been discussed in the preceding chapters, we perceive at once how many are the other possibilities of narrative, and, if we examine the story-telling of our own day, we shall find that most of them are illustrated in contemporary practice.

Story-telling has grown into a means of expression with a gamut as wide as that of poetry, which is as wide as that of humanity. 'It is literature,' says Wilde, 'that shows us the body in its swiftness and the soul in its unrest'; and the same art that helps us to laze away a summer afternoon is a key that lets us into the hearts of men we have never seen, and not infrequently opens our own to us, when, in the bustle of existence, we have gone out and found ourselves unable to return. It is a Gyges' ring with which, upon our finger, we can go about the world and mingle in the business of men to whom we would not bow, or who would not bow to us. It breaks the gold or iron collars of our classes and sets each man free as a man to understand all other men soever.

aus *Martin Eden* (London, 1927), 118-119; 123-124; 197-198, 247-249; 318-319. - Ein autobiographischer Roman, erstmals veröffentlicht im Jahre 1910.

[He] must write. He must earn money. He had had no acceptance. Two score of manuscripts were travelling the endless round of the magazines. How did the others do it? He spent long hours in the free reading-rooms, going over what others had written, studying their work eagerly and critically, comparing it with his own, and wondering, wondering about the secret trick they had discovered which enabled them to sell their work. ...

He was puzzled by countless short stories, written lightly and cleverly, he confessed, but without vitality or reality. Life was so strange and wonderful, filled with an immensity of problems, of dreams, and of heroic toils, and yet these stories dealt only with the commonplaces of life. He felt the stress and strain of life, its fevers and sweats and wild insurgences - surely this was the stuff to write about! He wanted to glorify the leaders of forlorn hopes, the mad lovers, the giants that fought under stress and strain, amid terror and tragedy, making life crackle with the strength of their endeavour. And yet the magazine short stories seemed intent on glorifying the Mr. Butlers, the sordid dollar-chasers, and the commonplace little love-affairs of commonplace little men and women. Was it because the editors of the magazines were commonplace? he demanded. Or were they afraid of life - these writers and editors and readers? ...

He read to her a story, one that he flattered himself was among his very best. He called it "The Wine of Life," and the wine of it that had stolen into his brain when he wrote it stole into his brain now as he read it. There was a certain magic in the original conception, and he had adorned it with more magic of phrase and touch. ...

Out of life he had captured something big and attempted to imprison it in the story. It was the big thing out of life he had read to her, not sentence structure and semicolons. He wanted her to feel with him this big thing that was his, that he had seen with his own eyes, grappled with his own brain, and placed there on the page with his own hands in printed words. Well, he had failed, was his secret decision. Perhaps the editors were right. He had felt the big thing, but he had failed to transmute it. He concealed his disappointment, and joined so easily with her in her criticism that she did not realize that deep down in him was running a strong undercurrent of disagreement.

He went farther in the matter. Reading the works of men who had arrived, he noted every result achieved by them, and worked out the tricks by which they had been achieved - the tricks of narrative, of exposition, of style, the points of view, the contrasts, the epigrams; and of all these he made lists for study. He did not ape. He sought principles. He drew up lists of effective and fetching mannerisms, till out of many such, culled from many writers, he was able to induce the general principle of mannerism, and, thus equipped, to cast about for new and original ones of his own, and to weigh, and measure, and appraise them properly. ... He sought always for the principle that lay behind and beneath. He wanted to know how the thing was done; after that he could do it for himself. ...

He wanted to know why and how. His was deliberate creative genius, and, before he began a story or poem, the thing itself was already alive in his brain, with the end in sight, and the means of realizing that end in his conscious possession. Otherwise the effort was doomed to failure. On the other hand, he appreciated the chance effects in words and phrases that came lightly and easily into his brain, and that later stood all tests of beauty and power, and developed tremendous and incommunicable connotations. Before such he bowed down and marvelled, knowing that they were beyond the deliberate creation of any man. ...

Encouraged by his several small sales, Martin went back to hack-work. Perhaps there was a living in it, after all. Stored away under his table were the twenty storyettes which had been rejected by the newspaper short-story syndicate. He read them over in order to find out how not to write newspaper storyettes, and, so doing, reasoned out the perfect formula. He found that the newspaper storyette should never be tragic, should never end unhappily, and should never contain beauty of language, subtlety of thought, nor real delicacy of sentiment. ...

Having learned such precautions, Martin ... proceeded to mix according to formula. The formula consisted of three parts: (1) A pair of lovers are jarred apart; (2) by some deed or event they are reunited; (3) marriage bells. The third part was an unvarying quantity, but the first and second parts could be varied an infinite number of times. ... In quantity, the formula prescribed twelve hundred words minimum dose, fifteen hundred words maximum dose.

Before he got very far along in the art of the storyette Martin worked out half a dozen stock forms, which he always consulted when constructing storyettes. These forms were like the cunning tables used by mathematicians, which may be entered from top, bottom, right and left, which entrances consist of scores of lines and dozens of columns, and from which may be drawn, without reasoning or thinking, thousands of different conclusions, all unchallengably precise and true. Thus, in the course of half an hour with his forms Martin could frame up a dozen or so storyettes, which he put aside and filled in at his convenience. He found that he could fill one in, after a day of serious work, in the hour before going to bed. ... The real work was in constructing the frames, and that was merely mechanical.

He had no doubt whatever of the efficacy of his formula, and for once he knew the editorial mind when he said positively to himself that the first two he sent off would bring cheques. And cheques they brought, for four dollars each, at the end of twelve days.

Martin began, that morning, a story which he had sketched out a number of weeks before, and which ever since had been worrying him with its insistent clamour to be created. Apparently it was to be a rattling sea-story, a tale of twentieth-century adventure and romance, handling real characters, in a real world, under real conditions. But beneath the swing and go of the story was to be something else - something that the superficial reader would never discern, and which, on the other hand, would not diminish in any way the interest and enjoyment for such a reader. It was this, and not the mere story, that impelled Martin to write it. For that matter, it was always the great universal *motif* that suggested plots to him. After having found such a *motif*, he cast about for the particular persons and particular location in time and space wherewith and wherein to utter the universal thing. "Overdue" was the title he had decided for it, and its length, he believed, would not be more than sixty thousand words - a bagatelle for him with his splendid vigour of production. On this first day he took hold of it with conscious delight in the mastery of his tools. He no longer worried for fear that the sharp, cutting edges should slip and mar his work. The long months of intense application and study had brought their reward. He could now devote himself, with sure hand, to the larger phases of the thing he shaped; and as he worked hour after hour, he felt, as never before, the sure and cosmic grasp with which he held life and the affairs of life. "Overdue" would tell a story that would be true of its particular characters and its particular events; but it would tell, too, he was confident, great vital things that would be true of all time, and all sea, and all life - thanks to Herbert Spencer, he thought, leaning back for a moment from the table. ...

He was conscious that it was great stuff he was writing. ... At last he was turning out the thing at which the magazines would jump. The whole story worked out before him in lightning flashes. He broke off from it long enough to write a paragraph in his notebook. This would be the last paragraph in "Overdue," but so thoroughly was the whole book already composed in his brain that he could write, weeks before he had arrived at the end, the end itself. ...

47. HERBERT GEORGE WELLS —— 1911

aus "Introduction" zu *The Country of the Blind and Other Stories* (London, 1911), [iii]-ix.

The task of selection and revision brings home to me with something of the effect of discovery that I was once an industrious writer of short stories, and that I am no longer anything of the kind. I have not written one now for quite a long time, and in the past five or six years I have made scarcely one a year. The bulk of the fifty or sixty tales from which this present three-and-thirty have been chosen dates from the last century. This edition is more definitive than I supposed when first I arranged for it. In the presence of so conclusive an ebb and cessation an almost obituary manner seems justifiable.

I find it a little difficult to disentangle the causes that have restricted the flow of these inventions. It has happened, I remark, to others as well as to myself, and in spite of the kindliest encouragement to continue from editors and readers. There was a time when life bubbled with short stories; they were always coming to the surface of my mind, and it is no deliberate change of will that has thus restricted my production. It is rather, I think, a diversion of attention to more sustained and more exacting forms. It was my friend Mr. C. L. Hind who set that spring going. He urged me to write short stories for the *Pall Mall Budget*, and persuaded me by his simple and buoyant conviction that I could do what he desired. There existed at the time only the little sketch, "The Jilting of Jane," included in this volume - at least, that is the only tolerable fragment of fiction I find surviving from my pre-Lewis-Hind period. But I set myself, so encouraged, to the experiment of inventing moving and interesting things that could be given vividly in the little space of eight or ten such pages as this, and for a time I found it a very entertaining pursuit indeed. Mr. Hind's indicating finger had shown me an amusing possibility of the mind. I found that, taking almost anything as a starting-point and letting my thoughts play about it, there would presently come out of the darkness, in a manner quite inexplicable, some absurd or vivid little incident more or less relevant to that initial nucleus. Little men in canoes upon sunlit oceans would come floating out of nothingness, incubating the eggs of prehistoric monsters unawares; violent conflicts would break out amidst the flower-beds of suburban gardens; I would discover I was peering into remote and mysterious worlds ruled by an order logical indeed but other than our common sanity.

The 'nineties was a good and stimulating period for a short-story writer. Mr. Kipling had made his astonishing advent with a series of little blue-grey books, whose covers opened like window-shutters to reveal the dusty sun-glare and blazing colours of the East; Mr. Barrie had demonstrated what could be done in a little space through the panes of his *Window in Thrums*. The *National Observer* was at the climax of its career of heroic insistence upon lyrical brevity and a vivid finish, and Mr. Frank Harris was not only printing good short stories by other people, but writing still better ones himself in the dignified pages of the *Fortnightly Review*. *Longman's Magazine*, too, represented a *clientèle* of appreciative short-story readers that is now scattered. Then came the generous opportunities of the *Yellow Book*, and the *National Observer* died only to give birth to the *New Review*. No short story of the slightest distinction went for long unrecognised. The sixpenny popular magazines had still to deaden down the conception of what a short story might be to the imaginative limitation of the common reader - and a maximum length of six thousand words. Short stories broke out everywhere. Kipling was writing short stories; Barrie, Stevenson, Frank Harris; Max Beerbohm wrote at least one perfect one, "The Happy Hypocrite"; Henry James pursued his wonderful and inimitable bent; and among other names that occur to me, like a mixed handful of jewels drawn from a bag, are George Street, Morley Roberts, George Gissing, Ella d'Arcy, Murray Gilchrist, E. Nesbit, Stephen Crane, Joseph Conrad, Edwin Pugh, Jerome K. Jerome, Kenneth Graham, Arthur Morrison, Marriott Watson, George Moore, Grant Allen, George Egerton, Henry Harland, Pett Ridge, W. W. Jacobs (who alone seems inexhaustible). I dare say I could recall as many more names with a little effort. I may be succumbing to the infirmities of middle age, but I do not think the present decade can produce any parallel to this list, or what is more remarkable, that the later achievements in this field of any of the survivors from that time, with the sole exception of Joseph Conrad, can compare with the work they did before 1900. It seems to me this outburst of short stories came not only as a phase in literary development, but also as a phase in the development of the individual writers concerned.

It is now quite unusual to see any adequate criticism of short stories in English. I do not know how far the decline in short-story writing may not be due to that. Every sort of artist demands human responses, and few men can contrive to write merely for a publisher's cheque and silence, however reassuring that cheque may be. A mad millionaire who commissioned masterpieces to burn would find it impossible to buy them. Scarcely any artist will hesitate in the choice between money and attention; and it was primarily for that last and better sort of pay that the short stories of the 'nineties were written. People talked about them tremendously, compared them, and ranked them. That was the thing that mattered.

It was not, of course, all good talk, and we suffered then, as now, from the *à priori* critic. Just as nowadays he goes about declaring that the work of such-and-such a dramatist is all very amusing and delightful, but "it isn't a Play," so we had a great deal of talk about *the* short story, and found ourselves measured by all kinds of arbitrary standards. There was a tendency to treat the short story as though it was as definable a form as the sonnet, instead of being just exactly what any one of courage and imagination can get told in twenty minutes' reading or so. It was either Mr. Edward Garnett or Mr. George Moore in a violently anti-Kipling mood who invented the distinction between the short story and the anecdote. The short story was Maupassant; the anecdote was damnable. It was a quite infernal comment in its way, because it permitted no defence. Fools caught it up and used it freely. Nothing is so destructive in a field of artistic effort as a stock term of abuse. Anyone could say of any short story, "A mere anecdote,"just as anyone can say "Incoherent!" of any novel or of any sonata that isn't studiously monotonous. The recession of enthusiasm for this compact, amusing form is closely associated in my mind with that discouraging imputation. One felt hopelessly open to a paralysing and unanswerable charge, and one's ease and happiness in the garden of one's fancies was more and more marred by the dread of it. It crept into one's mind, a distress as vague and inexpugnable as a sea fog on a spring morning, and presently one shivered and wanted to go indoors. ... It is the absurd fate of the imaginative writer that he should be thus sensitive to atmospheric conditions.

But after one has died as a maker one may still live as a critic, and I will confess I am all for laxness and variety in this as in every field of art. Insistence upon rigid forms and austere unities seems to me the instinctive reaction of the sterile against the fecund. It is the tired man with a headache who values a work of art for what it does not contain. I suppose it is the lot of every critic nowadays to suffer from indigestion and a fatigued appreciation, and to develop a self-protective tendency towards rules that will reject, as it were, automatically the more abundant and irregular forms. But this world is not for the weary, and in the long-run it is the new and variant that matter. I refuse altogether to recognise any hard and fast type for the Short Story, any more than I admit any limitation upon the liberties of the Small Picture. The short story is a fiction that may be read in something under an hour, and so that it is moving and delightful, it does not matter whether it is as "trivial" as a Japanese print of insects seen closely between grass stems, or as spacious as the prospect of the plain of Italy from Monte Mottarone. It does not matter whether it is human or inhuman, or whether it leaves you thinking deeply or radiantly but superficially pleased. Some things are more easily done as short stories than others and more abundantly done, but one of the many pleasures of short-story writing is to achieve the impossible.

At any rate, that is the present writer's conception of the art of the short story, as the jolly art of making something very bright and moving; it may be horrible or pathetic or funny or beautiful or profoundly illuminating, having only this essential, that it should take from fifteen to fifty minutes to read aloud. All the rest is just whatever invention and imagination and the mood can give - a vision of buttered slides on a busy day or of unprecedented worlds. In that spirit of miscellaneous expectation these stories should be received. Each is intended to be a thing by itself; and if it is not too ungrateful to kindly and enterprising publishers, I would confess I would much prefer to see each printed expensively alone, and left in a little brown-paper cover to lie about a room against the needs of a quite casual curiosity. And I would rather this volume were found in the bedrooms of convalescents and in dentists' parlours and railway trains than in gentlemen's studies. I would rather have it dipped in and dipped in again than read severely through. Essentially it is a miscellany of inventions, many of which were very pleasant to write; and its end is more than attained if some of them are refreshing and agreeable to read. I have now re-read them all, and I am glad to think I wrote them. I like them, but I cannot tell how much the associations of old happinesses gives them a flavour for me. I make no claims for them and no apology; they will be read as long as people read them. Things written either live or die; unless it be for a place of judgment upon Academic impostors, there is no apologetic intermediate state.

aus "The Contemporary Novel" in *An Englishman Looks at the World* (London, 1914), 148-169. - Dieser Essay wurde als Vortrag vor dem Times Book Club London im Mai 1911 unter d. T. "The Scope of the Novel" gehalten; gedruckt in *Fortnightly Review* (Nov. 11, 1911) und *Atlantic Monthly* (Jan. 12, 1912).

The novel has been treated as though its form was as well-defined as the sonnet. Some year or so ago, for example, there was a quite serious discussion, which began, I believe, in a weekly paper devoted to the interests of various nonconformist religious organisations, about the proper length for a novel. The critic was to begin his painful duties with a yard measure. The matter was taken up with profound gravity by the *Westminster Gazette*, and a considerable number of literary men and women were circularised and asked to state, in the face of "Tom Jones", "The Vicar of Wakefield", "The Shabby-Genteel Story", and "Bleak House", just exactly how long the novel ought to be. Our replies varied according to the civility of our natures, but the mere attempt to raise the question shows, I think, how widespread among the editorial, paragraph-writing, opinion-making sort of people is this notion of prescribing a definite length and a definite form for the novel. ...

That was obviously a half-forgotten echo of Edgar Allan Poe's discussion of the short story. Edgar Allan Poe was very definite upon the point that the short story should be finished at a sitting. But the novel and short story are two entirely different things, and the train of reasoning that made the American master limit the short story to about an hour of reading as a maximum, does not apply to the longer work. A short story is, or should be, a simple thing; it aims at producing one single, vivid effect; it has to seize the attention at the outset, and never relaxing, gather it together more and more until the climax is reached. The limits of the human capacity to attend closely therefore set a limit to it; it must explode and finish before interruption occurs or fatigue sets in. But the novel I hold to be a discursive thing; it is not a single interest, but a woven tapestry of interests; one is drawn on first by this affection and curiosity, and then by that; it is something to return to, and I do not see that we can possibly set any limit to its extent. The distinctive value of the novel among written works of art is in characterisation, and the charm of a well-conceived character lies, not in knowing its destiny, but in watching its proceedings. For my own part, I will confess that I find all the novels of

Dickens, long as they are, too short for me. I am sorry they do not flow into one another more than they do. ...

The confusion between the standards of a short story and the standards of the novel which leads at last to these - what shall I call them? - *Westminster Gazettisms*? - about the correct length to which the novelist should aspire, leads also to all kinds of absurd condemnations and exactions upon matters of method and style. The underlying fallacy is always this: the assumption that the novel, like the story, aims at a single, concentrate impression. From that comes a fertile growth of error. Constantly one finds in the reviews of works of fiction the complaint that this, that or the other thing in a novel is irrelevant. Now it is the easiest thing, and most fatal thing, to become irrelevant in a short story. A short story should go to its point as a man flies from a pursuing tiger: he pauses not for the daisies in his path, or to note the pretty moss on the tree he climbs for safety. But the novel by comparison is like breakfasting in the open air on a summer morning; nothing is irrelevant if the writer's mood is happy, and the tapping of the thrush upon the garden path, or the petal of apple-blossom that floats down into my coffee, is as relevant as the egg I open or the bread and butter I bite. And all sorts of things that inevitably mar the tense illusion which is the aim of the short story - the introduction, for example, of the author's personality - any comment that seems to admit that, after all, fiction is fiction, a change in manner between part and part, burlesque, parody, invective, all such things are not necessarily wrong in the novel.

49. ARNOLD BENNETT ———————————————————— 1914

aus *The Author's Craft* (London, 1914), 76 f.

One reason why a play is easier to write than a novel is that a play is shorter than a novel. On the average, one may say that it takes six plays to make the matter of a novel. Other things being equal, a short work of art presents fewer difficulties than a longer one. ... Some years ago we had an enormous palaver about the "art of the short story," which numerous persons who had omitted to write novels pronounced to be more difficult than the novel. But the fact remains that there are scores of perfect short stories, whereas it is doubtful whether anybody but Turgenev ever did write a perfect novel. A short form is easier to manipulate than a long form, because its construction is less complicated, because the balance of its proportions can be more easily corrected by means of a rapid survey, because it is lawful and even necessary in it to leave undone many things which are very hard to do, and because the emotional strain is less prolonged. The most difficult thing in all art is to maintain the imaginative tension unslackened throughout a considerable period.

50. BARRY E. O. PAIN — 1914

aus *The Short Story* (London, o.J. [1914]), 33 f.; 36-38; 41-46; 48.

Comedy as well as tragedy lie in the field of the short story. We must get rid of this false idea that to be artistic a short story must be grim and depressing. The range of the short story is as wide as the range of the novel. Its length is less. And it is indirectly due to this, that sometimes we find in the artistic short story a special quality - a quality which is very rarely found in the novel in the same degree of intensity - a very curious, haunting, and suggestive quality.

Rules have been laid down for the construction of the short story. The short story, I have been confidently told, is to consist of a single episode and close the door behind it - and so on. ...

In fact, it is a little dangerous to lay down rules and limits for artists.

But some limitation of plot there must be. The idea that a short story can be or should be "a novel in a nutshell" is absurd. There are good short stories by Henry James which, from the point of view of the editor of a popular magazine, contain no plot at all. The first concern of the artistic writer of short stories, as of the artistic novelist, is with his characters. These must be real and living, for otherwise nothing that they do or suffer matters in the least to an intelligent and educated reader. Characters that are real and living get into the memory and stay there. We all remember Mulvaney, Ortheris, and Learoyd. We know just what kind of men they were. We do not remember with the same certain, easy accuracy the incidents in which they took part. Now the novelist has a hundred thousand words in which to create characters, while the writer of the short story may have only three thousand or less than that. Yet the characters in the short story must be just as real and convincing as the characters in the novel. It follows therefore that the short-story writer will not introduce too many characters or saddle himself with a complicated plot which requires to be developed through many incidents. It is hardly a question of art at all; the writer is practising much the same common sense that prevents a hostess from giving a very large dance in a very small room.

In practice, the limitation of space is not a limitation which the writer often feels. If he knows what the space is to be, he knows what will be needed to fill it; and, conversely, if he knows what his story will be, he knows what space it will take. The power to make these estimates with approximate and sufficient correctness is not a gift. It is no part of the writer's gift. It is a knack which is very rapidly and easily acquired in practice. ...

In the long novel a little redundancy and repetition, an occasional barren sentence, a few ill-chosen words, do not necessarily bring condemnation. But the writer of the short story cannot afford these lapses. He must look always for the most fertile word, the word which will be most prolific in the mind of the reader. It is quite correct to write in a story that somebody has taken prizes in Syriac as well as in several less difficult languages. It is plain statement. If that is all the author wants, it is right. But Stephen Crane - a veritable artist of the short story - wanted plain statement with a suggestion of humorous comment in it, and got it in one word. "Several less opaque languages", was what he wrote. ...

Every idea has a tendency to bring before the mind its associated ideas. It is part of the gift of the short-story writer to select detail which calls up to the mind many other details, to choose something salient and rich in association. A novelist working on a plain, large scale, as Zola did, will enumerate many details, and build up an entire scene, where the short-story writer in two lines has to suggest all. This gift of selection is rarely part of the writer's conscious equipment; I think it probable that those who use the gift to best effect are rarely conscious that they use it. I doubt if Stevenson, when he wrote that Pinkerton had "a grey eye as active as a fowl's," had any notion of selecting a salient detail, rich in association. Yet try to visualise such an eye in your mind; you cannot do it without visualising the rest of the face, and you may see more - movements of shoulders and hands. Nor can you think much about that phrase without knowing something about Pinkerton's character. This selective gift is of course common enough in novelists, but for the writer of the short story it is essential. ...

It may fairly be said that all these methods which are used by the artist of the short story are also open to the artist of the novel and are used by him. It is perfectly true. Many authors of the novel have also been authors of the short story, and have used much the same methods in both. But it is generally possible to say whether the author is primarily a novelist or primarily a writer of short stories. If his gift is for the large scheme in plot, if he marshals a great number of characters, if he works this theme right out and leaves no windows open, then he is a novelist, even if his choice of words, his appearance of truth in dialogue, and his selection of detail, seem to proclaim the short-story writer. The novel is a satisfaction: the short story is a stimulus. But if the author's gift is principally terse and vivid expression, if plot is definitely less to him than character, if the art of suggestion is obviously stronger in him than the art of working out a thesis, if no conscientious sub-editor can cut ten lines out of his two thousand words, without feeling that he has committed a silly crime, then that writer is a writer of the short story.

The novelist gives more to the reader and asks less of him. The short-story writer gives less and asks more. What is the trend of the reader's thought after he has finished a story? In the case of the novel, the thought goes back to what the reader has been told in the novel. He is satisfied. He has the information that he requires. He can turn it over in his mind. But the artist of the short story makes the reader's thought spring out of the story and open wide. He sends it out and beyond the actual facts recorded in the story into the facts suggested. Read that fine story of Conrad's, *A Smile of Fortune*. When you have finished it your thoughts are of the daughter of Jacobus, it is true, but you go with her outside the time-limits and scene-limits of the story - that is, if you are at all imaginative.

And just there begins the trouble for the artist of the short story. Nothing displeases the absolutely commonplace mind more than this richly suggestive art. His imagination is asleep and does not wish to be disturbed. The poor man says in his favourite phrase that he cannot make head or tail of it, and sends the book back to the library, noting perhaps the name of the author to prevent the recurrence of such mistakes in future. ...

Artistic work is rarely popular. Those who want everything done for them by the author, and not to find their own imagination set to work - those who cannot appreciate choice of words and suggestive selection of detail - those who are not responsive and widely sympathetic - these are the readers whom the artist of the short story cannot please - and they are many. And if, as in the case of Meredith, instant lucidity is sometimes lost and one must read the passage again, then the circle of appreciative readers becomes smaller still. If the most artistic work is that which makes the greatest demand on those to whom it is submitted, then no kind of literary work is more artistic than the short story.

aus einem Symposium mit dem Titel "Does character drawing or plot count more in fiction?", *The New York Sun*, LXXXII, 229 (April 17, 1915, Spring Literary Section), [o. S.]. - Dieser das Symposium einführende und auslösende Artikel war kurz zuvor in der *Saturday Evening Post* erschienen. Die Beiträge und Repliken anderer Autoren befassen sich zumeist mit dem Roman.

The short story is a work of art. It is not a segment of human experience. It is a finished product of a certain sort of skilled laborer, and it must be constructed according to established rules. As Aristotle pointed out in his poetics, the structure of all plots falls naturally into two divisions - the complication or building up, and the unravelling or denouement. By complication he meant, and we mean, all that extends from the beginning to the action and the part which marks the turning point of good or bad fortune. The unravelling is that which extends from the beginning of the change to the end.

Many poets, the Greeks said, tied the knot well, but unravelled it unskillfully. Both arts, however, they insisted, should be mastered. They advised one to make a sketch or general outline first and then fill the details.

It is not too much to say that before the writer begins his story he ought to be able to make a geometrical diagram of it which would show the proper proportions, just as an architect is able to make a diagram of the house he proposes to build, or the artist is able to make a drawing of the picture he proposes to paint. It is fatal to begin before that is done.

In order to be of universal interest to the reader the plot of the story, as the Greeks pointed out, must contain a surprise. It must be something to unravel. It must give the mind a problem. It must move from one incident or event to the other, the reader being interested in each of these movements until the whole conception of the story is before him. And as one thing happens after another in life and we do not realize the scope of an event as it begins to arrive, so in the construction of the story the reader must be led from one step to another, and these steps must be in proper sequence.

For the purpose of developing the situation, after constructing a plot that is mathematically correct in proportion the author must select characters and incidents. The plot is wholly an arbitrary thing; he must make it a complete unity, though in life nothing is complete. Having made the plot, he may take characters from life or he may modify them ...

The incidents must be assembled from life. They must be precisely as they occur in life. One cannot use any fabulous incident. He may use a fabulous design, but he must fill it with natural incident. One may build any kind of house he likes, but he must build it of material that is real. He must get his stone from the field and his wood from the forest.

The vital factor in the structure of a plot is to make it complete in itself. Events must speak for themselves. They must require no outside explanation. The thing should be a piece of mechanism so perfect that by virtue of its own structure it folds and unfolds itself, following the law of mechanics. Now it will be seen that the structure of a plot is an extremely difficult piece of work and not apt to be successfully done by any but by skilled workmen. For this reason the Greek said that a poet was primarily a maker of plots; and the short story writer of today - notwithstanding all pretensions to the contrary - is primarily a maker of plots.

This is what editors mean when they say they are looking for "a story" - "stuff that has a story in it"; for if there is no story - that is to say, no plot - no amount of skill and workmanship will avail. However, when the plot is finished one has not yet produced a short story. ...

It must be remembered that the story teller is not relating what has happened; he is relating what may happen. He is not reproducing life, he is using life for the purpose of producing art. And after he assembles all his elements from life he may undertake something better than nature produces.
...

The story turning on tragic incidents will affect the mind with greater influence if the events in it seem to move of themselves, with some sinister design. What old authorities said about tragedy is equally applicable now.

"Such an effect is best produced when the events come on us by surprise; and the effect is heightened when, at the same time, they follow as cause and effect. The tragic wonder will then be greater than if they happened of themselves or by accident; for even coincidences are most striking when they have an air of design. We may instance the statue of Mitys, at Argos, which fell on his murderer while he was a spectator at a festival and killed him. Such events seem not to be due to mere chance. Plots, therefore, constructed on these principles are necessarily the best."

A well constructed plot should be single in its issue. It should present one moving event in its complete unity. It should be so constructed that it unfolds itself or builds itself up by a natural and orderly moving of events. Every event should follow the preceding one in inevitable sequence and the explanation should appear suddenly. The element of surprise must come swiftly at the end. When the story has ended the reader will not wait for explanations. Everything he must know or ought to know should be given in it. ...

This is the great age of the short story. It is to the American people today what the drama was to the Greeks. We seek the same elements of interest that the Greeks found to be universal. If we would interest everybody in our publications, as they undertook to interest everybody in their open forums, we must give them a work of art following strictly the rules they pointed out.

We must work it out with characters agreeable to its intent; with sustained dialogue; with incidents assembled from life, and such descriptions as will make it a succession of vivid pictures. And we must do this all without a single line or word or idea or suggestion that is not organicaly [*sic*] essential to the whole design.

52. *SHERWOOD ANDERSON* — 1921

Erschienen als Vorwort zu *The Triumph of the Egg: A Book of Impressions from American Life in Tales and Poems* (New York, 1921), [o.S.]. - Dieses Gedicht wurde später noch in drei weiteren Publikationen Andersons unter dem Titel "The Story Teller" abgedruckt.

Tales are people who sit on the doorstep of the house of my mind.
It is cold outside and they sit waiting.
I look out at a window.

> The tales have cold hands,
> Their hands are freezing.

A short thickly-built tale arises and threshes his arms about.
His nose is red and he has two gold teeth.

There is an old female tale sitting hunched up in a cloak.

Many tales come to sit for a few moments on the doorstep and then go away.
It is too cold for them outside.
The street before the door of the house of my mind is filled with tales.
They murmur and cry out, they are dying of cold and hunger.

I am a helpless man - my hands tremble.
I should be sitting on a bench like a tailor.

I should be weaving warm cloth out of the threads of thought.
The tales should be clothed.
They are freezing on the doorstep of the house of my mind.

I am a helpless man - my hands tremble.
I feel in the darkness but cannot find the doorknob.
I look out at a window.
Many tales are dying in the street before the house of my mind.

53. *THEODORE DREISER* —— 1922

aus "The Scope of Fiction", *The New Republic*, XXX (April 12, 1922, Spring Literary Supplement), 8 f.

[The] problem of scope must ever be personal and individual. It is not for academic interpretation or fixation. We know, for instance, that for Eugêne Sue and his admirers five hundred thousand words and endlessly pieced together verbal canvases and tapestries are by no means sufficient to cause either himself or his followers to be excommunicated on the ground of unreasonable indulgence in scope. ... To those who like Richardson and his Pamela, and I confess myself one of his admirers, his epistolary flights, even unto four and five hundred thousand words are by no means too much. Because of the time in and of which he writes perhaps, I find myself following him with interest. Since scope, in part at least, might be assumed to predicate length or brevity as well as pleasure to the reader, I would have to confess that the scope of his work is satisfactory to me. ... In fact I accept the short story, Without Benefit of Clergy, as full and satisfactory a picture of life as The Brothers Karamazov, A Family of Noblemen, or Anna Karenina but no more so. Why? I will try to tell you.

Each suggests in its way, though the first may require but minutes and the other days to read, that unescapable and yet somehow pitiable finiteness in the midst of infinity which, think as we will, contrives to touch and move the understanding. Each suggests, in full, a land, a people, a period, a mood. Each etches the individual against a background of enormous possibilities and enormous limitations. Each conveys with moving completeness an all embracing understanding shot through with an enfolding and comforting pity. What more, pray, is it, that we ask of scope?

aus "Note" in *Thrifty Stock and Other Stories* (New York, 1923), 346-351.

It was, if memory may be relied upon, Aristotle who initiated the Greeks into the delights of classification, analysis and definition. Since then, the love of pasting names on things has become so universal that it may almost be classed as an instinct. ...

There would appear to be some need of more accurate classification and definition in the field of prose fiction. The word "novel" has come to be as capacious as an omnibus. A story of twenty thousand words is labelled "novelette" in a magazine; then makes its bow between boards as a full-fledged novel. This same confusion extends in the other direction; and it is not infrequent to see stories of twenty thousand words and upward called "short stories." ...

Now there is a difference between the novel and the story, and it is not a question of bulk at all. If this distinction were recognized and appreciated, there would be a distinct clarification of criticism, as a consequence. The novel, obviously enough, depends for its interest upon delineation and development of character, and presents a comprehensive picture of some phase, large or small, of the social system. There need be no plot; there is usually merely a chronology. The story, on the other hand, whatever its length, depends for its interest primarily upon incident and situation; it deals with conflicts and contrasts, with sacrifices and surrenders, with achievements and acquirements, with penalties and punishments, with sorrow and rescue, prosperity and disaster, and all the torment of obstructed passion. In short, with drama. There need be no social background; there need not even be any characters, in the strict sense of the word. It is perfectly possible to write an interesting story dealing simply with He and She. The thing has been done.

This distinction between novel and story is not a question of merit or demerit. As a matter of fact, it is obviously much more difficult to write a great story than it is to write a great novel. ...

Nor is the distinction a question of length, or bulk. ... The difference lies in the means which the writer has used, to stimulate and interest and arouse his reader. The story writer is like a violinist who plays a swift and ordered melody upon his instrument. The melody has form, and movement; it begins, it progresses, and it ends. The novelist, on the contrary, is like a 'cellist, who evokes from the strings beneath his fingers a series of resonant and throbbing tones and chords. They begin nowhere, they end nowhere; they give the impression of eternity.

There are many subdivisions in each of these categories. In American prose fiction, the short story is numerically the most important. "Short" is a comparative term, but if one asks "How short is a short story?" the answer must be, "The shorter the better." For the distinctive attribute of a short story is its brevity, and this is a circumstance too often overlooked. There are many qualities which a short story must have to be good, but unless it is short, it is not a short story at all. If it is possible to cut out or condense any substantial part of the story without weakening the effect produced by the whole, then the story is too long. ...

It is probably fair to say that a short story is harder to write, in proportion to its length, than any other form of fiction. The perfection of its structure requires as much consideration as though it were to be a novel of a hundred thousand words; the selection of incident, and the compression of events into the least possible scope consistent with their proper presentation demand a rigor which is not required in the production of any longer prose work. It is infinitely easier to tell a story in ten or fifteen thousand words than it is to tell the same story in five thousand; to bring that same tale below four thousand words is often as hard again. Yet if it may be done, it is worth doing; for it is an axiom of criticism that if a writer imposes upon himself limitations, and then works successfully within those limitations, the result justifies his pains. ... [If] he tells a story in brief that he might have told at length, and tells it adequately, the effect more than repays his effort.

A short story should be as short as possible; and it should be interesting. This is a statement apparently obvious; yet it is not so obvious as it seems. For a story should be interesting not to any one person, nor to any single group of persons, but to all persons. In so far as a story's theme lacks this universality of interest, it is foredoomed. Such a story may have its hour; it will never have its eternity. ...

Hence it is a fair generalization that the raw material of the drama is also the proper raw material of the short story. In every great short story there is a moment which would have been supremely effective upon the stage; in every dramatic situation there is a short story. No better text book on the short story has ever been written than William Archer's "Play-Making." It analyzes and expounds the science of Form, and Form, which is entirely unnecessary in the novel, is essential to the story, short or long.

A short story should be short, it should be interesting, it should have form, and finally, it should be intelligible. The first part of the task of making the reader understand is for the writer to understand. A novel may be written in a blind, leisurely, chronological fashion, a page at a time, the end never very definitely in view; but this is not true of the story, and particularly it is not true of the short story. The writer of a great short story conceives his story, not as a beginning, nor as a middle, but as a whole; each successive step toward the finished structure is clear to him before he begins to write; his means are weighed, his methods chosen before the perfunctory task of putting the result on paper is begun. This final whole is intelligible to him before he begins; it is intelligible to his reader when he has done. The actual writing is merely a task in transcription; and for this task, the old newspaper rule is the best guide. Write, while always striving for beauty, yet so clearly and simply that whoever can read what you have written can also understand.

These matters have been set down dogmatically; but they are not dogma. They are rather a creed, to which one may or may not subscribe. Brevity, interest, form and clarity; these are the ideals toward which, however haltingly, we strive.

55. JOHN GALSWORTHY ——— 1923

aus "Preface" zu *Quality and Other Stories* (= The Works of John Galsworthy. Manaton Edition, XIV, London, 1923), ix f.

One is often asked what are the canons of short-story writing. Frankly I do not know; but there are certainly these: "Write only what interests yourself," "From sentence to sentence grip your reader." The first is a matter of doing justice to your own temperament; the second a matter of technique, which can only be acquired through hard work, varied experiment, and repeated failure. In any case, the art of the short story is like that of the hundred yards race - the writer, like the runner, should be "all out" with every stride he takes.

Taken by and large the quite short story does not seem the happiest medium for English and American writers. I can think of none who can so compact poignancy into small space as De Maupassant, and only Katherine Mansfield who can catch a living moment so deftly as Tchekov. In Kipling, even at his best, there is mannerism, and philosophic arrest; in O. Henry, even at his best, a diction rather provincial, and a jocularity somewhat infernal. To concrete perfect fluency in the perfectly staccato, or the dramatic in brief fluency, seems to defeat Anglo-Saxon brains and languages.

English and Americans tend to attempt it in verse rather than prose. Half the educated young men and women in Anglo-Saxon countries would now seem to be poets. The development is intriguing, but all against the short story.

56. *KATHERINE FULLERTON GEROULD* —————————— 1924

aus "The American Short Story", *Yale Review*, N. S. XIII (July, 1924), 642-663.

One of the things sometimes said is that America has brought the short story to perfection. Not the novel, or the drama, or the lyric, or any other literary form; but the short story they do give us. I do not know whether these critics are right; but the short story has had a tremendous vogue in the U.S., and we have certainly produced it in enormous quantities. ...

It has long been obvious to the student of the form that the English and American demand on fiction in general and the short story in particular, is quite different from the French demand. Take Maupassant, for example. ... Maupassant remains the chief French artist in the *genre*. Take any of Maupassant's finest tales: "The Piece of String," "The Necklace," etc. Analyze them. What do you find? An extraordinary brevity, first of all. We all know how Maupassant achieved that brevity: paring down, and paring down, to fit the single column that he had to fill in the newspaper. ... What you find in the best Maupassant tales is an ironic event; an example of the lever-like workings of fate. ...

Now, the Anglo-Saxon demands, in fiction, a little more than this, and something a little different. We are a romantic folk, and we are incurably interested in human character. Maupassant, I think, was not. He did not create human individuals in his short stories; and, so far as I know, he never tried to. ... He gives you enough of the hero's or heroine's background or mood to make the initial gesture plausible. Beyond that, there is no characterization. Fate does the rest. Nor is the background itself dramatized. The only appeal to our imagination comes from the actual incident, and the almost Hellenic effect of inescapable doom. The tale is a mere skeleton, but that skeleton grins at you authentically.

Now, when an Englishman or an American tries to do this - usually he cannot. In spite of himself, he begins to round out his character, explain his background, enrich his canvas. We do not, perhaps, demand, as the French do, absolute perfection of form; but we do demand more imaginative human reference. ... We are as interested in human character as we are in straight incident. The incident, indeed, often interests us chiefly because it happened to that person, or a person of that sort. We have even developed the kind of story where no incident is discernible except by its reverberations in an individual mind or heart. Like much of the later Henry James. The ideal short story, from our point of view, is the one wherein interesting or dramatic things happen to clearly identified and differentiated people. Kipling is the great master of the type.

With the American short story, background has always been extremely important. Nearly all our considerable short story writers have dealt with peculiar atmospheres and special moods. ... The short story does not need a complex and traditional background so badly as the novel does. Since it must centre in one incident, we need to be prepared perfectly for that incident, but not for anything else. ... [The] variety of our American backgrounds has given us a specializing habit.

The terrifying younger generation would have nothing to say to Poe, or Hawthorne, no doubt, because these authors are so very "special" and exclusive. Poe is "special," indeed; yet Poe found the formula of artistic economy long since [in his review of Hawthorne's "Twice Told Tales".] ...

American literature is intensely local. This is due to two or three different facts. One is our diffused civilization, and our inevitable sectionalism. We have no large background; only an infinity of small ones. Then, too, since there is nothing new under the sun - especially no new plot - the nearest to a new thing we poor writers can get is a fresh background, which we are the first to exploit, or are particularly familiar with. Everyone stakes out a Wessex of his own. It need not be a place; it may be a peculiar human group, a social rather than a geographical atmosphere. But it is not mere diffusion and discouragement, I think, that make us so local. It is also, I believe, our tendency to demand that fiction should be reasonably informing.

Now, the demand that fiction should be informing is a perfectly legitimate demand, though it is more of a strain on the short story than on the novel. The business of fiction - *let us never forget it* - is to entertain; but fiction is not literature unless it also instructs. Literature, that is, to be worthy of the name, must give you vicarious experience. It must present to you dramatic events that have not occurred in your private history; it must present you with human beings who are not of your familiar acquaintance. I do not mean that great literature does not deal with experiences common to us all, and human beings such as we are, ourselves, or have ourselves apprehended. But I do mean this: that if a man had time and opportunity to experience in his own person all adventures and all human types, he would never read a novel or a short story. ...

Professor Bliss Perry long ago compared the writing of the novel and the writing of the short story to the running of a long race and the running of a short race. It is ten times as easy, he said, to write a short story as it is to write one ten times as long. Professor Perry only voiced the high-brow distrust of the type which prevailed at that time. Contrast this with the much wiser dictum of Mr. Ben Ames Williams... in a note appended to his recent volume of short stories, "Thrifty Stock"...

That, at least, is the other side of the shield. It would be a pity, too, to omit a metaphor which Henry James once used for the short story. In a forgotten preface, he refers to it as "the silver-shod, sober-paced, short-stepping, but oh so hugely nosing, so tenderly and yearningly and ruefully sniffing, gray mule of the 'few thousand words.'" There was no question in *his* mind of its potential significance.

The fact at least is that the novel and the short story are radically different methods of treating material. The experienced author would look at a human situation and decide which treatment would bring out its high lights best. Naturally, I do not mean that the stuff of any novel could be treated in the short story, even by Kipling. But surely we could get the essence of half the novels written, if they had been done as short stories by the right person. In many, if not most, great short stories, a novel lies implicit. ... [There] are many *données,* as the French say, which can be treated either in the novel or the short story. It is for the author to choose his method: that is all. The two methods are absolutely different; the arrangement of material, the perspective, the stresses - everything is different. But it is not a mere question of its being easier to write a short story than a novel.

The criticism one is tempted to make of the average, clever American short story is that it is not close-packed enough. ... When one reads a short story, one likes to feel that the author knew enough concerning the people involved to have written a whole book about them, had he chosen. The reason why the short story is discredited as a literary form is, I believe, that most of our stories are not so significant as that. They centre in one incident which means nothing; which has no context in the rest of the hero's life, no power of revealing a whole personality. Yet the short story, rightly taken, is an important and impressive *genre*. ...

The short story has three formal elements: situation, suspense, and climax. Generally speaking, the story should begin as near the end in point of time as possible, in order to give us the sense of dramatic speed. (No one but Maupassant could manage lapse of time as he did; wave ten - or fifty - years away in one graceful gesture, give you the full value of the interval, and not wear you out with the sense of having lived through a generation. ...) Situation, suspense, and climax: those are the necessary elements, and most of our clever short stories have them, duly proportioned. The average American story in the average American magazine is well composed. I don't say well written, for I think we have very few writers who have a vital knowledge of English style. But an astonishing number of people have learned the trick - in so far as it is a trick - of the short story.

The difference between the first-rate short story writer and these others lies most often (style apart) in the quality of the moment he selects on which to make the whole thing hinge. The first-rate short story writer chooses a moment that is not simply exciting in itself, but is also of a profound significance to the person or people involved - according to the old metaphor of the stone flung and the ripples spreading from shore to shore. ...

Not only must your curiosity have been excited about what is going to happen, but you must feel that that thing, when it does happen, is important - either to the protagonist or to some one else. The event need not be either gruesome or tragic; it may be a happy event; it may even be an amusing event. ... The event may not be the major crisis of a life; it may be only a turning-point. It may be a mere vivid illustration of the kind of thing that happens on any summer day - made vital by its universality or its symbolism. ...

Technically speaking, some of the earliest and greatest narratives we possess - I mean the narratives of the Old Testament - are short stories, in every subtle detail of form and scope. The last verses of the ninth chapter of II Kings compose into a great short story. The fifth chapter of Daniel, which begins "Belshazzar the king made a great feast unto a thousand of his lords, and drank wine before the thousand," is a great short story. So is the fourth chapter of Judges, and so is the thirty-seventh chapter of Genesis. No sane critic condemns a poet for writing only lyrics, provided those lyrics are the best. The lyric is as important a poetic form as the narrative poem or the elegy. The same is true - as Poe long ago declared - of the tale, the short story. It is a perfectly valid criticism of life; and some of the most serious human situations can be treated better in this form than in the novel form. The difference is one of method, not of intrinsic importance.

57. *SHERWOOD ANDERSON* —— 1924

aus *A Story Teller's Story*, Book VI, Note I, (New York, 1924; 1951), 347-365.

I walked about the city of New York looking at people. I was not too young any more and could not make myself over to fit a new city. No doubt certain characteristics of my own nature had become fixed. I was a man of the mid-western towns who had gone from his town to the mid-western cities and there had gone through the adventures common to such fellows as myself. Was there some salt in me? To the end of my life I would talk with the half slovenly drawl of the middle-westerner, would walk like such a middle-westerner, have the air of something between a laborer, a man of business, a gambler, a race horse owner, an actor. If I was, as I then fully intended, to spend the rest of my life trying to tell such tales as I could think and feel my way through, I would have to tell the tales of my own people. Would I gain new power and insight for the telling by having come East, by consorting with other story-tellers? Would I understand better my own people and what had made the tragedies, the comedies and the wonders of their lives? ...

My own position was something like this: there were in my head certain tales I knew but could not yet tell and certain others I had told but felt I had told badly or haltingly. Was there a certain formula one could learn that might help one out of the difficulty? ...

There was a notion that ran through all story-telling in America, that stories must be built about a plot and that absurd Anglo-Saxon notion that they must point a moral, uplift the people, make better citizens, etc. The magazines were filled with these plot stories and most of the plays on our stage were plot plays. "The Poison Plot," I called it in conversation with my friends as the plot notion did seem to me to poison all story-telling. What was wanted I thought was form, not plot, an altogether more elusive and difficult thing to come at.

The plots were frameworks about which the stories were to be constructed and editors were inordinately fond of them. One got "an idea for a story." What was meant was that a new trick had been thought out. Nearly all the adventure stories and the well-known American western stories were so constructed. A man went into the redwood forests or into the deserts and took up land. He has been a rather mean, second-rate chap in civilization but in the new place a great change comes over him. Well, the writer had got him out where there was no one looking and could do as he pleased with the fellow. Never mind what he had been. The forests or the deserts had changed him completely. The writer could make a regular angel of him, have him rescue downtrodden women, catch horse thieves, exhibit any kind of bravery required to keep the reader excited and happy.

A word of good sense dropped in anywhere would have blown the whole thing to pieces but there was no danger. In all such writing all consideration for human beings was thrown aside. No one lived in such tales. Let such a writer begin to think of human beings, care a little for human beings, and his paste-board world would melt before his eyes. ...

In certain moods one became impregnated with the seeds of a hundred new tales in one day. The telling of the tales, to get them into form, to clothe them, find just the words and the arrangement of words that would clothe them - that was a quite different matter. ...

For such men as myself you must understand there is always a great difficulty about telling the tale after the scent has been picked up. The tales that continually came to me in the way indicated above could of course not become tales until I had clothed them. Having, from a conversation overheard or in some other way, got the tone of a tale, I was like a woman who has just become impregnated. Something was growing inside me. At night when I lay in my bed I could feel the heels of the tale kicking against the walls of my body. Often as I lay thus every word of the tale came to me quite clearly but when I got out of bed to write it down the words would not come.

I had constantly to seek in roads new to me. Other men had felt what I had felt, had seen what I had seen - how had they met the difficulties I faced? My father when he told his tales walked up and down the room before his audience. He pushed out little experimental sentences and watched his audience narrowly. There was a dull-eyed old farmer sitting in a corner of the room. Father had his eyes on the fellow. "I'll get him," he said to himself. He watched the farmer's eyes. When the experimental sentence he had tried did not get anywhere he tried another and kept trying. Beside words he had - to help the telling of his tales - the advantage of being able to act out those parts for which he could find no words. He would frown, shake his fists, smile, let a look of pain or annoyance drift over his face.

These were his advantages that I had to give up if I was to write my tales rather than tell them and how often I had cursed my fate. ...

[An] American painter, Mr. Felix Russman, had taken me one day into his workshop to show me his colors. He laid them out on a table before me ... It had been one of the most exciting moments of my life. I shifted the little pans of color about, laid one color against another. I walked away and came near. Suddenly there had flashed into my consciousness, for perhaps the first time in my life, the secret inner world of the painters. Before that time I had wondered often enough why certain paintings, done by the old masters, and hung in our Chicago Art Institute, had so strange an effect upon me. Now I thought I knew. The true painter revealed all of himself in every stroke of his brush. ...

Very well then, the words used by the tale-teller were as the colors used by the painter. Form was another matter. It grew out of the materials of the tale and the teller's reaction to them. It was the tale trying to take form that kicked about inside the tale-teller at night when he wanted to sleep.

And words were something else. Words were the surfaces, the clothes of the tale. I thought I had begun to get something a little clearer now. I had smiled to myself a little at the sudden realization of how little native American words had been used by American story-writers. When most American writers wanted to be very American they went in for slang. ...

Would the common words of our daily speech in shops and offices do the trick? Surely the Americans among whom one sat talking had felt everything the Greeks had felt, everything the English felt? Deaths came to them, the tricks of fate assailed their lives. I was certain none of them lived felt or talked as the average American novel made them live feel and talk and as for the plot short stories of the magazines - those bastard children of De Maupassant, Poe and O. Henry - it was certain there were no plot short stories ever lived in any life I had known anything about.

58. *SHERWOOD ANDERSON* ——— 1925

aus *The Modern Writer* (San Francisco, 1925), 22-24; 39 f.

Life ... is a complex delicate thing. Anything may happen in life. We all know that. People hardly ever do as we think they should. There are no plot short stories in life. All the clever tricks by which effects are to be got on the printed page are in reality a selling out of ourselves. ... If it is your desire to be that kind of a writer, to grow rich and be successful by writing and if you have a natural talent that can be made to serve your purpose, stay just as far away as possible from any real thinking or feeling about actual men and women. Stay in the pasteboard world. Believe in your heroic cowboys and lumberjacks. Go to the movies all you can. Read the magazines. Go to the short story schools and learn the bag of tricks. Spend your time thinking up plots for stories and never by any chance let the plots grow naturally out of the lives and the hopes, joys and the sufferings of the people you are writing about. That is the road to success. ...

Consider for a moment the materials of the prose writer, the teller of tales. His materials are human lives. To him these figures of his fancy, these people who live in his fancy should be as real as living people. He should be no more ready to sell them out than he would sell out his men friends or the woman he loves. To take the lives of these people and bend or twist them to suit the needs of some cleverly thought out plot to give your readers a false emotion is as mean and ignoble as to sell out living men or women. For the writer there is no escape, as there is no real escape for any craftsman. If you handle your materials in a cheap way you become cheap. The need of making a living may serve as an excuse but it will not save you as a craftsman. Nothing really will save you if you go cheap with tools and materials. Do cheap work and you are yourself cheap. That is the truth.

59. [ANONYMUS] ——— 1925

aus "The Modern Short Story", *The Times Literary Supplement* (Jan. 29, 1925), 61 f.

The present age is frequently, and with some justice, stigmatized as the misbegotten child of superficiality and hustle. The democratization of literature has been attended by many manifest evils. The vast increase of literacy, with no numerically proportionate increase in intelligence, has resulted in a lowering of the literary average. This signifies, however, that the commercialists are busy rather than that the artists are all dead. The production of good art is fairly constant, though its forms change. We can no longer with any confidence hope for long leisurely novels of such solid build and ample scope as the older masters delighted in; the spirit of the times is not friendly to epic poetry; and we have no imaginative periodical literature worthy of the name. This is the age of Snap, a brisk little deity with a squint, who manifests himself ubiquitously in short sentences, short gossiping paragraphs, and short stories.

Herein is no cause for despair, though much, perhaps, for disquietude.

Literature, which cannot afford to be "a thing enskied and sainted," is capable of surviving these perils and even of profiting by them. The artist has always contrived to "make his cross his crutch." Just as the poet turns the discipline of strict form to good account, so the writer of fiction may be led to new triumphs in the process of satisfying a popular demand for brevity. Just as cinematography, which began largely as a diversion for the brainless, now shows signs (in Germany) of becoming a genuine and independent art, so the short story, whose origin is more respectable but whose present commercial vogue is due to similar causes, is in a fair way to effect technical innovations that will be a permanent acquisition to English fiction. The short story, whether we like it or not, has come to stay; the man in the street is a man in a hurry; he has a train to catch, business letters to write, and probably a garden that demands his attention. Until he is supplied with something better, but equally brief, he will continue to corrode his brains with the scandalously bad fiction to be found in our monthly magazines. And until the most characteristic literary form of the age is taken seriously, by writers and critics alike, its artistic advance will remain imperceptible.

Definitions are out of favour. In our fear of seeming to impose a system of rules upon art we shrink from using even the most innocent of delimiting phrases. The instinct is a healthy one; the crippling of criticism and stultification of drama by the pseudo-Aristotelian dogma of the dramatic unities are a sufficient warning. It is possible, however, that the reaction from scholiastic pedantry has carried us too far into a luminous fog of tendencies and atmospheres. The short story, though periodically boomed by interested persons, has never, in England, been closely examined as a form. Indeed, one brilliant practitioner has denied that it possesses a distinctive form. In the 'nineties, complains Mr. Wells (in his introduction to "The Country of the Blind"),

> we suffered ... from the *a priori* critic. Just as nowadays he goes about declaring that the work of such-and-such a dramatist is all very amusing and delightful, but "it isn't a Play," so we had a great deal of talk about *the* short story, and found ourselves measured by all kinds of arbitrary standards. There was a tendency to treat the short story as though it was as definable a form as the sonnet, instead of being just exactly what anyone of courage and imagination can get told in twenty minutes' reading or so.

"A great deal of talk" we may have had; but if there was any critic who believed the short story to be "as definable a form as the sonnet" it is noteworthy that he made no attempt to supply the definition. And Mr. Wells's own attempt avails us little. Elsewhere in the same essay he delivers an even more positive pronouncement: - "The short story is a fiction that may be read in something under an hour." And again: - "The art of the short story ... the jolly art of making something very bright and moving; it may be horrible or pathetic or beautiful or profoundly illuminating, having only this essential, that it should take from fifteen to fifty minutes to read aloud." If this dictum were accepted, the penny novelette, Lamb's "Dream Children," and the synopses of "Ivanhoe" and "Esmond" in such popular compilations as "The World's Great Books," would henceforward have to be regarded as short stories. Without erecting vicious arbitrary standards, there is surely more to be said than this. With volumes by Stevenson, Wells, Kipling, Katherine Mansfield, De la Mare, and Coppard on our shelves, we cannot believe that the short story of to-day is not to be distinguished in kind from the anecdote, the fictional sketch, or the mere novel in knickerbockers.

This last point must be insisted upon. The connexion between the novel and the modern short story is extremely dubious. Historical connexion there is none. The newer form is not a development or offshoot of the older, any more than the lyric is an offshoot of the narrative poem. It would be roughly true to say that the short story is to the novel what the lyric is to the narrative poem, or - perhaps a better analogy - what Tragedy is to Epic. "Of all plots," said Aristotle, writing of Tragedy, "the episodic are the worst." And this is as true of the short story as it is untrue, as a generalization, of the novel. There is obviously much common ground where the two techniques overlap; but the differences are our present concern, and an examination of them will bring us as near the desired definition as we are likely to get. Setting aside Scott, who produced at least one fine work in this kind, it is not to the early novelists that we owe the short story; in their day it did not, as a distinctive form, exist, and they contributed little or nothing to its invention. In America, with Poe and Hawthorne, begins its legitimate history. Poe delighted, as only the insensitive can delight, in horror so crude as to amount to indecency; it is arguable that much of his fiction is more neurotic than imaginative; but these personal blemishes, and the Gothic excesses in his style, must not obscure for us the fact that he was the first considerable writer of English to use prose fiction, as the poet uses lyric and the essayist the essay, primarily for the expression of his own moods and fancies. He was, good or bad, a poet; he looked in his heart and wrote. His power of characterization was negligible; each of his best tales objectifies an emotional idea, creates a strongly flavoured psychological atmosphere - generally, as it happens, that of horror or fear. This has some relevance to our inquiry, for we shall find that, though other writers in this form immeasurably excel Poe in the creation of men and women, a certain close unity of treatment and atmosphere is one distinguishing feature of the short story. This unity, which is essential, may inhere in the very nature of the plot, or it may be imposed by some such device as that of mediate narration, whose singular virtue is that it can fuse into a brief unity events discontinuous in time and space, and at the same time enrich these events with the colours of the interpolated and (more or less) alien personality.

The creation of people, which is of first importance in the novel, remains important in the short story, but it takes second place. That is why the often clever character sketches that are sometimes presented as tales fail to satisfy us. The study of a young man shaving, or a young woman buying a dress, may be amusing and delightful, but it does not suffice. If we are interested in these people, and if it is for their sake alone that the narrative exists, it is disconcerting to be deprived so soon of their company. We demand more: we demand drama, whether external or of the mind; we demand movement to and from a crisis of illumination that shall be the significant pivot of the whole. In fine, we ask of the short story that it shall have a point, not a moral lesson, not an opinion on this or that - nothing, indeed, that can be stated in paraphrase, but a something to communicate that can be communicated only in this way. Of the novel we do not make quite this demand; it is sufficient that it have vitality, that its people are strong with life and that the world they live in (whether our own world or some other) is consistent with itself. After reading Dickens or Fielding, we rise stimulated by the excellent company we have kept, whereas from a tale by Katherine Mansfield or by Mr. de la Mare (both poets, it is significant to note, and both masters of the short story) we carry away, not a host of memorable friends, but a poetic emotion, a savour, a moment of illumination. If we examine those tales which yield us most potent aesthetic pleasure, we shall find that each of them exists for the sake of this illuminated and illuminating moment, of beauty or of terror, of wonder or of sheer surprise, all that precedes and follows that moment being in the nature of an orchestral prelude and postlude, the first to seduce our minds to the enchantment, the second to release us from it without shock. This moment, which may do its work in us even though itself remain undetected, is what the short story writer gives us; it is this that we retain. The characters may, and often do, linger in the memory; but memory cherishes them, not for their own sakes, but for the sake of what they contribute to the total significance. At their best they are more immediately (though subtly) symbolic than are the creatures of the novelist. Seaton's Aunt, with her suave mockeries, her secret life, her surmised commerce with the undying dead that infest her house, is less a woman than a living symbol of power and malignancy. ...

[The] difference in length between the novel and the short story is of practical rather than critical significance. "The Turn of the Screw," for example, is more purely a short story (or *conte*, as we may prefer to call it) than is "Rip Van Winkle," the fact that the first contains forty thousand words, while the second is completed in a trifle over six thousand, being irrelevant. Economy, essential to the short story, but to the novel no more than an additional grace, is not to be confused with brevity, though it is clear that in practice the two will generally go together. Washington Irving's admired tale has charm and many specific good qualities, but it lacks the particular quality or treatment that is the subject of our present inquiry. A quarter of his space, and that the first quarter, is devoted to a description of the Kaatskill mountains, Rip Van Winkle, his wife and his cronies. We have to swallow two thousand words of past-indefinite narration before the story proper begins, and another dose of the same medicine when the curtain falls. The result is in no legitimate sense a short story; it is rather the synopsis of a novel that the author had no time, or no inclination, to write.

Henry James's long tale, on the other hand, is admirably to our purpose. After an introduction, which is no more than the genial patter of one who is secretly planning to scare us out of our wits, the story begins in the middle of things and drives forward, with no break in continuity and no considerable variation in speed, to the end: there is no long lapse into the past-indefinite, no digression, and no characterization for characterization's sake such as in a novel we should welcome; above all, there is a steady pulsing movement. Only for the purposes of sale can "The Turn of the Screw" be termed a novel and "Rip Van Winkle" a short story. Evidently new terms are needed. The short story tends to brevity as the lyric tends to brevity and, as we have seen, for a similar reason. Because its characters are the life of a novel, we demand length, in order to see as much of them as possible. Because the short story must sustain a single mood, present one dominant flavour to the tongue, it cannot be protracted indefinitely without disaster. Brief, therefore, it is in general, but brevity is not of its essence.

In concluding, we must anticipate the inevitable contention that the larger form contains the smaller, that the novel is a complex unity and the short story a simple one, and that there is no other difference. But we are describing here, not stories that happen to be short, but something, reached by induction, that for want of a less ambiguous term we must call, with apologies to Mr. Wells, *the* Short Story, an ideal form whose characteristic quality is indeed to be found in a few modern novels as well as in brief tales. It is true that in certain novels ... chapters exist having in some degree the perfection and unity of this ideal form; but it is true also, and significant, that no such novels were written before Poe. The question of historical precedence, however, is of slight account. Admittedly there are transitional types; admittedly, too, there are works of fiction that have one foot in each category; admittedly, cast-iron categories are vicious. Between verse and prose there is a similar No Man's Land, yet verse and prose continue to exist as separate forms. What could more eloquently testify to the dearth of formal criticism than the fact that we have no term by which to designate this short story quality? Of a narrative poem we are permitted to say, "This has (or has not) a powerful lyrical element." But we cannot say, without tiresome paradox, "Here is a novel rich in the quality of the short story." By this we should mean: "It is written with unusual economy of diction and in a convention more austere than that of the novelist. It suggests more than it states; it is intense, continuous, and incandescent; above all, it differs in *tempo* from the normal novel."

The greatest creative novelists present to us a world of their own. There is, further, a common region of the imagination where their memorable personages dwell together with feasting and copious laughter, with sublime speeches, or with tragic gestures. To their company the short story writer can scarcely hope to add. His is a smaller world, and his are comparatively pygmy creatures. Each tale, indeed, is a bead of light in which we see one aspect of the author's vision of life - an emotion, a poetic idea, a one-act drama - reflected in exquisite miniature. Each tale is rounded and complete, a self-luminous bubble containing and confining the little figures that exist only to serve it. The world of the novel is not only larger; it is less ordered, less artificial, a world of vigorous and wilful people only a tithe of whose doings and sayings are recorded in the book where we first meet them. The novel is a window through which we see - idealized or caricatured, always more or less delicately distorted - the men and women who throng the busy street. The short story is a tiny glowing stage, microcosm of our mortal existence, across which, from one invisibility to another, pass the little people of the play.

aus "Telling a Short Story" in *The Writing of Fiction* (New York & London, 1925), 33-58.

Like the modern novel, the modern short story seems to have originated - or at least received its present stamp - in France. English writers, in this line, were slower in attaining the point to which the French and Russians first carried the art. ...

Though the critic no longer feels that need of classifying and sub-classifying the *genres* which so preoccupied the contemporaries of Wordsworth, there are, in all the arts, certain local products that seem to necessitate a parenthesis. ...

One of the chief obligations, in a short story, is to give the reader an immediate sense of security. Every phrase should be a sign-post, and never (unless intentionally) a misleading one: the reader must feel that he can trust to their guidance. His confidence once gained, he may be lured on to the most incredible adventures - as the Arabian Nights are there to show. ...

It is sometimes said that a "good subject" for a short story should always be capable of being expanded into a novel.

The principle may be defendable in special cases; but it is certainly a misleading one on which to build any general theory. Every "subject" (in the novelist's sense of the term) must necessarily contain within itself its own dimensions; and one of the fiction-writer's essential gifts is that of discerning whether the subject which presents itself to him, asking for incarnation, is suited to the proportions of a short story or of a novel. If it appears to be adapted to both the chances are that it is inadequate to either.

It would be as great a mistake, however, to try to base a hard-and-fast theory on the denial of the rule as on its assertion. Instances of short stories made out of subjects that could have been expanded into a novel, and that are yet typical short stories and not mere stunted novels, will occur to every one. General rules in art are useful chiefly as a lamp in a mine, or a hand-rail down a black stairway; they are necessary for the sake of the guidance they give, but it is a mistake, once they are formulated, to be too much in awe of them.

There are at least two reasons why a subject should find expression in novel-form rather than as a tale; but neither is based on the number of what may be conveniently called incidents, or external happenings, which the narrative contains. There are novels of action which might be condensed into short stories without the loss of their distinguishing qualities. The marks of the subject requiring a longer development are, first, the gradual unfolding of the inner life of its characters, and secondly the need of producing in the reader's mind the sense of the lapse of time. Outward events of the most varied and exciting nature may without loss of probability be crowded into a few hours, but moral dramas usually have their roots deep in the soul, their rise far back in time; and the suddenest-seeming clash in which they culminate should be led up to step by step if it is to explain and justify itself. There are cases, indeed, when the short story may make use of the moral drama at its culmination. If the incident dealt with be one which a single retrospective flash sufficiently lights up, it is qualified for use as a short story; but if the subject be so complex, and its successive phases so interesting, as to justify elaboration, the lapse of time must necessarily be suggested, and the novel-form becomes appropriate.

The effect of compactness and instantaneity sought in the short story is attained mainly by the observer of two "unities" - the old traditional one of time, and that other, more modern and complex, which requires that any rapidly enacted episode shall be seen through only one pair of eyes. Sicht

It is fairly obvious that nothing is more retarding than the marking of a time-interval long enough to suggest modification in the personages of the tale or in their circumstances. The use of such an interval inevitably turns the short story into a long tale unduly compressed, the bald scenario of a novel. ... [A] third, and intermediate, form of tale - the *long* short-story - is available for any subject too spreading for conciseness yet too slight in texture to be stretched into a novel. ...

It remains to try to see what constitutes (in any permanent sense) the underlying norm of the "good short story."

A curious distinction between the successful tale and the successful novel at once presents itself. It is safe to say (since the surest way of measuring achievement in art is by survival) that the test of the novel is that its people should be *alive*. No subject in itself, however fruitful, appears to be able to keep a novel alive; only the characters in it can. Of the short story the same cannot be said. Some of the greatest short stories owe their vitality entirely to the dramatic rendering of a situation. Undoubtedly the characters engaged must be a little more than puppets; but apparently, also, they may be a little less than individual human beings.

In this respect the short story, rather than the novel, might be called the direct descendant of the old epic or ballad - of those earlier forms of fiction in all of which action was the chief affair, and the characters, if they did not remain mere puppets, seldom or never became more than types - such as the people, for instance, in Molière. The reason of the difference is obvious. Type, general character, may be set forth in a few strokes, but the progression, the unfolding of personality, of which the reader instinctively feels the need if the actors in the tale are to retain their individuality for him through a succession of changing circumstances - this slow but continuous growth requires space, and therefore belongs by definition to a larger, a symphonic plan.

The chief technical difference between the short story and the novel may therefore be summed up by saying that situation is the main concern of the short story, character of the novel; and it follows that the effect produced by the short story depends almost entirely on its form, or presentation. Even more - yes, and much more - than in the construction of the novel, the impression of vividness, of *presentness*, in the affair narrated, has to be sought, and made sure of beforehand, by that careful artifice which is the real carelessness of art. The short-story writer must not only know from what angle to present his anecdote if it is to give out all its fires, but must understand just *why* that particular angle and no other is the right one. ...

[The] short-story writer's first concern, once he has mastered his subject, is to study what musicians call the "attack." The rule that the first page of a novel ought to contain the germ of the whole is even more applicable to the short story, because in the latter case the trajectory is so short that flash and sound nearly coincide. ...

The arrest of attention by a vivid opening should be something more than a trick. It should mean that the narrator has so brooded on this subject that it has become his indeed, so made over and synthesized within him that, as a great draughtsman gives the essentials of a face or landscape in a half-a-dozen strokes, the narrator can "situate" his tale in an opening passage which shall be a clue to all the detail eliminated.

The clue given, the writer has only to follow. But his grasp must be firm; he must never for an instant forget what he wants to tell, or why it seemed worth telling. And this intensity of hold on his subject presupposes, before the telling of even a short story, a good deal of thinking over. Just because the limits of the form selected prevent his producing the semblance of reality by elaborating his characters, is the short-story writer the more bound to make real the adventure in itself. ...

The precious instinct of selection is distilled by that long patience which, if it be not genius, must be one of genius's chief reliances in communicating itself. On this point repetition and insistence are excusable: the shorter the story,the more stripped of detail and "cleared for action," the more it depends for its effect not only on the choice of what is kept when the superfluous has been jettisoned, but on the order in which these essentials are set forth. ...

It has been often, and inaccurately, said that the mind of a creative artist is a mirror, and the work of art the reflection of life in it. The mirror, indeed, is the artist's mind, with all his experiences reflected in it;but the work of art, from the smallest to the greatest, should be something projected, not reflected, something on which his mirrored experiences, at the right conjunction of the stars, are to be turned for its full illumination.

61. *RUTH SUCKOW* ——— 1927

aus "The Short Story", *The Saturday Review of Literature*, IV (Nov. 19, 1927), 317 f.

Because I myself write short stories of a certain type does not in the least mean to me that that is the way in which all short stories must be written - it means simply that I have found it the way best suited to my own intention. I admit a preference but not a theory. It seems unprofitable to me to attack one type of short story for the benefit of another. It is definition and formulae themselves that I deny: the generalization of the specific. The definition formulated by Mr. Edgar Allan Poe defined *a* short story very well - the special kind of short story, of course, which he himself was bent upon writing. The trouble came when it was utilized to define *the* short story. ... The doctrine of The Short Story has had, does have, a blighting influence upon the production of short stories in America. ...

The rigidity of the definition is usually charged to the commercialization of popular magazines. That may explain its persistence, but not, I think, its origin. Many of the magazines themselves have been by-products of the definition. They owe their existence to The Short Story, and they have shown themselves very properly grateful. Commercialization does not explain even the persistence of the definition in the schools, outside of those "courses in The Short Story" that deal in marketable patterns with price-tag attached. It grew out of an aspiration and was held as an ideal. But, like most Americans ideals, it has been found a very profitable means of making money, preserving prosperity, and keeping the young people in line. ...

It was the chaos, the unevenness, the diversity of American life that made short stories such a natural artistic expression in the first place. Roving, unsettled, restless, unassimilated, here and gone again - a chaos so huge, a life so varied and so multitudinous that its meaning could be caught only in fragments, perceived only by will-o'-the-wisp gleams, preserved only in tiny pieces of perfection. It was the first eager, hasty way of snatching little treasures of art from the great abundance of unused, uncomprehended material. Short stories were a way of making America intelligible to itself.

Within this chaos, two factions were and are forever struggling, both for an ideal which they call by the same name, each with an opposing conviction of the means of attainment. The ideal is called American culture, American art. Both struggle for standards. But one faction seeks to bring in these standards from the outside, the other to develop them from within. One is colonial-minded, and the other national-minded. One is very timid, and the other recklessly brave. Short stories are about the only form of literature in America which did not have their origin in England - as a form, that is, not a variation. There was, therefore, no external, ready-made standard to be applied to them. Poe, an originator even though a classicist, in the very fierceness of his originality was impelled to state his own standard as well as to write his own stories. He did so partly because nobody but himself believed in it. In this manner, Poe, the original artist, became the originator of the barren negation of original art that goes under the heading of The Short Story. ...

Short stories? - A running commentary upon life; fireflies in the dark; questions and answers; fragments, or small and finished bits of beauty; whatever, in fact, their author has the power to make of them --- But The Short Story? - A fundamental stupidity.

aus "The Folk Story in America", *South Atlantic Quarterly*, XXXIII (Jan., 1934), 10-19.

Now that I can look back on the whole scale of my story interests, I can see that I had always liked the folk story better than any other, the sort of story I heard my own ancients telling, the sort I learned very early to draw up out of incident and anecdote going on about me, and learned to run down in footnote and reminder among my elders. But the sort of story that was prevalent at the time, along in the early nineties when I began to be explicitly interested in the story as a literary medium, was very different from that in which other young people were then interested. I had slipped into the limitation of Washington Irving, when he said "I consider the story merely a frame on which I stretch my materials.It is the play of thought and sentiment and language, the weaving of characters, lightly yet expressively, delineated, the familiar and faithful delineation of scenes of common life. ..." But the popular story of that period was not in the least like that. What editors of that day wanted was "reading matter, next to which" advertisements could expediently be placed, of which the salient ingredient was what went by the name of local color. ...

But my own notion was that color was something you ought to find already on the reader's hands. What I wanted was a background completely existent, such as you find taken for granted in fairy tales... The people were simply there with a given pattern of reactions, and the story happened. But the mode of the hour was that authors went to no end of trouble to account for and describe, until the whole atmosphere was so completely drenched with local color that you couldn't get into the story any way but by getting yourself thoroughly sloshed about in it.

There was an excuse for that, perhaps, in the circumstance that the fashion of life in any particular locality in the United States varied to a degree that induced variations in behavior, which had to be fully explained before the track of the story could be securely plotted amid them. But what I wanted was a certain solidity and alikeness of the underpinning of all stories, which you could take in a measure for granted, the way you could the universality of motive and behavior in a story like Cinderella. ...

[A] little later when I came to the story telling habits of Indians, among whom tales are often told quite competently in sign talk, I began to understand that the whole story business consists in the creation of assorted patterns of selected single behaviors.

When I speak of Indian stories as patterns, I mean realistic stories, not myths, which are patterns of thought and ideation plotted on the constitution of life as it is understood among Indians. All Indians have both kinds; stories of the movement of invisible forces at work on the stuff of life, and stories of how life itself gets accomplished. Myth stories are patterned by the Indian's notion of how the invisible life forces are supposed to work, and realistic tales relate what takes place among the visible activities of behavior.

By the Piutes, among whom I was initiated into the real stories, they were called One Smoke stories, being chiefly the sort of tales that get told around the fire in the intervals between ceremonial rituals, while the company relaxes itself with the little cornhusk cigarets filled with native tabac. One tells while the rest smoke, and then the next one in the circle leaves off smoking and tells another, short and explicit and packed with reality. ...

I had a realizing dissatisfaction with the current American form of Indian legends, made over as most of them were, on the plan of the existing European folk tale. Whole volumes of Indian stories, as published formerly, have the disability that they have been remade and distorted out of their original form, to bring them into European resemblances, so that they lose all freshness and variety. ...

What I had finally to discover was that the economy of style which characterized the two modes of telling was no mere trick of words, but the essential item of the teller's grip on the quality of life out of which the story issued. If one were to tell Indian tales, or sheepherder's, or cowboy's, or bear hunter's - any sort of distinctively folk stories - they must be the sort of tales such people told each other with complete adjustments of the mode of life and the environment involved. The environment had absolutely to disappear into the story, with nothing left over. The story itself would have to be completely resolved, every item so satisfyingly disposed of that no question remained to be asked, nor explanation offered. ...

Of minor technicalities, besides the skill with which the story is completely swallowed in the environment, there are two or three that cannot be omitted. ... In telling, the mood of the incident is struck almost immediately, within the first two or three sentences, and it is always the mood of the story and not of the teller. ... With the aboriginal, before the story is offered to an audience, its umbilical cord has always been cut. ...

[It] is indispensable to the primitive teller that the story should stand to the hearer in place of an experience, which is the primary reason why it should be told at all.

I have used the term "realistic," the thing that happens, to describe the sort of story that gets called Folk Tale as distinguished from the Myth, in which things figurative and imaginative, are made to do duty for realities not physically apprehended. But one has to remember that, for the primitive, many things get credit for actually happening which really occur in that borderland between things that have a palpable existence, and other things which have only a psychic reality; dreaming true, talking animals, mountains that walk, dead that return, and Gods that appear and hold converse. All of these things have a kind of believable reality to the Indian, on a plane from which he draws the note of mystery in dealing with them. One finds the same thing in Negro tales...

I do not mean to say that here in the Southwest the whole color and pattern of this rich folk literature is lost. Perhaps we are catching it in time to keep the original color and flavor of that portion of it which has shed its extra sacred quality, as it is actually told to Indian children. ... Much of it has already passed by the process of osmosis, in contact around the camp fires of the desert. Something of the Indian method has been taken over by the Spanish speaking population, just as something of the legendary lore of Saints has been taken up from the Spanish by the Indians, something of the terseness and figurative quality has gone from the Indian to the cowboy and prospector. Will Rogers has served to slither the dry alertness of Indian humor into the American occasion. I recall with interested amusement that it was *The Mercury,* the smartest, forwardest of American magazines, that began first to publish my One Smoke Stories, and that other magazines were not too long in following with the Short, Short Story which is the true Indian *genre*.

One of the factors which works unconsciously in the mind to hasten the use of the native American folk tale, is the felt need of generically American expressiveness, figures, illustrations for the native quality of our national life which shall have an intrinsically American significance, things seen or remembered which take only native color, give back only a truly American resonance, something more valid than the faded hues of European myth.

aus "The Short Story", in *The League of Frightened Philistines and Other Papers* (New York, 1945), 136-148. - Dieser Essay wurde 1935 auf dem ersten amerikanischen Schriftstellerkongress verlesen.

I believe that revolutionary criticism has been particularly negligent in the field of the short story, and not without cause. For the short story does not lend itself readily to that species of over-politicalized and ideologically schematized criticism that has been too dishearteningly frequent in the literary sections of revolutionary journals. The short-story writer, because of the obvious limitations of space, does not possess the same liberties as does the novelist. Consequently he often discovers that the short story does not permit him to say all he has to say, and that he is limited to dealing in compressed experiences and single, or at best, a few impressions. Hence he must often rely on a technique of indirection, and he must utilize implicit, rather than explicit, methods. ...

Putting aside esthetic considerations for the moment and considering the development of literary traditions, we can note the tendency to develop in terms of a succession of patterns, elements of one pattern tending to be assimilated into the succeeding pattern, while other elements are rejected, and so on, in a continuous process.

For purposes of illustration, I might refer, in passing, to the Negro in American writing. One pattern of the Negro in American writing is the Uncle Remus story of the dark-skinned Southern Handy Andy. This pattern presents a vaudevilized conception of the Negro, portrays him as obsequious, shiftless, childishly humorous and simple, and makes him a subject of comedy which, as we know, slurs and distorts the story of the tragic history of the Negro in capitalist America. This pattern established a norm of types, habits, characteristics, language, a residuum of conceptions, attitudes, and the like, which was assumed to be the "spirit" of the Negro. Even to this date the Uncle Remus pattern of the Negro has not worn thin in American popular writing and in many American conceptions of the Negro. ...

To continue, another pattern of the Negro in American writing might be termed that of the American primitive, presented in such characterizations as those found in the writings of Julia Peterkin and DuBose Heyward, and in Marc Connelly's play, *Green Pastures*. A third pattern is the Harlem Negro, found in novels like Carl Van Vechten's *Nigger Heaven*; in Rudolph Fischer's rather inept treatment of Harlem's middle class and its intellectuals, *The Walls of Jericho*; and in Claude McKay's story of a Pullman porter, *Home to*

Harlem. A fourth pattern, now in the offing, is that of the Negro proletariat; a forerunner of this literary development is Langston Hughes.

These patterns of the Negro in American writing follow a shifting in class relationships and social conditions in which the Negro is a factor, and they reveal these changes and shiftings. And if we view American writing as a whole, it will be obvious, I think, that there has been a diversity of such patterns. Furthermore, we will find that there is an irregularity in their development, influence, efficacy or lack of efficacy, and we will note that they intersect and become a kind of kaleidoscope. In addition, these patterns condition the manner in which we apprehend and perceive characters and events in the American scene. For instance, inane and inept patterns still persist and are often more influential determining factors in the crystallization and reinforcement of popular attitudes than we should like them to be.

Besides the external or social factors conditioning and qualifying the development of literature, there are also the internal, or literary, ones. And just as we are able to note the unevenness and irregularity in the development and life of social patterns, so are we able to perceive a corresponding unevenness of literary influences. ...

One of the influencing factors in American writing that requires some mention here is the plot short story, which was, until fairly recently, a dominant American literary form. The plot short story was built upon a mechanical formula, and as such it was extremely constricting. It demanded that life, as represented in the short story, be so ordered and arranged that it meet the requirements of the form rather than that the form be adapted to reveal the aspects of life a writer chose to utilize. The central demand in this form was that of conflict, based upon rising action and a clash of opposing views, which created a mounting suspense and was resolved in the denouement. The highest type of conflict for the plot short story was often conceived to be moral conflict. Frequently in plot short stories the characters were not convincing as human beings, but rather they impressed one as appendages to moral codes and points of view, and these codes and points of view were rooted in the ideology which is the intellectual bodyguard of capitalist democracy.

It is perhaps more than a mere fortuity that the revolt from the plot short story developed and attained some popularity at a time when there was an increasingly apparent contradiction between the hopes of the American dream and the manner in which human destinies unraveled in actual life. In other words, the contradictions between ideals and activity began to be apparent in American life, and people began to perceive that they were being betrayed by the American dream. The first works in that literature of realism and social protest which has come to be the dominant literary tradition in twentieth-century American writing, began a literary process of upsetting and overturning familiar patterns in American social thought and in literature. The happy ending became the unhappy ending. The plot short story became the plotless short story. ...

This literary revolt opened the floodgates for an inundation of new literary material that permitted, and still does permit, us to see many aspects of American life and American experience as if with new eyesight. What this writing has done, basically, is to assess the cost of American capitalist democracy in terms of human destinies and human suffering and frustrations. It has given expression to social pressures - the social pressures of new racial and class groupings seeking self-expression, self-understanding - that seeks to publicize a sense of its life, its sufferings, its problems, its aspirations, desires. Although we can see this development more clearly in the novel than in the short story, it is apparent in both forms. In the short story, we catch glimpses, states of mind, pictures of scenes, environments, atmospheres, the language of this life that hitherto had been unexpressed or unsatisfactorily expressed in American writing.

64. [ANONYMUS] —————————————————————— 1936

aus "The Short Story To-Day: Discoveries and Anticipations", *The Times Literary Supplement* (Aug. 8, 1936), 637 f.

The short story, to-day as ever, defies a formula; it is a growing, as it is a living, form, and its life is in its growth. To write of it is like trying to describe each of the waves tossed up from and falling back into a restless sea; yet there are, here as there, beneath the multitudinous individual manifestations, tides and currents which carry the vessel of one's inquiry this way and that, and which perhaps may be discerned and indicated, however crudely. ...

The vision of imagination - the perception of abiding perspectives - comes easily to none and abundantly to few, and few are those who can sustain it beyond the instant. The average contemporary novel has all too often its instants only; for the rest the reader must travel a road less of art than of a kind of cursory photography which is the pitfall of an unvitalized realism. The great bulk of short stories, even of artistic ambition, rise no higher; but the effort is less mixed, the result purer. The felicitous short story mirrors without padding the moment when all life runs to a single point of intense consciousness; it seizes upon the sheer living instant, and bodies it forth in unburdened symbols adequate to its specific intensity. Naturally, it has its degrees. It may be anything from a vaudeville performance to a prayer before an altar, and yet even when the former it will be something of the latter too, as in a very famous short story the Tumbler of Our Lady worshipped the Blessed Virgin with such service as he knew. The great short stories may more obviously reach towards universalities, the lesser be content to deal in aspects only; but even the figures of the microcosm will suggest the design of the macrocosm, and either in its kind will be, just so far as it is vital, a step upon the path to that truer, completer vision.

Plainly, though, the large bulk of currently printed short stories are steps to nowhere at all, save oblivion. But that is , in regard to literature, a fact more evident than important. The short story, inclusively considered, has always been an essentially popular form. It flourishes upon every news-stand; it is the staple of the ubiquitous magazine. But only a quantitatively very small proportion of this immense activity has anything more than a passing social and commercial significance. The distinction between the short story as art and the short story as commerce may be deplorable, but it cannot be avoided or diminished merely because art can sometimes prove a financially very valuable property, or because it is admitted that the survival factor of either is its ability to entertain. In truth, entertainment is a word of dual aspect. Its universal essence is engrossment, a selfless concentration upon the object displayed, *but* - a concentration which may be directed to either illumination of or distraction from one's world and one's self. In a healthy state of being men seek illumination objective and subjective; the whole widening history of the race affirms that. It is only where a general and personal sickness of the soul prevails that they turn from the vision which in its truthfulness shows their diseases all too plain, towards the distraction which conceals and denies. Caliban rages to see his own face in the glass, demanding to be Adonis, and, failing the transformation, figures himself instead as the Tired Business Man, who must be taken anywhere but home to himself. It is for him, and for all, male and female, of whom he is the prototype, that the commercial writer caters, bent primarily upon amusing without perturbing, and dealing therefore with essentially standardized situations, characters, and emotions, seeking not like the artist to explore life but instead to reduce it to a series of familiar and accepted attitudes. The demand of art for a total fidelity to one's vision admits of no such conformity; its very life is in the new, the unique, the unpredictable. It is not suggested, of course, that the mass of successful writers of the commercial short story do not write often, perhaps generally, with a perfect honesty; what must be doubted is whether they can be, or can remain, under such conditions, authentic artists, more than trivially originative minds.

65. ELIZABETH BOWEN ——— 1936

aus "Preface" zu *The Faber Book of Modern Short Stories* (London, 1936). - Hier zitiert nach *Collected Impressions* (London, 1950), 38-46.

The short story is a young art: as we now know it, it is the child of this century. Poetic tautness and clarity are so essential to it that it may be said to stand at the edge of prose; in its use of action it is nearer to drama than to the novel. The cinema, itself busy with a technique, is of the same generation: in the last thirty years the two arts have been accelerating together. They have affinities - neither is sponsored by a tradition; both are, accordingly, free; both, still, are self-conscious, show a self-imposed discipline and regard for form; both have, to work on, immense matter - the disorientated romanticism of the age. The new literature, whether written or visual, is an affair of reflexes, of immediate susceptibility, of associations not examined by reason: it does not attempt a synthesis. Narrative of any length involves continuity, sometimes a forced continuity: it is here that the novel too often becomes invalid. But action, which must in the novel be complex and motivated, in the short story regains heroic simplicity.

An art having behind it little tradition is at once impetuous and halting, and is very affectable. Its practitioners are still tentative, watching each other: some positive and original mind is wanted to renew impetus, or to direct it. The short story as an art has come into being through a disposition to see life in a certain way. But the writer himself may stay unaware of this new disposition if he have not already seen it made evident elsewhere in art: only the rare writer does not look for a precedent. In England, the limitations of narrative prose with its *longueurs*, its conventions dangerous to truth, had appeared for a long time to be impassable: oblique narration, cutting (as the cinema), the unlikely placing of emphasis, or symbolism (the telling use of the object both for its own sake and as an image) were unknown. The short story was once the condensed novel; it needed a complex subject and depended for merit on the skill with which condensation had been effected. The short stories of James and Hardy show, in their excellence, a sober virtuosity: they are *tours de force* by practised executants, side-issues from the crowded imagination. They show, *qua* the short story, no urgent aesthetic necessity; their matter does not dictate their form. Their shortness is not positive; it is non-extension. They are great architects' fancies, little buildings on an august plan. They have no emotion that is abrupt and special; they do not give mood or incident a significance outside the novelist's power to explore. Their very excellence made them a dead end: they did not invite imitation or advance in any way a development in the short story proper. That impetus that it needed, the English short story had to get from abroad. Rumour, the translation and easier circulation of foreign books, also a widening curiosity, brought Tchehov and Maupassant into the English view.

The influences of two foreign masters on an affectable new form have necessarily run counter to one another. Tchehov stands (or stands with us) for an emancipation of faculties, for a romantic distension of the form of the story to let in what might appear inchoate or nebulous. Maupassant stands for astringency, iron relevance. ...

The Irish Sea makes a bigger break in sentiment than the Atlantic, and Irish and American writers of the short story have - for all their differences in temper - strong common qualities. Extraverted coldness in art, objectivity, may be the fruit of a life that is, or has been lately, physically exciting or uncertain, life that is quick, rough or lived at high nervous tension, in which either sexual or political passion makes society unsafe. Precipitate feeling makes for hard form in art. The younger Irish writers have almost all carried arms; American civilization keeps the Americans, nervously, armed men: fact there overtops fantasy. There is a state of living in which events assault the imagination, stunning it: such a state of living enforces its own, a now no longer unique, literature. Amazement - involuntary and to a degree fathomed - is part of poetry. In the short story, semi-poetic, amazement is not only not fathomed but not stated; but has to be made evident. The writer must so strip fact of neutralizing elements as to return to it, and prolong for it, its first power: what was in life a half-second of apprehension must be perpetuated. The

extraverted short story - bare of analysis, sparse in emotional statement - is the formula for, never the transcript of, that amazement with which poetry deals. The particular must be given general significance. Narration is bound to be exact and impassive. This method, which was Maupassant's, is now in the hands of the Irish, the Americans, some of the younger English. Liam O'Flaherty, Hemingway have perfected it. It has dangers, which are now becoming apparent - style may be too much deflated, feeling is threatened with an over-simplification that makes it savage and dull.
...

The commercial short story writer had his own, hard-learnt, competence: the new, non-commercial story, if it is to be important, should be able to make its way, any distance, on its intrinsic merits - it still has to be, in one sense or another, subsidized. Subsidy dishonours what ought to be, in the great sense, a popular art. At present, a very large number of free stories lack verisimilitude, are pompous, dissatisfying - they are not up to the mark. But what is the mark?

The mark is, the completeness, or spherical perfection, latent in any story that is projected rightly; a completeness to which any story having the germ of real life should be capable of expanding, but which too few reach - at an indefinable moment the writer's purpose slackens, or some adventitious emotion starts to deform the story. The first necessity for the short story, at the set out, is *necessariness*. The story, that is to say, must spring from an impression or perception pressing enough, acute enough, to have made the writer write. Execution must be voluntary and careful, but conception should have been involuntary, a vital fortuity. The sought-about-for subject gives the story a dead kernel, however skilfully words may have been applied: the language, being *voulu*, remains inorganic. Contrived, unspontaneous feeling makes for unquickened prose. The story should have the valid central emotion and inner spontaneity of the lyric; it should magnetize the imagination and give pleasure - of however disturbing, painful or complex a kind.The story should be as composed, in the plastic sense, and as visual as a picture. It must have tautness and clearness;it must contain no passage not aesthetically relevant to the whole. The necessary subject dictates its own relevance. However plain or lively or unpretentious be the manner of the story, the central emotion - emotion however remotely involved or hinted at - should be austere, major. The subject must have implicit dignity. If in the writer half-conscious awe of his own subject be lacking, the story becomes flooded with falseness, mawkishness, whimsicality or some ulterior spite. The plot, whether or not it be ingenious or remarkable, for however short a way it is to be pursued, ought to raise some issue, so that it may continue in the mind. The art of the short story permits a break at what in the novel would be the crux of the plot: the short story, free from the *longueurs* of the novel is also exempt from the novel's conclusiveness - too often forced and false: it may thus more nearly than the novel approach aesthetic and moral truth. It can, while remaining rightly prosaic and circumstantial, give scene, action, event, character a poetic new actuality. It must have had, to the writer, moments of unfamiliarity, where it imposed itself. ...

The short story, within its shorter span than the novel's, with its freedom from forced complexity, its possible lucidness, is able, like the poetic drama, to measure man by his aspirations and dreads and place him alone on that stage which, inwardly, every man is conscious of occupying alone.

66. *JAMES T. FARRELL* ——— 1937

aus "Preface" zu *The Short Stories of James T. Farrell* (Garden City, N. Y., 1937; 1954), XIII-XXV. - Das Vorwort trägt das Datum des 10. August 1937.

In our time, perhaps, more nonsense has been written about the short story than about any other literary form. Commentators long ago popularized the conceit that the short story is the typical American literary form. There was a time when short stories of a certain plot pattern were in great demand and, for that matter, we are not yet out of that period. The short story has been conceived by persons with "literary" aspirations as a means of making a good living...

The short story, then - that so-called typical American literary form - became a business. And just as there are schools to teach accounting, stenography, salesmanship, hotel-keeping, and the like, so are there institutions teaching short-story writing. ... A whole series of guides to short-story writing, handbooks on the short story, treatises on narrative technique with special emphasis on the short story, household hints in the production and marketing of the short story, tips, suggestions, charts, outlines, diagrams, maps, and prospectuses have flooded the market. ...

In many instances, these books were written in order to keep flourishing the notion that the art and/or the technique of short-story writing could be learned, and that once it was mastered, it could be the means of a profitable and relatively easy livelihood. N. Bryllion Fagin's book, *Short*

Story-Writing, An Art or a Trade? (a sincere and clever protest against such tactics), points out clearly that the ease of mastering the short-story technique (so-called) was stressed because of such reasons. ...

Upon examination, most of the short-story handbooks reveal that they are largely expansions and extensions of what the late Brander Matthews wrote some years ago in his *The Philosophy of the Short-story*. And it must be added that he wrote next to nothing of real literary worth, insight, or suggestiveness. ...

To repeat, most of the latter-day books on short-story writing are largely derivative from Matthews. They follow his definitions and demarcations of the story in terms of form. But that is only a prelude, a breaking of ground for the real stuff - the charts, the formulae, the outlines, the plot diagrams, the analyses of methods of obtaining effects, the breaking up of narrative technique into its assumedly component parts, the presentation of an entire cabalistic ritual of writing. For example, there is one Stewart Beach, former Lecturer on Short-Story Writing at New York University. In his book, *Short-Story Technique*, he outlines a method that is particularly important for the neophyte. It is "the X-ray method." It "demands unity of focus" and "it is an ingeniously simple scheme which depends for its success upon the author's borrowing one leaf from the book of the theater and another from the clinical notes of the doctor. Instead of *telling* (italics in original) a story about a group of characters or about something which happened to some one, the author places one character under the X-ray and allows his readers to see his thoughts as well as his actions." ...

Then there is Professor E. A. Cross, whose *A Book of the Short Story* is full of a cabalistic lore all its own. ... His most notable contribution to this esoteric science, however, is to be found in his diagrams of plots. He is the man who has *demonstrated* the plot diagrams of stories. Thus, *The Piece of String* has a "stair-step" plot, and many of O. Henry's plots, when diagrammed, are of the "rocket" design.

It is to be noticed in all these views that something called *form* is stressed. In other words, it can be said that the positive value here is that of *structure*. The philosophy of the short story, as outlined, is one in which structure is given positive value. ... We discover here the weakness in all approaches to literature that are purely formal. Form becomes a philosophy, a value. In the traditional American short story, this is precisely what has happened. A writer whose sole gift is technical facility will rise to the top.... When form and structure become predominant values in literature, the material from life on which literature draws is falsified. Inevitably, there is a loss of concern with content. Content is altered - but not to gain that more concentrated effect and meaning which literature strives to achieve. It is changed, pieced together, in order to make it fit into an arbitrary structure. Life is falsified. A literature of hollow and straw men is produced. ...

The history of the revolt against the traditional short story ... is part of the general revolt in American literature that has resulted in the realism to be found in the works of our leading fiction writers of this era. ... Besides overturning popular myths, the revolt in American writing threw overboard the plot conception of the short story and the happy ending, the traditional patterns of the English Victorian novel. It introduced new phases and new emphases of experience into our fiction. ...

Most of the writing in this so-called revolt is usually described as realism, or as realism and naturalism. Naturalism in literature can be described as an attempt to embody scientific method in so-called creative writing. One of the foremost exponents of naturalism was Zola, who based his naturalism on an earlier view of materialism, a view that juxtaposed matter and spirit, environment and character. Theodore Dreiser has exemplified a similar naturalism in this country. This revolt, particularly in its earlier stages, involved the attempt to treat character as the product of environment. ...

The revolt in American literature, and the revolt of the short-story writer, which was part of the more general revolt, have been, to a certain degree, victorious. We have beheld the introduction of profound changes in the form, so-called, and in the content, so-called, in the American short story. There is now the basis for a tradition in our short story which runs counter to that of the O. Henry and Bret Harte story, and, more generally, to that of the plot story. ...

We come now to the question: "What is a short story?" There are definitions piled on top of other definitions, and I shall cite some. Professor Beach, the apostle of "the X-ray method" of writing short stories, has this definition: "The short story, in so far as its scope is concerned, is the simplest form of fiction. Unlike the novel, it lacks space to unfold a complex situation." ... Professor Cross, he who invented the "stair-step" and the "rocket" plot diagrams, says: "Like the novel, the short story is a piece of fiction producing a unified effect. Unlike the novel, the single effect is usually an *impression* (italics in original - J. T. F.), instead of a deliberate marshaling together of a large number of diverse elements into a unity. ... The short story is a cross section of life ... but of a single life or at most of the thread of life where it crosses and becomes entangled with one or two other subordinated threads - a section through the knot." Professor Cross also quotes Clayton Hamilton, another adept at this recondite wisdom. ... Edith Mirrielees, in *Significant Contemporary Stories*, ... states: "In the first fraction of the twentieth century, a shor story is a fiction in prose of a shomewhat limited magnitude - that and no more." In her *Writing the Short Story* she has this definition: *"A short story is a brief prose narrative, primarily imaginative, which, by means of the adhesion of every part to one central purpose, renders a coherent and interpretative account of some phase of action, character, or mood."* (Italics in original - J. T. F.) Blanche Colton Williams ... has her definition: "The short-story is a prose narrative artistically presenting character in a struggle or complication which has a definite outcome. If the action occurs in a brief time and a closely circumscribed place, the story approaches the extreme or ultimate form." Which of these definitions is best suited to the stories of Chekhov? - in my opinion the greatest short-story writer who ever lived. Or which one is most applicable to the stories in Joyce's *Dubliners*? To [Sherwood Anderson's] *Winesburg Ohio*? Amen. And again - *amen*!

To anyone concerned with the evaluation and appreciation of literature, it is not crucial whether a particular work be a novel, a condensed novel, a novelette, a story, a tale, a sketch, an anecdote, an incident, a dramatic dialogue or whatever other term be applied. What does matter is whether a specific piece of writing provides the reader with an *experience*, whether it increases his or her understanding, intensifies his or her consciousness, provides the reader with pleasure and refreshment. All of the definitions with which I am familiar are arbitrary. And when we refer them to our actual experience in reading, we readily perceive how arbitrary they are. For instance, some of the experts tell us that the short story creates a *single* or a *unified* impression. What is the meaning here of single? Of unified? When we look at a work of art, we learn that there are not just *single* impressions to be gathered from it. ...

Fiction ... is a great sea of human experience, and part of that sea is the novel, part of it other forms. Into it is poured a complexity of human experience. The manner of presenting this experience is determined by many factors. There are, for instance, many impressions that do not, in terms of the writer's purposes, talents, values, way of seeing and feeling life, etc., merit being translated into more than a short piece of fiction, a story, anecdote, tale, incident, sketch, or whatever else it may be called. Form and content are functions of each other mutually interdependent, mutually related. They cannot be separated. If we approach shorter works of fiction with definitions and peer through these definitions as lenses, we shall turn literature into a parlor game of recognition. New writers will come along and smash our definitions - and we shall have to add new ones.

67. ELIZABETH BOWEN ——— 1939

aus "Gorki Stories" in *Collected Impressions* (London, 1950), 153-156. - Zuerst veröffentlicht in *The New Statesman and Nation* (1939) als Rezension von *A Book of Short Stories. By Maxim Gorki.*

The craft (it may be no more) of the short story has special criteria; its limitations are narrow and definite. It is in the building-up of the short story that the craftsman side of the artist has to appear. Very close demands on the writer's judgment are made; the short story is not a mere ease for the passing fancy; it offers no place for the unobjectified sentiment, for the impulsive start that could not be followed through. It must have implications which will continue when the story is done. It may be a *tour de force*, but it must not be a by-product; if it reads like a by-product it is so much waste. Its disadvantages are, an emotional narrowness that the writer would not permit himself in a longer work, a necessary over-simplification of characters, and a rather theatrical tensing-up of the dialogue - if there be dialogue. The writer who rates above all things verisimilitude and the all-round view, or who cannot sustain one mood till the writing rounds itself off, does better to leave the short story alone. It must be recognized that even in the short story of the greatest integrity there has to be a sort of concealed trick.

aus "Introduction" zu *Teller of Tales* (1939). - Hier zitiert nach *Selected Prefaces and Introductions of W. Somerset Maugham* (London, 1963), 86-117.

It is natural for men to tell tales, and I suppose the short story began in the night of time when the hunter, to beguile the leisure of his fellows when they had eaten and drunk their fill, narrated by the cavern fire some marvellous incident of which he had heard. In cities of the East you can to this day see the story-teller sitting in the market place, surrounded by a circle of eager listeners, and hear him tell the tales that he has inherited from an immemorial past. But I chose to start with the nineteenth century because it was then that the short story acquired a character and a currency that it had not had before. Of course short stories had been written: there were the religious stories of Greek origin, there were the edifying narratives popular in the Middle Ages, and there were the immortal stories of *The Thousand and One Nights;* throughout the Renaissance, in Italy and Spain, in France and England, there was a great vogue for brief narrative. The *Decameron* of Boccaccio and the *Exemplary Tales* of Cervantes are its unperished monuments. But with the rise of the novel the vogue dwindled. The booksellers would no longer pay good money for a collection of short tales, and the authors soon came to look askance on a form of fiction that brought them neither profit nor renown. When from time to time, conceiving a theme that they could adequately treat in a little space, they wrote a short story, they did not quite know what to do with it; and so, unwilling to waste it, they inserted it, sometimes, one must admit, very clumsily, into the body of their novels.

But at the beginning of the nineteenth century a new form of publication was put before the reading public which very soon acquired an immense popularity. The result shows that the authors welcomed with delight the chance thus offered to them for disposing to advantage of the brief pieces which for one reason or another they had occasion to write. This was the annual. It seems to have started in Germany. It was a miscellany of prose and verse; and in its native land offered its readers substantial fare, for we are told that Schiller's *Maid of Orleans* and Goethe's *Hermann and Dorothea* first appeared in periodicals of this character. But when their success led English publishers to imitate them they relied chiefly on short stories to attract a sufficiency of readers. The annual soon found its way to America and gave American authors an opportunity they had long been looking for. ...

Now at the beginning of the nineteenth century the annuals and keepsakes offered writers a means of introducing themselves to the public by way of the short story, and so short stories, serving a better purpose than merely to give a fillip to the reader's interest in the course of a long novel, began to be written in greater numbers than ever before. More especially was this the case in America where the lack of a copyright law made it difficult for American authors to find a publisher to publish their novels. English novels were pirated and the competition was too severe for the American author to meet; he was almost forced to write short stories, and fortunately for him, the public, which was content to read of foreign people and foreign scenes in novels, insisted in briefer narratives on native themes and native authors. Many hard things have been said of the annual and the lady's book, and harder things still of the magazine which succeeded them in the public favour; but it can scarcely be denied that the rich abundance of short stories that were produced in the nineteenth century was directly occasioned by the opportunity which these periodicals afforded. In America they gave rise to a school of writers so brilliant and so fertile that some persons, unacquainted with the history of literature, have claimed that the short story is an American invention. That is not so; but it may very well be admitted that in none of the countries of Europe has this form of fiction been so assiduously cultivated as it has been in the United States; nor have its methods, technique and possibilities been elsewhere more attentively studied. ...

It did not seem unreasonable then, when I set out to show the development of the short story, to start with the nineteenth century. ... But when I embarked upon the serious reading that my aim involved I made a most inconvenient discovery. ... I could not escape the conclusion that the short story which was written at the beginning of my period was as finished, well constructed, sophisticated and accomplished as any that were written during the last ten years. ...

The more I read the more was it forced upon my notice that in essentials the short story has changed little; what was a good story at the beginning of the nineteenth century is a good story today. I could not in face of this continue with the instructive intention with which I had started. I was obliged to relinquish my aim of showing the same sort of development in the brief narration as the biologist can show you in the development of the horse. It has been a disappointment to me. ...

I have had to abandon some of the notions I held before. The first of these concerns the nature of the short story. Now I should warn the reader at once that a writer treating of the art he pursues is biassed. He very naturally thinks his own practice best. He writes as he can, and as he must, because he is a certain sort of man; he has his own parts, and his own idiosyncrasy, so that he sees things in a manner peculiar to himself, and he gives his vision the form that is forced upon him by his nature. ...

I have said all this to clear the ground. I like best the sort of story I can myself write. This is the sort of story that many people have written well, but no one more admirably than Maupassant, so I cannot do better, to show exactly what its nature is, than to discuss one of his most famous productions, *The Necklace*. At the base of it is an anecdote. It relates an incident which is curious, striking and original. But of course it is much more than an anecdote, for when you know this you can read the story with as much interest as before. The scene is set before you with brevity, as the medium requires, but with clearness; and the persons concerned, the kind of life they lead and their deterioration, are shown you with just the amount of detail that is needed to make the circumstances of the case plain. You are told everything that you should know about them. From this appears the second excellence of this sort of story; when you have read it to find out what happens you can read it again for the cleverness of the telling. *The Necklace* is not from its own standpoint perfect, for this kind of narrative should have a beginning, a middle and an end; and when the end is reached the whole story should have been told and you should neither wish nor need to ask a further question. Your crossword is filled up. But in this case Maupassant satisfied himself with an end that was ironic and effective. The practical reader can hardly fail to ask himself, what next? It is true that the unfortunate couple had lost their youth and most of what makes life pleasant in the dreary years they had passed saving money to pay for the lost necklace; but when they discovered that it was worthless they might very well have claimed the real one with which they had replaced it and then found themselves in possession of a small fortune. In the aridity of spirit to which their sacrifices had brought them, it might very well have seemed a satisfactory compensation. It is a tribute to Maupassant's skill that few readers remain so self-possessed that the objection occurs to them. This brings me to the third characteristic of this kind of story. The author does not copy life; he arranges it in order the better to interest, excite, and surprise. He demands from you a willing suspension of disbelief.

This has caused the sort of narrative with which I am now dealing to fall of late years into some discredit. People say that in real life things do not happen with this neatness; real life is an affair of broken threads and loose ends; to arrange them into a pattern falsifies. Such an author as

Maupassant does not mind; he is not aiming at a transcription of life, but at a dramatization of it. He is willing to sacrifice plausibility to effect, and the test is whether he can get away with it: if he has so shaped the incidents he describes and the persons concerned in them that you are conscious of the violence he has put on them, he has failed. But that he sometimes fails is no argument against the method. I am disposed to think that the desire to tell stories and to listen to them is inherent in the human race. At some periods readers exact a close adherence to the facts of life as they know them - it is then that realism is in fashion; at others, indifferent to this, they ask for the strange, the unusual, the marvellous - these are periods that historians of literature call romantic; and then, so long as they are held, readers are willing to accept pretty well anything. They are willing to accept *Sinbad the Sailor* and *Monsieur Beaucaire*. In fiction probability changes with the inclinations of the time; it is what you can get your readers to swallow. No one has stated the canons of the kind of story which I am now discussing with more precision than Edgar Allan Poe. But for its length I would quote in full his review of Hawthorne's *Twice-Told Tales;* it says everything that is to be said on the matter. ...

I think it is possible to frame a definition of what Poe meant by a good short story: it is a piece of fiction, dealing with a single incident, material or spiritual, that can be read at a sitting; it is original, it must sparkle, excite or impress; and it must have unity of effect or impression. It should move in an even line from its exposition to its close. ...

Now the critic does not prescribe laws for the artist; he takes note of his common practice and from this deduces rules; but when an original talent breaks them, the critic, though he may jib like the devil, in the end is forced to change his rules to accommodate the novelty. It is evident that there are other ways than Poe's of writing a good story. ...

To write a story in accordance with the principles laid down by Edgar Allan Poe is not so easy as some think. It requires intelligence, not perhaps of a very high order, but of a special kind; it requires a sense of form and no small power of invention. But it is plain that this manner of story no longer carries conviction. The modern story fulfils a spiritual need in the modern reader which the old story cannot satisfy. The technique and the outlook of the writers of today differ a good deal from those of the masters of the nineteenth century; but before I go into this I must mention a circumstance that has forced itself upon my attention and that has caused me a certain perplexity; this is that so many of these stories might have been written by the same hand. It looks as though there were something in the method of the modern short story that submerges the personality of the author. The stories of Henry James, of Maupassant and of Chekhov could only have been written by themselves. You may not like the personality of these authors, but there it is, manifest to the grossest sense, in their every page. For my part I have always thought that just this, the personality of the creator, was what gave a work of art its lasting interest; it does not matter if it is a slightly absurd one, as with Henry James, a somewhat vulgar one, as with Maupassant, or a grey, melancholic one, as with Chekhov: so long as he can present it, distinct and idiosyncratic, his work has life. The short-story writers of our time seem to lack this curious power. Violent though they often are, hard, ruthless and devoid of sentimentality, they seldom manage to impress their special individuality upon their work. They are communal writers. They remind one of the decorative painters in the eighteenth century who painted flower pieces to put over doors or let into panels above the chimneypiece; it is a pleasant art, but its merit owes more to a period than to a personal gift.

The writers of the present time, unless I am mistaken, are more interested in social circumstances, in the injustice of modern conditions, in the relation of persons to their environment, in short, than in their relations to one another. The result of this is that they are likely to suffer from a certain shortage of material. ... The only subject that is inexhaustible is man. You can go on writing all your life and touch no more than the fringe of it. The difficulty of the writer who eschews a plot - and a plot, I should add, is no more than the pattern that is imposed upon the conduct of the various persons with whom you are dealing - in favour of a narration of the circumstances offered by a certain environment is that, getting nearer and nearer to life as we know it is lived, avoiding surprise, thrill, unexpected yet logical accident, which are the essential characteristics of the formal story, he has nothing to offer the reader that the narrator of actual facts cannot give him with greater force. He has ceased to be a writer of fiction; he has become a reporter. ...

There is a certain amount of fiction that it becomes every well-bred man to have read; it belongs to the culture of the world, and so far as culture is a part of knowledge it must be regarded as essential to everyone's education. But there is not much of it. I think a bookcase that held twenty books would be large enough to contain all the works of fiction that it would leave a man spiritually poorer not to have read. This bookcase would contain *Don Quixote*, *Wilhelm Meister*, *Pride and Prejudice*, *Le Rouge et le*

Noir, Le Père Goriot, Madame Bovary, War and Peace, David Copperfield, The Brothers Karamazov and *A la Recherche du Temps Perdu*: but I am not sure that it would contain any short stories. For the short story is a minor art, and it must content itself with moving, exciting and amusing the reader. There are a hundred stories in this book, and I do not think there is a single one that will fail to do at least one of these things, but also I do not think that there is any that will give the reader that thrill, that rapture, that fruitful energy which great art can produce. The most important short-story writers of the nineteenth century were not men who had it in them to achieve such effects. They had talent and they were artists; but Maupassant had some commonness in his nature, and Henry James, who took his calling with such an admirable seriousness, was defeated by a peculiar triviality of soul; Chekhov was neither trivial nor common, but as is evident when on occasion he indulges in general reflection, his mental capacity was mediocre. None of these writers impresses you by the power and fullness of his personality as you are impressed when you read Balzac or Tolstoy.

It is wise then to read short stories for the entertainment they provide. It is unreasonable to ask of them more than they can give you. But it would be foolish to despise them on that account. ...

English writers on the whole have not taken kindly to the art of the short story. They have felt the novel more congenial to their idiosyncrasy, for the English, though in conversation often tongue-tied, when they take a pen in their hands are inclined to prolixity. They have no natural instinct for succinctness, which is indispensable to the short story, nor a sense of form, which is essential to its significance. So the diffuseness of the national temper has found its most satisfactory literary expression in the long, unwieldy, shapeless novels of the Victorian Era which still remain the country's outstanding contribution to the world's fiction. English writers find it difficult to be brief without being trivial, and for the most part they have looked upon the short story as a thing of no great matter to be thrown off in their spare time in order to earn a few useful guineas without much expenditure of effort. I know only two English writers who have taken the short story as seriously as it must be taken if excellence is to be achieved, Rudyard Kipling, namely, and Katherine Mansfield. Miss Mansfield had a small, derivative, but exquisite talent; and her shorter pieces - for she had insufficient power to deal with a theme that demanded a solid gift of construction - are admirable. Rudyard Kipling stands in a different category. He alone among English writers of the short story can bear comparison with the masters of France and Russia.

aus *The Modern Short Story. A Critical Survey* (London, 1941). - Hier zitiert nach dem Neudruck (London, 1972), 15 f.; 18-21, 23-25; 214-216; 220; 222.

The basis of almost every argument or conclusion I can make is the axiom that the short story can be anything the author decides it shall be; it can be anything from the death of a horse to a young girl's first love affair, from the static sketch without plot to the swiftly moving machine of bold action and climax, from the prose poem, painted rather than written, to the piece of straight reportage in which style, colour, and elaboration have no place, from the piece which catches like a cobweb the light subtle iridescence of emotions that can never be really captured or measured to the solid tale in which all emotion, all action, all reaction is measured, fixed, puttied, glazed, and finished, like a well-built house, with three coats of shining and enduring paint. In that infinite flexibility, indeed, lies the reason why the short story has never been adequately defined. ...

It is only when Mr. Ellery Sedgewick asserts, in his extremely perceptive essay written fo American schools, "So it is that the short story has become all sorts of things, situation, episode, characterization, or narrative - in effect a vehicle for every man's talent,"[1] that we come back again to the sensible conclusion that the short story, whether short or long, poetical or reported, plotted or sketched, concrete or cobweb, has an insistent and eternal fluidity that slips through the hands.

This is, and has always been, my own view. The impression that the short story has something of the indefinite and infinitely variable nature of a cloud is one which sooner or later must be forced on anyone who not only reads, but attempts to break down analytically, the work of writers differing so vastly as Turgenev and Hemingway, Sherwood Anderson and O. Henry, George Moore and Stephen Crane, Kipling and Katherine Mansfield. Is the cumulus or the cirrus more beautiful? The thunder-cloud or the flotilla of feathers? The calm blue and white of noon, or the savagery of sunset? There is no definition, no measure, which will aptly contain the structure, effect, and beauty of them all. As the sky is not made of bricks, so it is worth remembering that stories are not put together with plumb-line and trowel.

---

[1] Sedgewick and Dominovitch: ed. *Novel and Story* (Atlantic Monthly Press).

There is one other thing which these many and varied definitions all have in common. All omit to point out the advantages of elasticity, in both choice of character and use of time, which the short story holds over the novel. The novel is predominantly an exploration of life: reflecting and describing in some form the impact, entanglement, fruition, destruction or fulfilment of human emotions and desires. "Characters begin young; they grow old; they move from scene to scene, from place to place," said Virginia Woolf. This development of character, this forward movement of time, have always been and perhaps always will be the pulse and nerve of the novel. But in the short story time need not move, except by an infinitesimal fraction; the characters themselves need not move; they need not grow old; indeed there may be no characters at all. A novel without characters would be a tiresome affair; but a novel with characters who never spoke a word would surely be more tiresome still. Yet many a good short story has characters who never open their lips. A novel whose characters were never named, whose location and time were never stated, might well impose on its readers a strain that they would justifiably refuse to bear. Yet many a short story has characters which bear no more marks of identification than the anonymous and universal label of "boy" or "girl," "man" or "woman," "the traveller" or "the commercial traveller," "the barmaid" or "the soldier," and no more topographical exactitude than "the street," "the field," "the room," or any seashore between Brighton and Botany Bay.

"The Novel," said Edward Garnett, "can be anything according to the hands which use it" - a truth far more widely applicable to the short story. For the short story remains plastic, and continues to increase its plasticity, as long as human nature remains the infinitely plastic and variable thing it is. ...

In its various stages of development the short story has frequently been compared with some other literary form, sometimes with some artistic form outside literature. It is thus declared to have affinities with the drama; with the narrative ballad; with the lyric and the sonnet. In the last thirty years it has shown itself, as in fact much other writing has, to be pictorial rather than dramatic, to be more closely allied to painting and the cinema than to the stage. Mr. A. E. Coppard has long cherished the theory that short story and film are expressions of the same art, the art of telling a story by a series of subtly implied gestures, swift shots, moments of suggestion, an art in which elaboration and above all explanation are superfluous and tedious. ...

The evolution of the short story may ... have something to do with the evolution of the general reader. We must be wary of condemning Dickens, when it would be more just, perhaps, to condemn an age more confined to compartments of class, place, and prejudice than our own. Dickens, often publishing a novel in monthly parts, found it necessary to devote some hundreds of words, and if necessary repeat those words a month later, to a single character. In 1920 Sherwood Anderson remarked simply that "she was a tall silent woman with a long nose and troubled grey eyes"; in 1930 Mr. Ernest Hemingway in a moment, for him, of unusual expansion, said, "He wore a derby hat and a black overcoat buttoned across his chest. His face was small and white and he had tight lips. He wore a silk muffler and gloves." In 1940 Mr. V. S. Pritchett writes, "He had a cape on, soaked with rain, and the rain was in beads in his hair. It was fair hair. It stood up on end."

Anderson took up fourteen words, Mr. Hemingway thirty-one, Mr. Pritchett twenty-six. Between Dickens and Mr. Pritchett, then, something has happened. Is it only the evolution of the short story? May it not also be, perhaps, the parallel evolution of the reader? Education, travel, wider social contact, the increased uniformity of life, dress, and manners have made us all familiar with things that were once remote enough to need to be described. To-day all of us have seen Sherwood Anderson's woman, the tragic, anonymous representative of a whole inarticulate class; we have seen Mr. Hemingway's tough with the black overcoat and bowler hat; we know Mr. Pritchett's type with its fair hair that stands up on end. The widening of social contact, among other things, has relieved these three writers, and their generation, of an oppressive obligation. It is no longer necessary to describe; it is enough to suggest. The full-length portrait, in full dress, with scenic background, has become superfluous; now it is enough that we should know a woman by the shape of her hands.

In this way the short story can be seen not as a product evolved by generations of writers united in a revolutionary intention to get the short story more simply, more economically, and more truthfully written, but as something shaped also by readers, by social expansion, and by what Miss Bowen calls "peaks of common experience." ...

A writer's method is, on a final assessment, himself. Yet if he is a writer of stories or a writer of poems he must accept the imposition and limitation of form. In choice of subject, like the novelist, he is free; unlike the novelist, who is so lightly held by restrictions that he can express himself in any length between a hundred and fifty pages and a thousand and five hundred and even in several volumes ... , the short-story writer and the poet must accept certain restrictions of length. For centuries the poet even had to accept a certain numerical restriction in the matter of syllables; the sonnet in particular held him in chains; the heroic couplet threatened to make a mockery of his art. The short story, not so rigidly confined as a sonnet yet superficially more restricted than a novel, stands nearer the drama than either. It is at once restricted, yet free; its range of time, place, and movement is necessarily limited, and like the drama it is forced back on the use of suggestion, implied action, indirect narration, and symbolism to convey what might otherwise be conveyed by a plain catalogue of solid words. ... [It] is free in a sense that the drama is never free - it may describe, in natural detail, the things that may never happen on the stage: an undraped woman, a road crash, an air-battle, and countless others. Or it is free of description at all, and may rely, as Hemingway's *Hills Like White Elephants* relies, almost entirely on conversation and the ability of the reader to draw the appropriate descriptive and emotional conclusions from that conversation. Or there may be no conversation, but only description, and indirect description at that. Or there may be description and conversation, both direct and suggestive, with a coherence of action and an obedience to the unities such as would satisfy the most academic dramatist. In short, once the short story has accepted a certain light restriction of length (say between a hundred and fifty words, which is roughly the length of *The Prodigal Son,* and fifteen thousand words, which is somewhere near the length of Tolstoy's *Family Happiness*), the short-story writer is the freest of all artists in words: far freer than the dramatist, infinitely freer than the poet, and in reality far freer than the novelist, since he is offered a wealth of subjects which it is unprofitable, undignified, or otherwise not worth the novelist's while to touch. ...

Critical jargon will talk about them [i.e. stories] and round them all, but critical jargon has no word for that quality, which might be described as balance, which is the expression of the instinctive part of the writer's self. A story must, so to speak, be weighed in the hands, to a fine and intuitive test. Its balance will collapse under a superfluous sentence, even a superfluous word. To see a writer building up his tale, piece by piece, as one builds up a toy tower of match-sticks, and to feel that he knows both instinctively and consciously which match-stick must be last and exactly when the tower will bear no more, is an experience which can become, also, a general critical test of form. For the story which passes the application of that simple test, whether it is a story of smart plot, subtle inflections, action or symbolism, fact or fantasy, or anything else, may be said to have passed all tests. And as prime examples of that balanced perfection, which gives the reader the imcomparable feeling of being slightly lifted off the earth, I would say that certain Biblical stories, notably *Ruth, The Prodigal Son, Susannah,* and *Jonah,* certain stories of Hans Andersen, notably *The Princess and the Pea,* and a few modern stories such as *Boule de Suif,* Tchehov's little sketch *The Beauties,* Gorki's *Twenty-six Men and a Girl,* Bierce's *A Horseman in the Sky,* and Joyce's *The Dead* are, with a very few others, supreme. ...

More short-story writers are to-day writing in England and America, and moreoever writing better stories, than ever before. That fact is no accident. A particular artistic form does not flourish in a particular age because of a happy accident, but because certain cultural, inventive, revolutionary, or popular forces combine to stimulate its growth: so that finally, perhaps, it becomes the most necessary and natural expression of the age. This was notably true of the drama in Elizabethan times, the heroic couplet in the eighteenth century, the novel in the nineteenth century, and in a lesser but increasing way is true of the short story to-day. The war of 1914-18 prepared the ground for a new story; the intermediate period of distrust and dislocation fostered it; and it would not surprise me very much if the literature of the second war, and its inevitable aftermath of still more distrustful dislocation, found in the short story the essential medium for whatever it has to say. For it is certain that, as Hemingway has proved of Spain, if no other good comes out of wars, stories will.

70. [ANONYMUS] —— 1942

aus "An Art without Traditions? The Short Story's Claim to New Freedom. Democracy of Writer and Reader", *The Times Literary Supplement* (Jan. 17, 1942), 30. - Dieser Artikel ist eine Rezension der Monographie von H. E. Bates, *The Modern Short Story. A Critical Survey* (London, 1941).

The spirit bloweth where it listeth, but there are often practical and prosaic reasons why one form of literature flourishes at a particular time and another does not. The level of taste or education of the reading public, or of disparate sections of the reading public, may have a good deal to do with the popularity of this or that literary form. So may the status of the author in society and the economic rewards of authorship generally. And the material and technical development of publishing, of course, has always been a determining influence. Without the magazine Press of the last half-century, for instance, it is most unlikely that the short story could have attained its present variety or degree of popularity. The form of the short story is no doubt as old as any form of literature, but - with only a few classic exceptions - the professional practice of the short story is new. Allowing for the necessary fore-runners, the modern short story, in fact, is the short story of not much more than the past half-century.

Much has been written of its appeal and technique in recent years, though seldom at great length and most often by way of criticism of individual short-story writers or as introduction to an anthology of new work. Mr. Bates's is the latest critical survey, and one of the fullest. He is acute and unfailingly enthusiastic; he writes with lively imagination, and in combining criticism with literary history he is able to put forward a view of the evolution of the short story that carries wide and pointed suggestion. For a writer who himself writes short stories, who is indeed among the half-dozen most richly endowed short-story writers in this country to-day, Mr. Bates has almost too many theories on the subject of the short story and its prospects; together with what may be inferred from two or three extravagant likes and dislikes that he professes they seem to account for some of his own weaknesses of style. But there is generous and penetrating good sense in many of his critical judgments, which in the end seem to provide sound backing for his belief that, just as the complex of contemporary social influences stimulated the drama in the Elizabethan age, the heroic couplet in the eighteenth century, and the novel in the nineteenth century, so to-day it favours the art of the short story.

Perhaps Mr. Bates rates the short story as a literary form too highly, or at all events feels for it too jealous a love. After all, though it may be true that the public as a whole consistently undervalues the modern short story, it remains a common experience that even the most accomplished short stories have a way of being aesthetically unsatisfying. Except in the case of the very greatest, the truly poetical short-story writers, who are possibly fewer than the number of fingers to be counted on both hands, the short story necessarily lacks the abundance and diversity of the novel. There is substance, when all is said, in the novel-reader's prejudice. The truth, for all that it may seem a platitude of the mistaken sort, is surely that the short story tends to be a minor variety of prose fiction, whose major achievement is the novel. Tolstoy wrote short stories - stories of great light and power - but is it not a little absurd to set Tolstoy down in a book on the short story, as Mr. Bates does, as a short-story writer? The fact is that a great or good novelist appears almost always to have had it in him to write great or good short stories. It is not a matter of using up a scrap of material left over in the novelist's workroom. The aim is admittedly different, the method is radically different in one way or another; but Tolstoy and Flaubert, Henry James and Conrad, Mr. Maugham and Mr. Forster in this respect have all demonstrated the same thing. Writers of successful short stories, on the other hand, have only rarely exhibited a similar capacity for the novel.

71. *KATHERINE ANNE PORTER* —— 1942

aus "No Plot, My Dear, No Story" in *The Days Before* (New York, 1952), 133-136. - Zuerst erschienen 1942.

[A] short story [needs] *first* a *theme*, and then a point of view, a certain knowledge of human nature and strong feeling about it, and style - that is to say, his own special way of telling a thing that makes it precisely his own and no one else's. ... The greater the theme and the better the style, the better the story, you might say.

You might say, and it would be nice to think you would.Especially if you are an author and write short stories. Now listen carefully: except in emergencies, when you are trying to manufacture a quick trick and make some easy money, you don't really need a plot. If you have one, all well and good, if you know what it means and what to do with it. ...

First, have faith in your theme; then get so well acquainted with your characters that they live and grow in your imagination exactly as if you saw them in the flesh; and finally, tell their story with all the truth and tenderness and severity you are capable of; and if you have any character of your own, you will have a style of your own; it grows, as your ideas grow, and as your knowledge of your craft increases.

72. L. A. G. STRONG —— *1945*,1947

aus "The Art of the Short Story", *Essays by divers hands. Being the transactions of the Royal Society of Literature of the United Kingdom*, N. S. XXIII (1947), 37-51. - Zuerst als "The Wedmore Memorial Lecture," gehalten am 6. Juni 1945.

That admirable craftsman Arnold Bennett, confronted with the suggestion that it was harder to write a good short story than a good novel, replied with characteristic vigour that it wasn't. He had tried both, and he knew.

The writing of a novel, he pointed out, was a feat of manual labour. It called for a stamina and an endurance not exacted by the short story. And he went on to denounce the suggestion as yet another instance of the tendency to disparage professional hard work in the arts, and to exalt above it those flashes of inspiration beloved of the amateur.

I think that Bennett was right, but I would make two reservations. First, the amount of work needed to produce an artistic result is neither here nor there: nothing matters but the quality of the result. To moralize judgments on art, to prefer the work which has taken longer and cost the most pains, can be left to schoolmasters - and schoolmistresses. Second, the short story form is forbiddingly difficult to all except those with a natural bent for it, and difficult to exasperation even for them. Anyone afraid of hard work is advised to leave it alone. What is more, good novels are commoner than good short stories. Many novelists cannot write a short story at all. The spread, the leisure, the discursiveness of the novel are fatal to the short story, which has more in common with the lyric poem or with the verse epigram than with any other literary form, for it is as ruthless as either in its compression, its completeness, its rhythmic advance to a climax. These are qualities - one might compare them to the swift economies of the caricaturist - in which our prose writers do not commonly excel. They leave speed of apprehension and certainty of suggestion to the poets. A large number of our short story writers come of Celtic stock: many, too, are poets. The weight of the English literary tradition is still against the short story. Its history among us is short. For a variety of reasons we are self-conscious and undecided about it. We do not know where to place it, or what to think about it. Those of us who are obliged to think about it try to solve our perplexities in typical English fashion by narrowing down the definition, and refusing the title of short story to any work of which we disapprove. Of the various cleavages of opinion, the widest, and to the outsider the most perplexing, is that between the editors of popular magazines and those short story writers whom the critics and the learned weeklies seem to like best. Perhaps this will be our most promising point of departure in an attempt, limited strictly by time, to consider this fascinating and exacting art. It is exacting, there is no doubt of that. One may learn readily enough to manufacture short stories up to a certain level of utility and entertainment, but the good short story, the short story as a work of art, comes seldom and by a miracle. It is with the short story as an art form that we are here concerned; but to consider it, to isolate it for inspection, we shall be obliged to glance also at the manufactured products, "trade goods" as Mr. H. G. Wells has called them, by which, like a diamond in a heap of powdered glass it is surrounded. ...

"Nothing morbid or depressing" is the continuous cry of editors, theatre managers, and film producers; and by morbid and depressing the British public means anything that confronts it with a situation it cannot alter to its liking.

Thus we like our artists to provide us with an escape, to show us situations in which people take action of which we approve in order to change conditions of which we disapprove. That such action should transcend our own powers does not distress us, especially if the characters who take it resemble us so much in other respects as to make us believe that we, too, might possibly react as nobly, as resourcefully. This characteristic is to be borne in mind if we are to understand the development of the British short story, for it has done much to direct its course. It explains why the British short story, after a lusty beginning, in which it pleased all types of reader, experienced a violent split, branching one way into an esoteric, minority form which was restless, experimental, and self-conscious, and the other way into a popular form which, apart from notable improvements in the manner of its presentation, has remained virtually unchanged for some forty years. ...

What these four quite dissimilar writers [i.e. Rudyard Kipling, H. G. Wells, W. W. Jacobs, Conan Doyle] did to the British short story was to give it an immense energy, to make it move rapidly in one direction, and force upon it the one thing which all their stories shared - a plot. Plot is not an easy word to define; but we are on safe ground if we say that the essence of it is the statement and solution of a problem. Plot dangles before the reader a number of coloured threads, crosses and interweaves them, and ties them neatly in a knot at the end. It is a way of achieving what must always be the end of the short story, what distinguishes it from the episode, the anecdote, the sketch; that is, that it shall somehow give the reader a sense of completed experience. British and American readers, because of their inherent love of action, get this sense of completion more readily from a plot, from the active solution of a specific problem, than in other ways. ...

Such, then, was the British short story when a new star arose in the East, the star of Tchekov. The stories of Tchekov seemed at first sight to be unlike any others. To readers brought up on the Western type of story they appeared casual, anecdotal, mere episodes. Manifestly, they had no plot. Writers were quick to recognize their excellence, but not all realized to what they owed it. The more superficial saw only that a master story-teller had proved the possibility of writing a short story without a plot. They proceeded to celebrate the discovery by producing innumerable episodes, sketches, anecdotes. What they did not see was that the stories of Tchekov derived their power, their communication to the reader of a sense of completed experience, from the tremendous imaginative groundwork which had preceded the writing of them. Like rocks just visible above the tide, their foundations were out of sight. The slightest Tchekov story - 'The Head of the Family,' for example - rests on a secure base of understanding and psychological groundwork. As in the one-act plays of Synge, a background of deep experience enabled the writer to present his characters so clearly that every gesture is a revelation, every sentence a confession. Each character, in the short time of appearing before us, is his own epitome.

So came the first open division of the short story. If I may be allowed an over-simplified phrase, from a story where things happened *to* the characters, there branched off a new kind of story where things happened *in* the characters. From conflict of circumstance we came to conflict of thought and feeling; from a physical completeness to a psychological; from a statement to a question; from a structural rounding-off, a grand Amen, which left nothing to the reader's imagination, to an unresolved composition for which his imagination must supply the final chord. Writers became interested in character and atmosphere for their own sakes. Hitherto, both had been adjuncts to the story; atmosphere had been a stage setting, a property. In the same way, character had been a personal setting, had given colour and piquancy to the things that happened. I am speaking, needless to say, of the more popular type of story, the type demanded by editors. A few experimenters had been working in obscurity, groping their way towards the story based on happenings in the inner life, some of them by way of Henry James; though here, again, superficial imitators had failed to see that the psychological detail of James's stories grew from theme and character as leaves from the parent stem, whereas the detail with which they loaded their stories was irrelevant, detail for its own sake, and could be transferred from one story to another without anyone's being the wiser.

So came the split. So the serious short story grew away from the popular, commercial short story. It was a difference not in degree but in kind. We must be clear about this. It was not that the popular stories were bad examples of a thing which the serious writers were doing well. However bad they were - and some were so bad as to command a kind of awe - they were examples of something quite different. The bad stories of the new type were just as lamentable in their way. Their subject matter had a veneer of intelligence, but, taking them all round, they were even less well written. They were structureless, invertebrate. They had neither beginning, middle, nor end. Nine-tenths of them were embryonic slabs from novels which their authors had neither the persistence nor the power to write. ...

Technique is the means to achieve harmony between intention, medium and material. But the skilled tradesman knows how to make the most effective use of what he has got. Very often it is lies, or nonsense; but he knows how to put it across. This is because the competition among popular short stories has been severe, because they fell into easily recognized types, and are always busy conforming to them and copying their originals. On the other hand, I am continually reading stories by serious writers who do not know how to put their stuff across. Here is the one department in which the popular story has something to teach its superior, its very far superior, relation. ...

Starting from H. G. Wells's definition, that it shall not take more than half an hour to read, I repeat my claim that, to be a short story, each piece of short prose fiction should give the reader a sense of completed experience, and that it can best do this by rigid economy and undeviating progress in one direction towards its climax. No admission except on business: that is the warning that must be given to every character, every property, every idea, every sentence. Failure to be ruthless in this respect spoils nine out of ten of the more intelligent short stories; a fault into which the commercial short story writer, with his rigidly prescribed aim, falls far less often.

I know no other rules, and I am glad. If there were more, the art of the short story would be in danger of being standardized. A young form, still in process of growth, having passed from a lusty infancy to a troubled adolescence, it needs all the freedom it can get.

73. ROSE MACAULAY ——— 1946

aus "The Future of Fiction" in *New Writing and Daylight* (London, 1946), 71-75.

The novel, as narrative entertainment, has always had formidable rivals - the ballad, the play, the short tale, the biography and autobiography, the memoir, the history. Until about two centuries ago, it put up a weakish fight against these competitors. Then it entered on its hey-day, and for a long time victoriously held the field. Now its position totters. To the formidable rivals is added another - the film drama. And two of its ancient competitors have grown of late in popularity among writers - the short story and the report of facts. There are obvious reasons for the strengthening hold of both of these on the writer. The short story, besides taking less time to write, and often making an interim appearance in some magazine, has grown in recent years far less exacting in form and content than of old. It used to be required to have a beginning and an end; it was supposed to be self-contained, to have a plot, a story; it ended with the closing of a door on the incident or situation depicted (sometimes with some sudden booby-trap of a surprise to fall on the reader's head, but not all writers attempted this.) So the form was exacting: it was a drama in miniature, cut out and sewn together without loose ends; it made more demands than a novel on the concentration, relevance, and story-telling deftness of the narrator. Take a short (or shortish) story by Henry James, Maupassant, Anatole France, Balzac, Kipling, O. Henry, W. W. Jacobs, Somerset Maugham, Aldous Huxley, - different as all these are, they all tell a tale, they begin with an opening and end with a climax; they do not just stop. But now a short story may be, and often is, quite different; it can be an odd length chopped off a piece; any bit of any novel-in-progress will do; you merely cut it off and serve. Your readers have a sense of dipping into the middle of some untold tale; they may like the fragment before them, or they may be annoyed by its vagueness, its unrelatedness, its lack of climax, sometimes its insignificance. It is often like sitting opposite travellers in a train; there they sit, doing nothing in particular, reading newspapers, eating chocolate, occasionally passing a remark; and there you sit opposite, waiting for one of them to jump out of the window, pull the alarm cord, say something interesting; but they don't. The train reaches your station; you get out, leaving them still sitting; you will never know why they are travelling, where they are going, or why your attention has been focused on them for perhaps half an hour. It is too easy, too dull; everyone can do it, there seems no reason why anyone should. All round the Danube, the Volga, the great ruminating regions of Central Europe, the natives sit writing like that. 'The sun was rising. In the yard my Uncle Mischa was killing pigs ... and so on, till the sun sets on the European day, and Uncle Mischa and the rest go to bed. It is sometimes good; often less so. The French, an impatient, unruminative, bustling people, do not write like that; they still like snap and point in their narratives. The British, lazier-minded, are largely adopting the unexacting form; it suits them. It suits them so well that it may drive out the novel altogether. There are, of course, practitioners of the short story to-day who use an art as deft and exacting as that of any novelist; indeed, more so; but they are exceptions.

74. *EUDORA WELTY* ———— *1947*,1949

aus *Short Stories* (New York, 1949). - Ein im August 1947 an der University of Washington unter dem Titel "Some Views on the Reading and Writing of Short Stories" gehaltener Vortrag. Teile daraus wurden im *Atlantic Monthly* (Feb. & March, 1949) abgedruckt.

[Our] experience tells us ... that each story is a specific thing, never a general thing - never. The words in the story we're writing now might as well never have been used before. They all shine. Stories are *new* things, stories make words new; that is one of their illusions and part of their beauty. ...

But although all stories in the throes of being written seem new and although good stories are new and persist, there'll always be some characteristics and some functions about them as old as time, as human nature itself, to keep them more or less alike, of a family; and there may be other things, undiscovered yet, in the language, in technique, in the world's body of knowledge, to change them out of our present recognition. Critics, historians, and scholars deal with these affairs - and keep good track of them - while for us, the practitioners, the writing of stories seems to simmer down - between stories - into some generalities that are, we all think from time to time, worth talking about. ...

They are entirely different states, composing a story and talking about the composing of stories. Makers of jelly will know what we mean and may feel with us. When the pot is cooking along, simmering, there's the generality, and there's time to gaze in and dip up and match experiences and speculate how this batch is going to turn out and the state of blackberries this year. But when it boils up! Then there's your state of active composing - there's a cauldron of heat and energy on your hands, and there's only one thing to do, attend to that jelly on the fire - do what's needed the best you can, get it tested and poured out in the glasses, and at the right instant, or you'll be sorry. It's changed from a matter of dreaming along and thinking of jelly - just jelly, abstractly - to a matter of now or never. A condition of crisis is at hand; and out of the past - hearsay or experience - a *practical* knowledge is all you can really use. That is, somebody could have told you to use a safer kind of test at one point, somebody else could have warned you how to keep the glasses from breaking, somebody can always come along and say "I'd have added a little lemon juice" - but that's about as far as outside aid can come - little things. ...

High principled persons here will say, But what about Communication? ... Yes, I think we write stories in the ultimate hope of communication, but so do we make jelly in that hope. ... Always in the back of our heads and in our hearts are such hopes, and attendant fears that we may fail - we do everything out of the energy of some form of love or desire to please. The writing of a story uses the *power* of this love or hope, of course, and not its simple, surface form such as comes out - rather nicely - in jelly making.

During the writing of a story, all the energy we have is put to pressure and reaches a changed over state - so as to act for the sole and concentrated purpose of making our work excellent and to the pattern of some preconceived idea we have of beauty. ...

But the practical problems of the story at hand are, on the whole, minutiae. ... The little things get worked out - successfully or unsuccessfully, and possibly with the aid of outside criticism - and then they're done. One story's problem is no more than a nuisance. To get at general problems we have to go deeper, in fact, the deepest we can go, into the act of writing itself. ...

We work by the story - by the piece. The next story will always be a different thing. There are no two days alike - time moves. There are no two stories alike - *our* time moves. We were in one story and now we are in another - two worlds - and there are many more, though the thought neither helps nor hinders us any in the one where we now struggle.

How do we write a story?

Our own way.

Beyond that, I think it's hard to assign a process to it. ... [The] mind in writing a story is in the throes of imagination, and it is not in the calculations of analysis. There is a Great Divide in the workings of the mind - shedding its energy in two directions - it creates in imagination, and it tears down in analysis. ...

The fact that a story will reduce to elements, can be analyzed, does not necessarily mean it started with them, certainly not consciously. A story can start with a bird song.

Criticism, or more strictly, analysis, is an impossible way to learn how the story was written. Analysis is a one-way process, and is only good after the event. In the newsreel pictures when the dive is shown in reverse, a swimmer can come back out of the water, the splash is swallowed up, he rises in the air and is safe and dry back on the diving board. But in truth you can't come by way of analysis back to the starting point of inspiration. ...

Mr. E. M. Forster in his book on the novel makes the acute distinction between plot and narrative thread. A story is a "narrative of events arranged in their time-sequence. A plot is also a narrative of events, the emphasis falling on causality. 'The king died and then the queen died' is a story. 'The king died, and then the queen died of grief' is a plot." ...

[Plot] can throw its weight in any of several ways, varying in their complexity, flexibility, and interest: onto the narrative, or situation; onto the character; onto the interplay of same; and onto some higher aspects of character, emotional states, and so on, *per se,* which is where the rules leave off, if they've come with us this far, and the uncharted country begins. ...

When plot, whatever it does or however it goes, becomes the outward manifestation of the very germ of the story, then it is purest - then the narrative thread is least objectionable, then it is not in the way. When it is identifiable in every motion and progression of its own with the motions and progression of simple revelation, then it's at its highest use. Plot can be made so beautifully to reveal character, reveal atmosphere and the breathing of it, reveal the secrets of hidden inner (that is, "real") life, that its very unfolding is a joy. It is undoubtedly a joy that is more felt than conscious - a subtle satisfaction, that comes from where? Probably it comes from a deep-seated perception we all carry in us of the beauty of organization - of that less strictly definable thing, of form.

Where does form come from - how do you "get it?" My guess is that form is evolved. It is the residue, the thrown-off shape, of the very act of writing, as I look at it. It is the work, its manifestation in addition to the characters, the plot, the sensory impressions - it is the result of these, which comes to more than their mathematical total. It is these plus something more. This something more springs from the whole. It pertains to the essence of the story. From the writer's point of view, we might say that form is somehow connected with the process of the story's work - that form *is* the work. From the reader's point of view, we might say that form is connected with recognition, it is what makes us know, in a story, what we are looking at, what unique thing we are for a length of time intensely contemplating. It does seem that the part of the mind form speaks to and reaches is the memory.

In our stories today, form, as acutely and definitely as it may be felt, does not necessarily imply a formal structure. It is not accounted for by structure, rather. A story with a "pattern", an exact kind of design, may lack a more compelling over-all quality that is what we mean by form. Edgar A. Poe and other writers whose ultimate aim depended on pattern, on a perfect and dove-tailing structure (note the relation to puzzles and to detection and mystery here) might have felt real horror at a story by D. H. Lawrence first of all because of the unmitigated shapelessness of Lawrence's narrative. ... Lawrence's world of action and conversation is as far from the frozen perfection, the marblelike situations, of Poe as we can imagine ... It is the world of the senses that Lawrence writes in, works in, thinks in, takes as his medium - and if that is strange to us, isn't the loss ours? Through this world he will send his story - it is the plot too - it is his story's reason for being ...

We've seen that a story's major emphasis may fall on the things that make it up - on character, on plot, on its physical or moral world, in sensory or symbolic form. Now we see that perhaps the way this emphasis is let fall may determine the value of the story. May determine not how well it is written, for that is in the lap of other gods, but the worth of its being written.

Of course fashion and the habits of understanding stories at given periods in history may play their parts, unconsciously or wilfully. But mainly, I venture to think, the way emphasis falls, the value of a story is the thing nearest dependent upon the individual and personal factor involved, the writer behind the writing. ...

In conclusion to these scattering remarks, I think we had better say - it's safest - that a short story writer can try anything. He has tried anything - but presumably not everything. Variety is, has been, and no doubt will remain endless in possibilities, because the power and stirring of the mind never rest. It is what this power will try that will most pertinently define the short story. Not rules, not esthetics, not problems and their solution. It is not rules as long as there is imagination; not esthetics as long as there is passion; not success as long as there is intensity behind the effort that calls forth and communicates, that will try and try again.

aus "A Beginning on the Short Story (Notes)" in *Selected Essays of William Carlos Williams* (New York, 1954), 295-310. - Dieser Essay trägt das Datum des 15. Dezember 1949. Er wurde zuerst veröffentlicht als No. XVII der *Outcast Chapbooks* (Yonkers, N. Y., 1950).

The principal feature re the short story is that it is short - and so must pack in what it has to say (unless it be snipped off a large piece of writing as a sort of prose for quality of writing which might be justifiable)

It seems to me to be a good medium for nailing down a single conviction. Emotionally.

There's "Melanctha" (and there are the Poe stories), a means of writing, practice sheet for the novel one might *discover*, in it. But a novel is many related things, a short story one. ...

It isn't a snippet from the newspaper. It isn't realism. It is, as in all forms of art, taking the materials of every day (or otherwise) and using them to raise the consciousness of our lives to higher aesthetic and moral levels by the use of the art.

As in the poem it must be stressed, that the short story uses the same materials as newsprint, the same dregs - the same in fact as Shakespeare and Greek tragedy: the elevation of spirit that occurs when a consciousness of form, art in short, is imposed upon materials debased by dispirited and crassly cynical handling. What the newspaper uses on the lowest (sentimental) level, the short story had best elevate to the level of other interests.

This should make apparent that a mere "thrilling" account of an occurrence from daily life, a transcription of a fact, is not of itself and for that reason a short story. You get the fact, it interests you for whatever reason; of that fact you *make*, using words, a story. A thing. A piece of writing, as in the case of De Maup't, "A Piece of String."

In plainest words, it isn't the mere interest of the event that makes the short story, it is the way it raises the newspaper level to distinction that counts. ...

The finest short stories are those that raise, in short, one particular man or woman, from that Gehenna, the newspapers, where at last all men are equal, to the distinction of being an individual. To be responsive not to the ordinances of the herd (Russia-like) but to the extraordinary responsibility of being a person. ...

[The] real writing, the real short story will be written privately, in secret, despairingly - for the individual. For it will be the individual.

Thus and for that purpose, the great writer will use his materials formally, in his own style, the words, the choice and the mode of his words - like Boccaccio, Stein and Faulkner. ...

I cannot tell you how to write a short story, I can only tell you how you must write it.

It is not to place adjectives, it is to learn to employ the verbs in imitation of nature - so that the pieces move naturally - and watch, often breathlessly, what they *do*.

That is the enlargement of nature which we call art. The *additions* to nature which we call art.

You do not *copy* nature, you make something which is an *imitation* of nature - read your Aristotle again.

That is the *work* of the imagination, as the late Virginia Woolf pointed out. You have to work, you have to imagine the character, which is for your mind to *be* the creator.

Arrived at that condition, the imagination inflamed, the excitement of it is that you no longer copy but *make* a natural object. (Something comparable to nature: an other nature.) You yourself become the instrument of nature - the helpless instrument.

You must tell the truth. You can't lie because the moment you attempt to fall off you destroy yourself.

It *is* nature. I don't think you know in a short story what's coming out. That is the excitement of it. ...

Now what are some of the advantages of the short story as an art form - bearing what I have said, in mind.

It should be a brush stroke - as compared with a picture.

One chief advantage as against a novel - which is its nearest cousin - is that you do not have to bear in mind the complex structural paraphernalia of a novel in writing a short story and so may dwell on the manner, the writing. On the process itself. A single stroke, uncomplicated but complete. Not like a chapter or paragraph.

Thus, bearing a possible novel in mind, if you will, you can play with the words as materials. You can try various modes of writing - more freely.

Try all sorts of effects. The short story is a wonderful medium for prose experimentation. ...

What shall the short story be written about. Obviously not, if it is serious, the mere sentimental characters. How write about a poor Wop, a Polish gal in her kitchen, a foreign peasant who is barely articulate.

What then? Something that interests the writer seriously, as a writer (not necessarily a man for in that case the interest would be moral and perhaps best NOT as a short story). It is the way his interests, as a writer, impinge upon the material - graphically told.

The result is life, not morals. It is THE LIFE which comes alive in the telling. It is the life under specified conditions - so that it is relived in the reading - as it strikes off flashes from the material. The material is the metal against which a flint makes sparks.

Anything, thus anything can be used without fear of sentimentality. The THING we are writing, directing all our wit, our intelligence to discovering and setting down - is revealed as it hits against anything at all. That's the modern understanding - and I guess it is pretty hard to realize. Whatever that may be for each man who writes.

76. ALFRED E. COPPARD —— 1951

aus "Foreword" zu *The Collected Tales of A. E. Coppard* (New York, 1951), vii f.

[There] are just two things I really must say about short stories in general and their principles of manufacture. First, I want to crush the assumption that the short story and the novel are manifestations of one principle of fiction, differentiated merely by size, that the novel is inherently and naturally the substantial and therefore the important piece of work, the bale of tweed - you may suppose - out of which your golfer gets his plus-four suit, the short story being merely a remnant, the rag or two left over to make the caddie a cap. In fact the relationship of the short story to the novel amounts to nothing at all. The novel is a distinct form of art having a pedigree and practice of hardly more than a couple of hundred years; the short story, so far from being its offspring, is an ancient art originating in the folk tale, which was a thing of joy even before writing, not to mention printing, was invented. Put the beginning of English printing in the last quarter of the fifteenth century and you light on a date when the folk tale lost its oral or spoken form and issued as a printed short story. Moreover, it was only through that same device of printing that the novel became even a possibility; it did not materialize until the eighteenth century, its forerunners being *Pilgrim's Progress* and *Gulliver's Travels*.

The folk tale ministered to an apparently inborn and universal desire to hear tales, and it is my feeling that the closer the modern short story conforms to that ancient tradition of being spoken to you, rather than being read at you, the more acceptable it becomes. One of the earliest delights of childhood is to be told a tale, and the queer pleasure does not lessen or leave us until we ourselves are left in the grave. Cut off a person from all contact with tales and he will assuredly begin to invent some - probably about himself. I don't know why this is, or what is the curious compulsion that urges some to take to the job of telling the tale, that unconscionable lying which is styled the Art of Fiction, but for good or ill I seem to have been that sort of liar. It has been a pleasant business for me, and I hope it will not be too bad for those about to receive these fabrications.

The second principle I would like to urge is that unity, verisimilitude, and completeness of contour are best obtained by plotting your story through the mind or consciousness of only one of your characters, a process that I used to think might be the secret hinted at in Henry James's tale "The Figure in the Carpet."

Of course one does not adhere to literary principles any more than one does to political or moral ones - we accept them for guidance, not for use in dictatorship. As long as mine served and were not too difficult to embody, I was virtuous; whenever they became irksome or incurred some loss of interest, I took the primrose path and hoped for the best.

77. W. SOMERSET MAUGHAM ——— 1952

aus "Preface" zu der amerikanischen Ausgabe der *Complete Short Stories of W. Somerset Maugham, vol. I: East and West* (Garden City, N. Y., 1952). - Hier zitiert nach *Selected Prefaces and Introductions of W. Somerset Maugham* (London, 1963), 42-61.

My prepossessions in the arts are on the side of law and order. I like a story that fits. I did not take to writing stories seriously till I had had much experience as a dramatist, and this experience taught me to leave out everything that did not serve the dramatic value of my story. It taught me to make incident follow incident in such a manner as to lead up to the climax I had in mind. I am not unaware of the disadvantages of this method. It gives a tightness of effect that is sometimes disconcerting. You feel that life does not dovetail into its various parts with such neatness. In life stories straggle, they begin nowhere and tail off without a point. That is probably what Chekhov meant when he said that stories should have neither a beginning nor an end. It is certain that sometimes it gives you a sensation of airlessness when you see persons who behave so exactly according to character, and incidents that fall into place with such perfect convenience. The story-teller of this kind aims not only at giving his own feelings about life, but at a formal decoration. He arranges life to suit his purposes. He follows a design in his mind, leaving out this and changing that; he distorts facts to his advantage, according to his plan; and when he attains his object produces a work of art. It may be that life slips through his fingers; then he has failed; it may be that he seems sometimes so artificial that you cannot believe him, and when you do not believe a story-teller he is done. When he succeeds he has forced you for a time to accept his view of the universe and has given you the pleasure of following out the pattern he has drawn on the surface of chaos. But he seeks to prove nothing. He paints a picture and sets it before you. You can take it or leave it.

78. W. SOMERSET MAUGHAM —— 1952

aus "Introduction" zu *A Choice of Kipling's Prose* (London, 1952). - Hier zitiert nach *Selected Prefaces and Introductions of W. Somerset Maugham* (London, 1963), 118-146.

Kipling was widely accused of vulgarity: so were Balzac and Dickens; I think only because they dealt with aspects of life that offended persons of refinement. We are tougher now: when we call someone refined we do not think we are paying him a compliment. But one of the most absurd charges brought against him was that his stories were anecdotes, which the critics who made it thought was to condemn him (as they sometimes still do); but if they had troubled to consult the Oxford Dictionary they would have seen that a meaning it gives to the word is: 'The narration of a detached incident, or of a single event, told as being in itself interesting or striking.' That is a perfect definition of a short story. The story of Ruth, the story of the Matron of Ephesus, Boccaccio's story of Federigo degli Alberighi and his falcon are all anecdotes. So are *Boule de Suif, La Parure* and *L'Héritage*. An anecdote is the bony structure of a story which gives it form and coherence and which the author clothes with flesh, blood and nerves. No one is obliged to read stories, and if you don't like them unless there is something in them more than a story, there is nothing to do about it. You may not like oysters, no one can blame you for that, but it is unreasonable to condemn them because they don't possess the emotional quality of a beefsteak and kidney pudding. ...

Another fault found with him [i.e. Kipling] was that he had little power of characterization. I don't think the critics who did this quite understood the place of characterization in a short story. Of course you can write a story with the intention of displaying a character. Flaubert did it in *Un Coeur Simple* and Chekhov in *The Darling*, which Tolstoy thought so well of; though a purist might object that they are not short stories, but potted novels. Kipling was concerned with incident. In a tale so concerned you need only tell enough about the persons who take part in it to bring them to life; you show them at the moment you are occupied with; they are inevitably static. To show the development of character an author needs the passage of time and the elbow-room of a novel. Perhaps the most remarkable character in fiction is Julien Sorel, but how could Stendhal have shown the development of his complicated character in a short story? ...

The short story is not a form of fiction in which the English have on the whole excelled. The English, as their novels show, are inclined to diffuseness. They have never been much interested in form. Succinctness goes against their grain. But the short story demands form. It demands succinctness. Diffuseness kills it. It depends on construction. It does not admit of loose ends. It must be complete in itself. All these qualities you will find in Kipling's stories when he was at his magnificent best, and this, happily for us, he was in story after story.

79. FRANK O'CONNOR ——— 1953

aus "And It's a Lonely, Personal Art", *The New York Times Book Review*, LVIII (No. 15, April 12, 1953), 1 und 34.

Definitions are a nuisance, but they prevent misunderstandings. When E. M. Forster wrote a book on the novel, he accepted a French definition of it as "a prose fiction of a certain length" which was incontrovertible, like saying it was written on paper, but not very helpful, as it implied that practically everything "of a certain length" was a novel and consequently that there was nothing useful to be said about it. Anthologies of short stories also suggest that everything "of a certain length" is a short story - squibs by Dorothy Parker or Saki, articles, essays and plain shockers, and that nothing useful can be said about that, either. I don't share either view. I admit I am not at all clear what I mean by a short story, or else I should have much less trouble in writing it, but I am passionately clear about what I do *not* mean, and for me, anthologies are full of negative definitions.

A yarn, for instance, is not a short story, as - begging Mr. Forster's pardon - a medieval saga or romance is not a novel. Every literary form is, to a certain extent, a convention; it is what people generally mean when they use the word that defines it, exactly as when a man says, "I'll meet you with the car," you expect to be met with an automobile, not a perambulator. ... By convention, the novel and the short story have both come to mean stories of real people in real situations, rather than what I call "The Cat's Whisker," the sort of yarn, so popular with magazine editors, which ends, usually in italics "*The face was the face of Minkie, the cat, but the whiskers were the whiskers of Colonel Claude Combpyne.*" If we must have a word for the thing, let us call it a "tale," and not mix it up with Chekhov's "Lady With the Toy Dog," with which it has nothing whatever in common but the fact that it is "a prose fiction of a certain length."

For me, what makes the short story what it is, is its attitude to Time. In any novel the principal character is Time - "Ulysses," "The Informer" and "Mrs. Dalloway" notwithstanding. Even in inferior novels and in books which are not strictly creative literature, the chronological ordering of events establishes a rhythm, which is the rhythm of life itself, and I have known novelists who sometimes wrote hundreds of pages until the novel proper began. But what to the novelist is the most precious element in his work is a nightmare to the short-story writer. He is all the while trying to get round the necessity for describing events in sequence; the rhythm is too slow, and when novelists like Henry James and Hardy turn story-tellers and use the rhythms of the novel, he finds the result disastrous. Hardy will cheerfully waste three pages getting his hero up the hill before he even begins to reveal what his story is about. Time the collaborator has become Time the gasbag.

Every great short story represents a struggle with Time - the novelist's Time - a refusal to allow it to establish its majestic rhythms ("Chapter I, A Walk on the Heath"). It attempts to reach some point of vantage, some glowing center of action from which past and future will be equally visible. The crisis of a short story *is* the short story, and not, as in the novel, the logical, inescapable, result of everything preceding it, the mere flowering of events. I should almost say that in the story what precedes the crisis becomes a consequence of the crisis.

It is one of the weaknesses of the story-writer that, because of his awareness of the importance of the crisis, he tends to inflate it, to give it artificial, symbolic significance. In teaching the short story, I have had to warn students that anyone using symbolism would be instantly expelled from the class. Joyce, who was fascinated by the problem, did use symbolism, but being Joyce used it in such a remote form that he manages to conceal it from most readers. In "Ivy-Day in the Committee Room," a satirical comment on Ireland after Parnell, we meet a few political figures consumed with rancor for the want of a drink. Then some bottles of stout appear, and the tone of their sentiment at once becomes nobler, till, in a mock-heroic parody of a Hero's funeral, a sentimental poem takes the place of a Dead March and three bottles of stout, placed before the fire to open, that of the three volleys fired over the Hero's grave. ...

The short story is lyrical, not epic; that it springs from the heart of a situation rather than mounts up to and explains it. There is yet another way of expressing the same thing in relation to the novel. The novel, it is generally agreed, is the typical art of the middle classes which reached its highest development in the century of the middle classes, the nineteenth. The nineteenth-century novel in Europe had a peculiar geographical distribution. It is at its greatest in England, France and Russia.

The distribution of the short story is quite different. Here, the Russians have the field to themselves; the French with Maupassant are barely in sight, while the English are still hovering round the starting post, eagerly searching for the whiskers of Colonel Claude Combpyne. It is true that the great period of the short story didn't come until the decline of the novel, about 1880, but long before that Turgenev had done things with the short story which have never been bettered. This hints at a basic difference in approach between novel and story.

It is even more peculiar in our own times. Now, it is America which takes the place of Imperial Russia and produces both novels and short stories of the first rank. But Ireland, which has never produced a novel, had produced short stories of remarkable quality, and, in spite of Coppard and Pritchett, far superior to English short stories which still mainly investigate whiskers in italics. This suggests that the difference has something to do with the attitude that the two art forms impose on their writers. I have small doubt that the difference is in the attitude to society.

The thing which makes the Irish novel impossible is that the subject of a novel is almost invariably the relation of the individual to society, and Ireland does not have a society which can absorb the individual; as an

American critic has put it, every good Irish novel ends on a ship to England or America. But the emotion of Gabriel Conroy in "The Dead" is not conditioned by society, and the loneliness of the people in Winesburg, Ohio, is not likely to be changed by any change in their social condition. Their troubles "are from eternity and shall not fail."

In fact, the short story, compared with the novel, is a lonely, personal art; the lyric cry in face of human destiny, it does not deal as the novel must do with types or with problems of moment, but with what Synge calls "the profound and common interests of life"; the little servant girl so weary of her nursing that she smothers the baby; the cabman so obsessed by his son's death that when none of his busy customers will listen to his grief, he tells it to his old cab-horse. It is not for nothing that some of the great story-tellers like Gorki have been tramps. The story-writer is not a soldier in the field, but a guerilla fighter, fighting the obscure duels of a great campaign. He stands always somewhere on the outskirts of society, less interested in its famous and typical figures than in the lonely and gnarled and obscure individuals of Winesburg, Ohio, and Dublin, Ireland.

80. VICTOR S. PRITCHETT ——— 1953

"Short Stories", *Harper's Bazaar*, LXXXVII (July, 1953), 31 und 113. - Abgedruckt in Eugene Current-García and Walton R. Patrick (Eds.), *What is the Short Story?* (Glenview, Ill., 1961), 123 f.

For a long time the short story was the poor relation of the novel. It was the chapter left over, the anecdote to be tossed off in a spare moment. Even in the hands of genius, like those of Maupassant and Chekhov, the short story was thought to be the *pis aller* of writers who would have written novels if they had only known how, for Chekhov wasted two or three years trying and Maupassant is a failure as a novelist. We now think differently: the originating genius of Poe in America, of these French and Russian writers and (very late) of Kipling in Britain, has turned out to be decisive and, in this century, writers have had the excitement of a new, intensely individual prose art at their disposal. It is a hybrid. It owes much to the quickness, the objectivity and cutting of the cinema; it owes much to the poet on the one hand and the newspaper reporter on the other; something also to the dramatic compression of the theatre, and everything to the restlessness, the alert nerve, the scientific eye and the short breath of contemporary life. It is the art of the short expectation of life. It fulfills Poe's demand that works of art should be short and immediate in effect. It succeeds on condition that it gets off on the right foot and bears in mind what is said to be the motto of the Bank of England: never explain, never apologize.

If the short story is natural to our age, it makes one crucial requirement which many young writers who attempt this form fatally lack. Maxim Gorki, who inherited a natural power of storytelling from his grandmother, makes it clear in his autobiography that without personality - possibly without the right grandmother - the storyteller is sunk. He describes how his grandmother kept the simple Russian sailors on a ship captivated by her tales. One was about a goblin who ran a splinter in his paw and screamed out, "I can't bear it, little mice, it hurts so much." And, says Gorki, "She lifted her own foot in her hands and rocked comically, screwing up her face as if she actually felt the pain."

The good storyteller knows that, orally or writing, he is putting on a personal, individual act. A novelist can dispense with that. Trollope had almost no personality; quite a number of excellent modern novelists have an average personality common to them all. The novelist is able, for long periods, to rely on the cumulative weight and diffusion of his material. Not so the storyteller. A miniaturist like Colette, as delicate as a cat, a dramatist of nervous alarm and the inner precipice like Elizabeth Bowen, a reporter like Hemingway, intrepid travelers into the tropics of character like Eudora Welty and Carson McCullers owe the indispensable shock they give to the reader to their personality.

Moralists used to condemn even the greatest novels as dangerous, drugging daydreams. There was *something* in this argument. Their length, their inclusiveness, their shapelessness - despite all the efforts of Henry James and Flaubert - were bemusing. The story, on the other hand, wakes the reader up. Not only that; it answers the primitive craving for art, the wit, paradox and beauty of shape, the longing to see a dramatic pattern and significance in our experience, the desire for the electric shock. The modern reader is longing for a revival of the tale which the novel, in its complexity and sophistication, has so thoroughly repressed in the brief two hundred and fifty years of its life. But in stressing the "art" of the short story, I do not mean to convey something precious or nicely removed from life. Chekhov's stories form a passionate, indignant yet scientific record of Russian life in his time. Maupassant has described the Normandy peasant forever. All conscience spreads entangled from Conrad's tale of the Captain who hides the refugee in his cabin; all the fatality attending the rebel and the soldier is in Frank O'Connor's tale of the Irishmen playing cards with their British prisoners, while they wait orders to execute them. These stories are not missing chapters or scenarios for novels. Expanded, they would "explain," "apologize" and fail to pierce.

The modern nervous system is keyed up. The very collapse of standards, conventions and values, which has so bewildered the impersonal novelist, has been the making of the story writer who can catch any piece of life as it flies and make his personal performance out of it.

81. ANGUS WILSON ——— 1954

aus "The Short Story Changes", *The Spectator*, CXCVIII (Oct. 1, 1954), 401 f. - Dieser Artikel ist eine Rezension der Kurzgeschichtenbände von Margarete Lane (*A Crown of Convolvulus*), Jean Stafford (*Children are Bored on Sundays*), C. S. Forester (*The Nightmare*), Antonia White (*Strangers*) und Louis Auchincloss (*The Romantic Egoists*).

In a recent article in *The Times Literary Supplement* a critic quotes Miss Elizabeth Bowen as saying that the short story is 'in its use of action ... nearer to the drama than to the novel,' and then comments, 'if in some cases it is nearer to the drama than the novel, in others it is nearer to the poem.' This careful separation of the short story from the novel has, I suspect, been very influential among the more serious short story writers for the last twenty or so years. It has, of course, certain truths in it, but in searching for the more subtle aspects of form, it seems to me wilfully to disregard the obvious. Of course it is true that short stories like plays must be compressed in statement and depend for their aesthetic impact upon climax, surprise and other directly artful methods of presentation. The very tightness of form, too, means that the short story writer must make use of allusion, symbol and overtone to convey his meaning in a way that brings him closer to the poet than the novelist. Indeed some of the best short stories of today remind me directly of those combinations of drama and poetry we find in Browning's *Men and Women*. Given the change of moral mood, there is much in the stories, for example, of Miss Jean Stafford and Miss Margaret Lane, in their prepossession with the psychological significance of incidents and their suggestions of general moral truth by the peculiar or the macabre that recalls Bishop Blougram, or Holy Cross Day, or the Statue and the Bust. It is the moral atmosphere that is stressed and the significant moment that is caught to convey it. Nevertheless, for all these affinities between short stories, poetry and drama, the plain truth is that the development of the short story in this century has followed that of the novel. The classic short story of Mr. Maugham's era, with its emphasis on narrative and surprise, proved too tight to convey the flow of sensitivity which to Katherine Mansfield was the essence both of art and life. By injecting greater subtlety of mood and deeper levels of consciousness, she almost succeeded in destroying the form and reducing short stories to 'sketches.' Short story writers for the last fifteen years have been trying to tie the two threads together again. The history of the novel has not been dissilimar and, on the whole, the short story writers have been more successful than the novelists in restoring shape without losing subtlety. It would not be unfair, I think, to say that the success of the stories under review is in direct ratio to their power of maintaining form without losing suggestion and overtone.

82. *HOWARD NEMEROV* ———————————————— *1956*,1963

aus "Composition and Fate in the Short Novel" in *Poetry and Fiction: Essays* (New Brunswick, N. Y., 1963), 229-245. - Dieser Essay, der am 7. September 1956 als Vortrag vor dem English Institute der Columbia University gehalten wurde, erschien ursprünglich in *The Graduate Journal*, V (Fall, 1963).

The writer attempting for the first time a short novel must face, I should think, nothing but problems, the first, though probably the least, of which is, What are short novels? For the writer who is by habit of mind a novelist they must represent not simply a compression but a corresponding rhythmic intensification, a more refined criterion of relevance than the one he usually enjoys, an austerity and economy perhaps somewhat compulsive in the intention itself. For the writer who habitually thinks in short stories - a bad habit, by the way - the challenge is probably greater: he will have to learn as never before about the interstices of his action; he will have to think about a fairly large space which must be filled, not with everything (his complaint against the novelist), but with something definite which must be made to yield in a quite explicit way its most reserved and recondite ranges of feeling; he will have to think, for once, of design and not merely of plot. To both writers it must soon become apparent that a short novel is something in itself, neither a lengthily written short story nor the refurbished attempt at a novel sent out into the world with its hat clapped on at the eightieth page.

I am speaking, perhaps, ideally, and about the ideal; it is difficult not to. ...

I will try to suggest, without wasting time on attempts at unexceptionable definition, some of the things, other than length, which seem to set the novella apart from the short story and the novel. For the term "short novel" is descriptive only in the way that the term "Middle Ages" is descriptive - that is, not at all, except with reference to the territory on either side. And just as historians exaggerate the darkness of the Dark Ages and the brightness of the Renaissance, I shall exaggerate some elements of the short story and the novel, to make the middle term more visible.

The short story at present is a way of transacting one's fictional business which is shiny, efficient, and inexpensive; consequently it has become very attractive to non-artists. ... To write a fine short story may be harder now than it has ever been, but there is no indication that large numbers of short story writers are aware of the fact. ... Short stories amount for the most part to parlor tricks, party favors with built-in snappers, gadgets for inducing recognitions and reversals: a small pump serves to build up the pressure, a tiny trigger releases it, there follow a puff and a flash as freedom and necessity combine; finally a Celluloid doll drops from the muzzle and descends by parachute to the floor. These things happen, but they happen to no one in particular.

Of many possible reasons why this fate has overtaken the short story, one must be the vast quantity of such stuff produced every day of every week and published in newspapers and magazines, on radio and television (for those "dramas" are either adapted from short stories or made up with the same requirements in mind). ...

The contrast I want to bring out is this: for many novelists, all but the simplest element of compositional art (the plot) is destroyed by observation, by detail work, by reality, which keeps poking its head in. The leisure, the "warm earthy humanity," of the novel owes itself to this consideration: people read novellas, but they tend to live in novels, and sometimes they live there very comfortably indeed: thus you have descriptions which are nothing but descriptions, thus you have philosophical excursions, set-pieces, summaries, double plot, and full orchestration, not to mention that all the chairs are heavily upholstered and even the walls padded. Stendhal provided benches for the reader to sit down on, but many novelists erect hotels for the same laudable accommodation. ...

The most striking element shared by almost all the great pieces in this genre [of the short novel or novella] is their outright concentration upon traditional problems of philosophy, the boldness of their venture into generality, the evidence they give of direct and profound moral concern. We are not entitled to suppose, of course, that such works were composed from the point of view first of general ideas and philosophic problems and paradoxes ... What we may insist is that these works combine with their actions a most explicit awareness of themselves as parables, as philosophic myths, and almost invariably announce and demonstrate the intention of discursive profundity - the intention, it is not too much to say, of becoming sacred books: final instances, exhaustively analyzed, of a symbolic universe of whose truth we can be persuaded only by fictions. The result for composition is that problem becomes the center of the short novel, which with a peculiar purity dramatizes conflicts of appearance and reality (*Benito Cereno*), freedom and necessity (*Notes from the Underground*), madness and sanity (*Ward Number Six*)...

Whereas the short story tends to rest upon action, a combination of circumstances to which the characters must very readily conform, while the novel, especially in English, goes toward the opposite pole and tends to produce "characters" as an independent value, the short novel strikes a very delicate and exact balance between motive and circumstance; its action generally speaking is the fate of the agonists, and this fate is regarded as flowing demonstrably and with some precision and in great detail from their individual natures, which accordingly are developed at considerable length. ...

I have tried to describe the short novel, according to the examples I am most familiar with, not as a compromise between novel and short story, but as something like the ideal and primary form, suggestively allied in simplicity and even in length with the tragedies of antiquity, and dealing in effect with equivalent materials. No doubt in dealing with this subject I have slighted somewhat the complex novel and, even more, the short story; that has to do in part, as I said, with making the middle term visible, but perhaps in even greater part with my lasting delight in short novels, which I will even go so far as nearly to identify with tragic art in our fictional tradition.

83. *TRUMAN CAPOTE* — 1957

aus "Truman Capote" in *Writers at Work: The Paris Review Interviews*. With an Introduction by Malcolm Cowley (London, 1958), 253-267. - Ursprünglich erschienen in *The Paris Review* (Spring/Summer, 1957).

INTERVIEWER: What did you first write?

CAPOTE: Short stories. And my more unswerving ambitions still revolve around this form. When seriously explored, the short story seems to me the most difficult and disciplining form of prose writing extant. Whatever control and technique I may have I owe entirely to my training in this medium.

INTERVIEWER: What do you mean exactly by "control"?

CAPOTE: I mean maintaining a stylistic and emotional upper hand over your material. Call it precious and go to hell, but I believe a story can be wrecked by a faulty rhythm in a sentence - especially if it occurs towards the end - or a mistake in paragraphing, even punctuation. Henry James is the maestro of the semicolon. Hemingway is a first-rate paragrapher. From the point of view of ear, Virginia Woolf never wrote a bad sentence. I don't mean to imply that I successfully practise what I preach. I try, that's all.

INTERVIEWER: How does one arrive at short-story technique?

CAPOTE: Since each story presents its own technical problems, obviously one can't generalize about them on a two-times-two-equals-four basis. Finding the right form for your story is simply to realize the most *natural* way of telling the story. The test of whether or not a writer has divined the natural shape of his story is just this: after reading it, can you imagine it differently, or does it silence your imagination and seem to you absolute and final? As an orange is final. As an orange is something nature has made just right.

84. FRANK O'CONNOR — 1957

aus "Frank O'Connor" in *Writers at Work: The Paris Review Interviews*. With an Introduction by Malcolm Cowley (London, 1958), 145-163. - Ursprünglich erschienen in *The Paris Review* (Autumn/Winter, 1957).

INTERVIEWER: Why do you prefer the short story for your medium?

O'CONNOR: Because it's the nearest thing I know to lyric poetry - I wrote lyric poetry for a long time, then discovered that God had not intended me to be a lyric poet, and the nearest thing to that is the short story. A novel actually requires far more logic and far more knowledge of circumstances, whereas a short story can have the sort of detachment from circumstances that lyric poetry has.

INTERVIEWER: Faulkner has said, "Maybe every novelist wants to write poetry first, finds he can't, and then tries the short story, which is the most demanding form after poetry. And, failing at that, only then does he take up novel writing." What do you think about this?

O'CONNOR: I'd love to console myself, it's that neat - it sounds absolutely perfect except that it implies, as from a short-story writer, that the novel is just an easy sort of thing that you slide gently into, whereas, in fact, my own experience with the novel is that it was always too difficult for me to do. At least to do a novel like *Pride and Prejudice* requires something more than to be a failed B. A. or a failed poet or a failed short-story writer, or a failed anything else. Creating in the novel a sense of continuing life is the thing. We don't have that problem in the short story, where you merely suggest continuing life. In the novel, you have to create it, and that explains one of my quarrels with modern novels. Even a novel like *As I Lay Dying*, which I admire enormously, is not a novel at all, it's a short story. To me a novel is something that's built around the character of time, the nature of time, and the effects that time has on events and characters. When I see a novel that's supposed to take place in twenty-four hours, I just wonder why the man padded out the short story.

INTERVIEWER: Yeats said, "O'Connor is doing for Ireland what Chekhov did for Russia." What do you think of Chekhov?

O'CONNOR: Oh, naturally I admire Chekhov extravagantly, I think every short-story writer does. He's inimitable, a person to read and admire and worship - but never, never, never to imitate. He's got all the most extraordinary technical devices, and the moment you start imitating him without those technical devices, you fall into a sort of rambling narrative, as I think even a good story writer like Katherine Mansfield did. She sees that Chekhov apparently constructs a story without episodic interest, so she decides that if she constructs a story without episodic interest it will be equally good. It isn't. What she forgets is that Chekhov had a long career as a journalist, as a writer for comic magazines, writing squibs, writing vaudevilles, and he had learned the art very, very early of maintaining interest, of creating a bony structure. It's only concealed in the later work. They think they can do without that bony structure, but they are all wrong. ...

INTERVIEWER: What writers do you feel have influenced you in your own work?

O'CONNOR: It's very hard to say. The man who has influenced me most, I suppose, is really Isaak Babel, and again with that natural enthusiasm of mine for imitating everybody. "Guests of the Nation" and a couple of the other stories in that book are really imitations of Babel's stories in *The Red Cavalry* [*Konarmia*].

INTERVIEWER: What about working habits? How do you start a story?

O'CONNOR: "Get black on white" used to be Maupassant's advice - that's what I always do. I don't give a hoot what the writing's like, I write any sort of rubbish which will cover the main outlines of the story, then I can begin to see it. When I write, when I draft a story, I never think of writing nice sentences about, "It was a nice August evening when Elizabeth Jane Moriarity was coming down the road." I just write roughly what happened, and then I'm able to see what the construction looks like. It's the design of the story which to me is most important, the thing that tells you there's a bad gap in the narrative here and you really ought to fill that up in some way or another. I'm always looking at the design of a story, not the treatment. Yesterday I was finishing off a piece about my friend A. E. Coppard, the greatest of all the English storytellers, who died about a fortnight ago. I was describing the way Coppard must have written these stories, going around with a notebook, recording what the lighting looked like, what that house looked like, and all the time using metaphor to suggest it to himself, "The road looked like a mad serpent going up the hill," or something of the kind, and, "She said so-and-so, and the man in the pub said something else." After he had written them all out, he must have got the outline of his story, and he'd start working in all the details. Now, I could never do that at all. I've got to see what these people did, first of all, and *then* I start thinking of whether it was a nice August evening or a spring evening. I have to wait for the theme before I can do anything.

INTERVIEWER: Do you rewrite?

O'CONNOR: Endlessly, endlessly, endlessly. And keep on rewriting, and after it's published, and then after it's published in book form, I usually rewrite it again. I've rewritten versions of most of my early stories and one of these days, God help, I'll publish these as well.

INTERVIEWER: Do you keep notes as a source of supply for future stories?

O'CONNOR: Just notes of themes. If somebody tells me a good story, I'll write it down in my four lines; that is the secret of the theme. If you make the subject of a story twelve or fourteen lines, that's a treatment. You've already committed yourself to the sort of character, the sort of surroundings, and the moment you've committed yourself, the story is already written. It has ceased to be fluid, you can't design it any longer, you can't model it. So I always confine myself to my four lines. If it won't go into four, that means you haven't reduced it to its ultimate simplicity, reduced it to the fable.

INTERVIEWER: I have noticed in your stories a spareness of physical description of people and places. Why this apparent rejection of sense impressions?

O'CONNOR: I thoroughly agree, it's one of the things I know I do, and sometimes when I'm reading Coppard I feel that it's entirely wrong. I'd love to be able to describe people as he describes them, and landscapes as he describes them, but I begin the story in the man's head and it never gets out of the man's head. And in fact, in real life, when you meet somebody in the street you don't start recording that she had this sort of nose - at least a man doesn't. I mean, if you're the sort of person that meets a girl in the street and instantly notices the colour of her eyes and of her hair and the sort of dress she's wearing, then you're not in the least like me. I just notice a feeling from people. I notice particularly the cadence of their voices, the sort of phrases they'll use, and that's what I'm all the time trying to hear in my head, how people word things - because everybody speaks an entirely different language, that's really what it amounts to. I have terribly sensitive hearing and I'm terribly aware of voices. If I remember somebody, for instance, that I was very fond of, I don't remember what he or she looked like, but I can absolutely take off the voice. I'm a good mimic; I've a bit of the actor in me, I suppose, that's really what it amounts to. I cannot pass a story as finished unless I connect it myself, unless I know how everybody in it spoke, which, as I say, can go quite well with the fact that I couldn't tell you in the least what they looked like. If I use the right phrase and the reader hears the phrase in his head, he sees the individual. It's like writing for the theatre, you see. A bad playwright will "pull" an actor because he'll tell him what to do, but a really good playwright will give you a part that you can do what you like with. It's transferring to the reader the responsibility for acting those scenes. I've given him all the information I have and put it into his own life.

INTERVIEWER: What about adapting your own work to another medium - say, movies?

O'CONNOR: Well, I've tried it here and there and generally it's pretty awful. ... What I really enjoy doing is transferring stories to the air. Again, my sort of story is suitable for that. The ones I've seen on television, they don't impress me. Again, they become too precise. Also, of course, there is this awful business in television, even, certainly with the cinema, of the amount of money involved, so that everything has to be tested again, and again, and again; this thing's got to be submitted to So-and-so, and So-and-so, and they all lay down different laws and your script is being changed all the time. Finally, what comes over is nobody's job - it's a sort of accident and sometimes, by accident, you'll get a fairly decent movie or a fairly decent television show. But you never have that feeling you have in the theatre, or in the story, above all (that's the reason I like writing short stories) that you're your own theatre. You can control every bloomin' thing - if you say it's going to be twilight, it's going to be twilight and you're not askin' the advice of a lighting man who will say to you, "Well, you can't have a second twilight, you had twilight ten minutes ago, you can't have another one." You can do what you please and you're ultimately the only person responsible. To tell you the truth, I don't think any of these mass media is a satisfactory art form. The real trouble is, the moment you get a mass audience, commercial interests become involved. ...

INTERVIEWER: What is the greatest essential of a story?

O'CONNOR: You have to have a theme, a story to tell. Here's a man at the other side of the table and I'm talking to him; I'm going to tell him something that will interest him. As you know perfectly well, our principal difficulty at Harvard was a number of people who'd had affairs with girls or had had another interesting experience, and wanted to come in and tell about it, straight away. That is not a theme. A theme is something that is worth something to every body. In fact, you wouldn't, if you'd ever been involved in a thing like this, grab a man in a pub and say, "Look, I had a girl out last night, under the Charles Bridge." That's the last thing you'd do. You grab somebody and say, "Look, an extraordinary thing happened to me yesterday - I met a man - he said this to me - " and that, to me, is a theme. The moment you grab somebody by the lapels and you've got something to tell, that's a real story. It means you want to tell him and think the story is interesting in itself. If you start describing your own personal experiences, something that's only of interest to yourself, then you can't express yourself, you cannot say, ultimately, what you think about human beings. The moment you say this, you're committed.

I'll tell you what I mean. We were down on the south coast of Ireland for a holiday and we got talkin' to this old farmer and he said his son, who was dead now, had gone to America. He'd married an American girl and she had come over for a visit, alone. Apparently her doctor had told her a trip to Ireland would do her good. And she stayed with the parents, had gone around to see his friends and other relations, and it wasn't till after she'd gone that they learned that the boy had died. Why didn't she tell them? There's your story. Dragging the reader in, making the reader a part of the story - the reader is a part of the story. You're saying all the time, "This story is about you - *de te fabula* ..."

85. ANGUS WILSON —— 1957

aus "Angus Wilson" in *Writers at Work: The Paris Review Interviews*. With an Introduction by Malcolm Cowley (London, 1958), 225-238. - Ursprünglich erschienen in *The Paris Review* (Autumn/Winter 1957).

INTERVIEWER: What is the difference for you between a short story and a novel?

WILSON: Short stories and plays go together in my mind. You take a point in time and develop it from there; there is no room for development backwards. In a novel I also take a point in time, but feel every room for development backwards. All fiction for me is a kind of magic and trickery - a confidence trick, trying to make people believe something is true that isn't. And the novelist, in particular, is trying to convince the reader that he is seeing society as a whole.

This is why I use such a lot of minor characters and subplots, of course. It isn't wilful love of subplots for their own sake, wilful Victorianism, but because they enable me to suggest the existence of a wider society, the ripples of a society outside. And more important is this thing about fiction as trickery. The natural habit of any good and critical reader is to disbelieve what you are telling him and try to escape out of the world you are picturing. Some novelists try to make the magic work by taking you deep down inside one person. I try to multiply the worlds I put into the books - so that, like the ripples of the stone thrown into the brook, you feel the repercussions going farther and farther out, and at the same time bringing more in. ...

INTERVIEWER: What about short stories?

WILSON: You can't do this sort of thing with short stories. They have a kind of immediate ethical text. Many of mine have punning titles. I take a platitude - "the wrong set," for example: the point is that no one knows what the wrong set is, and one person's wrong set is another's right set. And you get the pay-off, which is something I like. A play is rather like this, but has more depth. And plays and short stories are similar in that both start when all but the action has finished.

aus *Faulkner in the University, Class Conferences at the University of Virginia 1957-1958*, hrsg. von Frederick L. Gwynn and Joseph Blotner (Charlottesville, Va., 1959), 48 f.; 207.

Q. Sir, in your novels, you said in one of the other classes that you begin with a character in mind or more than one character. In your short stories, do they - do you conceive of them the same way? Do you start with a person or do you - ?

A. Sometimes with a person, sometimes with an anecdote, but the short story is conceived in the same terms that the book is. The first job the craftsman faces is to tell this as quickly and as simply as I can, and if he's good, if he's of the first water, like Chekhov, he can do it every time in two or three thousand words, but if he's not that good, sometimes it takes him eighty thousand words. But they are similar, and he is simply trying to tell something which was true and moving in the shortest time he can, and then if he has sense enough stop. That is, I don't believe the man or the woman sits down and says, Now I'm going to write a short story, or Now I'm going to write a novel. It's an idea that begins with the thought, the image of a character, or with an anecdote, and even in the same breath, almost like lightning, it begins to take a shape that he can see whether it's going to be a short story or a novel. Sometimes, not always. Sometimes he thinks it'll be a short story and finds that he can't. Sometimes it looks like it's to be a novel and then after he works on it, he sees that it's not, that he can tell it in two thousand or five thousand words. No rule to it. ...

Q. Mr. Faulkner, you spoke about *The Sound and the Fury* as starting out to write a short story and it kept growing. Well now, do you think that it's easier to write a novel than a short story?

A. Yes sir. You can be more careless, you can put more trash in it and be excused for it. In a short story that's next to the poem, almost every word has got to be almost exactly right. In the novel you can be careless but in the short story you can't. I mean by that the good short stories like Chekhov wrote. That's why I rate that second - it's because it demands a nearer absolute exactitude. You have less room to be slovenly and careless. There's less room in it for trash. In poetry, of course, there's no room at all for trash. It's got to be absolutely impeccable, absolutely perfect.

Q. More like playwriting? ...

A. Yes'm, that's right. Of course playwriting has one more demand that you're not going to keep your audience that long. With a book you can read that a while and put it down and then go back and read it, but a play you can't.

87. W. SOMERSET MAUGHAM ——— 1958

aus "The Short Story" in *Points of View* (London, 1958), 142-188.

All art is escapist, Mozart's symphonies as well as Constable's landscapes; and do we read Shakespeare's sonnets or the odes of Keats for anything but the delight they give us? Why should we ask more from the novelist than we ask of the poet, the composer, the painter? In point of fact there is no such thing as a 'mere' story. When he writes a story, the author, sometimes without any more intention than to make it readable, willy-nilly offers a criticism of life. When Rudyard Kipling in his *Plain Tales of the Hills* wrote of the Indian civilians, the polo-playing officers and their wives, he wrote with the naive admiration of a young journalist of modest extraction dazzled by what he took for glamour. It is amazing that no one at the time saw what a damning indictment of the Paramount Power these stories were. You cannot read them now without realising how inevitable it was that the British sooner or later would be forced to surrender their hold on India. So with Chekhov. Objective as he tried to be, intent only on describing life with truth, you cannot read his stories without its being borne in upon you that the brutality and ignorance he wrote of, the corruption, the miserable poverty of the poor and the insouciance of the rich, must inevitably result in a bloody revolution.

I suppose most people read works of fiction because they have nothing much else to do. They read for pleasure, which is what they should do, but different people look in their reading for different kinds of pleasure. One is the pleasure of recognition. The contemporary readers of Trollope's *Barchester Chronicles* read them with an intimate satisfaction because he portrayed the sort of lives they led themselves. For the most part his readers belonged to the upper-middle class and they felt at home with the upper-middle class he dealt with. They felt the same pleasant glow of self complacency as they felt when dear Mr. Browning told them that "God's in his heaven - All's right with the world". Time has given these novels the attractiveness of *genre*. We find them amusing, and rather touching (how nice it was to live in a world in which life for the well-to-do was so easy and everything came out all right in the end!) and they have the same sort of charm as those anecdotic pictures of the mid-nineteenth century, with their bearded gentlemen in frock-coats and top-hats, and their pretty ladies in poke-bonnets and crinolines. Other readers seek in their novels strangeness and novelty. The exotic story has always had its votaries. Most people lead prodigiously dull lives, and it is a release from the monotony of existence to be absorbed for a while in a world of hazard and perilous adventure. I suspect that the Russian readers of Chekhov's stories found in them a very different pleasure from that found by readers of the Western World. They knew only too well the conditions of the people he so vividly described. English readers found in his stories something new and strange, horrible often and depressing, but presented with a truth that was impressive, fascinating and even romantic.

88. ELIZABETH BOWEN ——— 1959

aus "Preface" zu *Stories by Elizabeth Bowen* (New York, 1959). - Hier zitiert nach Elizabeth Bowen, *Afterthought* (London, 1962), 75-81.

Total impersonality in story-writing is, for me certainly, impossible - so much so that it would be a waste of time to wonder whether it would be desirable. And I doubt, actually, whether for any writer it is either desirable or possible for this reason: the short story is linked with poetry, and that, we know, cannot but bear a signature. The tale without lyricism or passion desiccates into little more than a document. The poet, and in his wake the short-story writer, is using his own, unique susceptibility to experience: in a sense, the susceptibility is the experience. The susceptibility, equally, is the writer, who therefore cannot be absent from what he writes. The short story is at an advantage over the novel, and can claim its nearer kinship to poetry, because it must be more concentrated, can be more visionary, and is not weighed down (as the novel is bound to be) by facts, explanation, or analysis. I do not mean to say that the short story is by any means exempt from the laws of narrative: it must observe them, but on its own terms. Fewer characters, fewer scenes, and above all fewer happenings are necessary; shape and action are framed for simplification. As against that, there are dangers and can be penalties: essentially, at no point in the story must the electrical-imaginative current be found to fail. Novels legitimately have 'slack' passages, which serve, like intermissions, to ease off the reader between crisis and crisis. But the short story revolves round one crisis only - one might call it, almost, a crisis in itself. There (ideally) ought to be nothing in such a story which can weaken, detract from, or blur the central, single effect.

This, I recognize, has been one idea I have kept before myself. In short-story writing it has been my main aim, and at least as an aim it has been continuous. I state it, though without deluding myself that I have realized it, succeeded in it, in any one story.

... To return to the matter of the personal, I repeat that one cannot wholly eliminate oneself for a second, and also sufficient, reason: any fiction (and surely poetry too?) is bound to be transposed autobiography. (True, it may be this at so many removes as to defeat ordinary recognition.) I can, and indeed if I would not I still must, relate any and every story I have written to something that happened to me in my own life. But here I am speaking of happenings in a broad sense - to behold, and react, is where I am concerned a happening; speculations, unaccountable stirs of interest, longings, attractions, apprehensions without knowable cause - these are happenings also. When I re-read a story, I re-live the moment from which it sprang. A scene burned itself into me, a building magnetized me, a mood or season of Nature's penetrated me, history suddenly appeared to me in some tiny act or a face had begun to haunt me before I glanced at it.

On the whole, places more often than faces have sparked off stories. To be honest, the scenes have been with me before the characters - it could have seemed to me, even, once or twice, as though the former had summoned up the latter. I do not feel, necessarily, that this is wrong: a story must come to life in its own order. Also, I re-assert what I said when discussing the art of Katherine Mansfield: I do not feel that the short story can be, or should be, used for the analysis or development of character. The full, full-length portrait is fitter work for the novelist; in the short story, treatment must be dramatic - we are dealing with man, or woman or child, in relation to a particular crisis or mood or moment, and to that only. Though (and as to this, law is stern) the crisis must be one in which such-and-such a character would be likely to be involved, or, still more, would be likely to precipitate; the mood must be one to which such-and-such a character would be likely to be prone, or still more, to heighten; the moment should essentially be the one which would, on the given character, act most strongly. Once a story truly germinates in my mind, the inevitable actors in it take form - and not only this, but they also take hold, to the point of remaining after the tale is told. I give, as examples, four stories in this selection: 'The Storm', 'Her Table Spread', 'Ivy Gripped the Steps',

'Mysterious Kôr'. Each of these arose out of an intensified, all but spell-bound beholding, on my part, of the scene in question - a fountain-filled Italian garden in livid, pre-thundery light; a shabbily fanciful Irish castle overlooking an estuary; an ivy-strangled house in a formerly suave residential avenue; or weird moonlight over bomb-pitted London. Each time I felt: 'Yes, this affects me - but it would affect "X" more.' Under what circumstances; for what reason? And who is 'X'? In each case, the 'X' I pondered upon became the key character in the resultant story. It could seem to me that stories, with their dramatis personae, pre-exist, only wait to be come upon. I know I do not invent them; I discover them. Though that does not mean that they are easily told. On me devolves the onus of narration.

Fantasy - another important element. One may, of course, say that any story (from any pen) is the exercise or working-out of a fantasy - that any author of fiction, to write at all, must have recourse to his or her dreaming faculty. But in Elizabeth Bowen stories, it may be found, fantasy is often present twice over; part as it is of the fabric of the actual plot, or governor of the behaviour of the characters. Looking through this selection I have made, I find fantasy strongly represented. Critics may possibly say, too much so? Yet these, I still maintain, are my better stories. If I were a short-story writer only, I might well seem to be out of balance. But recall, more than half of my life is under the steadying influence of the novel, with its calmer, stricter, more orthodox demands: into the novel goes such taste as I have for rational behaviour and social portraiture. The short story, as I see it to be, allows for what is crazy about humanity: obstinacies, inordinate heroisms, 'immortal longings'. At no time, even in the novel, do I consider realism to be my forte. Fortunately, however, there are many other writers; taken all-in-all we complement one another - literature is a compost to which we are each contributing what we have.

89. *HERBERT GOLD* —————————————————— 1959

aus "The Novel and the Story - The Long and Short of It" in *Fiction of the Fifties* (New York, 1959). - Hier zitiert nach *Recent American Fiction. Some Critical Views*, hrsg. von Joseph J. Waldmeir (Boston, 1963), 40-42.

What the novelist seems to be doing at his philosophical best is to explore possibility. He cuts loose from the expected and sees another possibility for an entire life - his own, his characters', everybody's. The mystery of personality, that unheard sound, always the most heavy presence in a place, works its way to some concrete clap of existence through the tangle of growth which is a successful novel. The great novelists, hearing new sounds, building new worlds in the jungle of the real world, are also great moralists by implication - committed, before all else, to an intense valuation of human experience in the here and now. They are also dangerous and destructive moralists. With angry shouts and kicks they clear away their place in the jungle before they build. They tear down our customary ways of looking at things. They stare into the sun of alternatives. They tell us: You can choose this, you can decide that. You are free! Or if not, you must seek to be free.

In the short story, a writer does something rather different in degree and therefore different in quality. Of course, some novels are merely long stories, and some stories are merely foreshortened novels, but in general the short story is work conceived with greater rigor than the novel. The short-story writer pretty much knows what he is about when he begins; he puts on the smoked glasses of a limited form before watching the eclipse of the sun. The novelist, bound to freedom, may end up blind, roasted, stupefied, and lonely. He sets out with only a hint of the end of the voyage on which he has embarked with no maps but the sealed secret orders of instinct and intelligence. He is as blind as a Secretary of State on the brink of - he knows not what. He is chronically in a bad way, dazzled and sunburned, and heading full steam up shiftless creek.

Because of this necessity of psychic confusion crystallizing out toward inexplicable and miraculous clarity in the important novel - "novel" means new, and the novel brings us unwanted news of the world - the short story is usually more reassuring both to read and to write. The agony of doubt is relieved. The destructive power of a total re-evaluation of experience is not risked. The writer can put down some of his moral baggage. ...

Part of the difference between the short story and the novel is the difference between a love affair and marriage. The first is piquant, exciting, less risky, but may cause beautiful troubles, such as wedlock. The second is long, complicated, noisy, unpredictable, very often unhappy, and absolutely prime to living on earth. The total commitment of marriage is very different from the lyrical joys of love. The novel is different from the story, and not merely because it is longer and heavier. The responsibility is total. "In dreams begin responsibilities" - in stories. "In the day responsibilities end, they end in responsibilities" - so the blessed total envelopment of a novel tells us. Those who read and write both forms treasure these two modes of experiencing fiction. And of course we love either a novel or a story as we love a girl - not for intelligence or virtue - but for the way it meets our gaze.

The short story, as it has developed since James Joyce, seems to be concerned with scene and incident, striking hot, like the lyrical poem. The novel since Dostoyevsky and Tolstoy has increasingly charged itself to make the whole man face the whole world - really the metaphysical enterprise, the bedrock sense of religious thought. ...

The difference between the short story and the novel can be expressed also through another partly parallel, overlapping set of categories. The short story tends to control and formalize experience (though the expressionistic story does not); the novel tends to set forward experience in documentary detail (though the Jamesian novel does not). Fiction can be divided this way into two types: First, that which seeks the ordered ranging and mastery of ideas; second, that which seeks the mastery of experience by passionate avowal. The first writer says: "This is what I can do with it!" The second says: "This is how it is - all of it!" The writers who Avow have the virtues of weight of Feeling, purgation by life, passion with its submissions and excesses. They run the risks of looseness, maudlin howling, self-indulgence. The writers who Control give the satisfactions of answering formal demands for order, of coming to an understanding of ends and causes and thus purging us of menace. They run the risks of a false, faked formalism, of giving us resolutions which do not resolve. ...

No writer of any lasting interest is purely one thing or the other. The best writers of the Fifties have both expressed the disasters of the times and given us some tentative notions of order. And the great writer, who has the chance of producing a masterpiece, certainly combines both of these irreconcilables, the Avowed and the Controlled - just as estranged metals can finally be fused under great heat. With fire, pressure, and continued intensity, the great artist rises to the peak of emotion and the pitch of resolution in the same work ...

90. FRANK O'CONNOR ——— 1963

aus *The Lonely Voice. A Study of the Short Story* (London, 1963), 14-23; 26 f.

[Even] from its beginnings, the short story has functioned in a quite different way from the novel, and, however difficult it may be to describe the difference, describing it is the critic's principal business.

"We all came out from under Gogol's 'Overcoat'" is a familiar saying of Turgenev, and though it applies to Russian rather than European fiction, it has also a general truth.

Read now, and by itself, "The Overcoat" does not appear so very impressive. All the things Gogol has done in it have been done frequently since his day, and sometimes done better. But if we read it again in its historical context, closing our minds so far as we can to all the short stories it gave rise to, we can see that Turgenev was not exaggerating. We have all come out from under Gogol's "Overcoat." ...

It [i.e. the story] uses the old rhetorical device of the mock-heroic, but uses it to create a new form that is neither satiric nor heroic, but something in between - something that perhaps finally transcends both. So far as I know, it is the first appearance in fiction of the Little Man, which may define what I mean by the short story better than any terms I may later use about it. Everything about Akakey Akakeivitch, from his absurd name to his absurd job, is on the same level of mediocrity, and yet his absurdity is somehow transfigured by Gogol. ... What Gogol has done so boldly and brilliantly is to take the mock-heroic character, the absurd little copying clerk, and impose his image over that of the crucified Jesus, so that even while we laugh we are filled with horror at the resemblance.

Now, this is something that the novel cannot do. For some reason that I can only guess at, the novel is bound to be a process of identification between the reader and the character. One could not make a novel out of a copying clerk with a name like Akakey Akakeivitch who merely needed a new overcoat any more than one could make one out of a child called Tommy Tompkins whose penny had gone down a drain. One character at least in any novel must represent the reader in some aspect of his own conception of himself - as the Wild Boy, the Rebel, the Dreamer, the Misunderstood Idealist - and this process of identification invariably leads to some concept of normality and to some relationship - hostile or friendly - with society as a whole. People are abnormal insofar as they frustrate the efforts of such a character to exist in what he regards as a normal universe, normal insofar as they support him. There is not only the Hero, there is also the Semi-Hero and the Demi-Semi-Hero. I should almost go so far as to say that without the concept of a normal society the novel is impossible. I know there are examples of the novel that seem to contradict this, but in general I should say that it is perfectly true. The President of the Immortals is called in only when society has made a thorough mess of the job.

But in "The Overcoat" this is not true, nor is it true of most of the stories I shall have to consider. There is no character here with whom the reader can identify himself, unless it is that nameless horrified figure who represents the author. There is no form of society to which any character in it could possibly attach himself and regard as normal. In discussions of the modern novel we have come to talk of it as the novel without a hero. In fact, the short story has never had a hero.

What it has instead is a submerged population group - a bad phrase which I have had to use for want of a better. That submerged population changes its character from writer to writer, from generation to generation. It may be Gogol's officials, Turgenev's serfs, Maupassant's prostitutes, Chekhov's doctors and teachers, Sherwood Anderson's provincials, always dreaming of escape. ... Always in the short story there is this sense of out-lawed figures wandering about the fringes of society, superimposed sometimes on symbolic figures, whom they caricature and echo - Christ, Socrates, Moses. ... As a result there is in the short story at its most characteristic something we do not often find in the novel - an intense awareness of human loneliness. Indeed, it might be truer to say that while we often read a familiar novel again for companionship, we approach the short story in a very different mood. It is more akin to the mood of Pascal's saying: *Le silence éternel de ces espaces infinis m'effraie*. ...

Clearly, the novel and the short story, though they derive from the same sources, derive in a quite different way, and are distinct literary forms; and the difference is not so much formal (though, as we shall see, there are plenty of formal differences) as ideological. I am not, of course, suggesting that for the future the short story can be written only by Eskimos and American Indians: without going so far afield, we have plenty of submerged population groups. I am suggesting strongly that we can see in it an attitude of mind that is attracted by submerged population groups, whatever these may be at any given time - tramps, artists, lonely idealists, dreamers, and spoiled priests. The novel can still adhere to the classical concept of civilized society, of man as an animal who lives in a community, as in Jane Austen and Trollope it obviously does; but the short story remains by its very nature remote from the community - romantic, individualistic, and intransigent.

But formally as well the short story differs from the novel. At its crudest you can express the difference merely by saying that the short story is short. It is not necessarily true, but as a generalization it will do well enough. If the novelist takes a character of any interest and sets him up in opposition to society, and then, as a result of the conflict between them, allows his character either to master society or to be mastered by it, he has done all that can reasonably be expected of him. In this the element of Time is his greatest asset; the chronological development of character or incident is essential form as we see it in life, and the novelist flouts it at his own peril.

For the short-story writer there is no such thing as essential form. Because his frame of reference can never be the totality of human life, he must be forever selecting the point at which he can approach it, and each selection he makes contains the possibility of a new form as well as the possibility of a complete fiasco. I have illustrated this element of choice by reference to a poem of Browning's. Almost any one of his great dramatic lyrics is a novel in itself but caught in a single moment of peculiar significance - Lippo Lippi arrested as he slinks back to his monastery in the early morning, Andrea Del Sarto as he resigns himself to the part of a complaisant lover, the Bishop dying in St. Praxed's. But since a whole lifetime must be crowded into a few minutes, those minutes must be carefully chosen indeed and lit by an unearthly glow, one that enables us to distinguish present, past and future as though they were all contemporaneous. ... Accordingly, the storyteller differs from the novelist in this: he must be much more of a writer, much more of an artist - perhaps I should add, considering the examples I have chosen, more of a dramatist. ...

Now, a man can be a very great novelist as I believe Trollope was, and yet be a very inferior writer. ... But I cannot think of a great storyteller who was also an inferior writer, unless perhaps Sherwood Anderson, nor of any at all who did not have the sense of theater.

This is anything but the recommendation that it may seem, because it is only too easy for a short-story writer to become a little too much of an artist. Hemingway, for instance, has so studied the artful approach to the significant moment that we sometimes end up with too much significance and too little information. ...

The ideal, of course, is to give the reader precisely enough information, and in this again the short story differs from the novel, because no convention of length ever seems to affect the novelist's power to tell us all we need to know. No such convention of length seems to apply to the short story at all. ... One can put this crudely by saying that the form of the novel is given by the length; in the short story the length is given by the form. There is simply no criterion of the length of a short story other than that provided by the material itself, and either padding to bring it up to a conventional length or cutting to bring it down to a conventional length is liable to injure it. I am afraid that the modern short story is being seriously affected by editorial ideas of what its length should be. (Like most storytellers, I have been told that "nobody reads anything longer than three thousand words.") All I can say from reading Turgenev, Chekhov, Katherine Anne Porter, and others is that the very term "short story" is a misnomer. A great story is not necessarily short at all, and the conception of the short story as a miniature art is inherently false. Basically, the difference between the short story and the novel is not one of length. It is a difference between pure and applied storytelling, and in case someone has still failed to get the point, I am not trying to decry applied storytelling. Pure storytelling is more artistic, that is all, and in storytelling I am not sure how much art is preferable to nature.

91. *KATHERINE ANNE PORTER* ——— 1963

aus "Katherine Anne Porter" in *Writers at Work*, Second Series, hrsg. von Van Wyck Brooks (New York, 1963), 87-114. - Ursprünglich erschienen in *The Paris Review* (Winter/Spring, 1963).

PORTER: ... Human life itself may be almost pure chaos, but the work of the artist - the only thing he's good for - is to take these handfuls of confusion and disparate things, things that seem to be irreconcilable, and put them together in a frame to give them some kind of shape and meaning. Even if it's only his view of a meaning. That's what he's for - to give his view of life. Surely, we understand very little of what is happening to us at any given moment. But by remembering, comparing, waiting to know the consequences, we can sometimes see what an event really meant, what it was trying to teach us.

INTERVIEWER: You once said that every story begins with an ending, that until the end is known there is no story.

PORTER: That is where the artist begins to work: with the consequences of acts, not the acts themselves. Or the events. The event is important only as it affects your life and the lives of those around you. The reverberations, you might say, the overtones: that is where the artist works. In that sense it has sometimes taken me ten years to understand even a little of some important event that had happened to me. Oh, I could have given a perfectly factual account of what had happened, but I didn't know what it meant until I knew the consequences.

If I didn't know the ending of a story, I wouldn't begin. I always write my last lines, my last paragraph, my last page first, and then I go back and work towards it. I know where I'm going. I know what my goal is. And how I get there is God's grace. ...

INTERVIEWER: Has a story never surprised you in the writing? A character suddenly taken a different turn?

PORTER: Well, in the vision of death at the end of "Flowering Judas" I knew the real ending - that she was not going to be able to face her life, what she'd done. ...

INTERVIEWER: That was in a fairly literal sense, a 'true' story, wasn't it?

PORTER: The truth is, I have never written a story in my life that didn't have a very firm foundation in actual human experience - somebody else's experience quite often, but an experience that became my own by hearing the story, by witnessing the thing, by hearing just a word perhaps. It doen't matter, it just takes a little - a tiny seed. Then it takes root, and it grows. It's an organic thing. That story had been on my mind for years, growing out of this one little thing that happened in Mexico. ...

INTERVIEWER: What about the technical problems a story presents, its formal structure? How deliberate are you in matters of technique? For example, the use of the historical present in "Flowering Judas"?

PORTER: The first time someone said to me, "why did you write 'Flowering Judas' in the historical present?" I thought for a moment and said, "Did I?" I'd never noticed it. Because I didn't *plan* to write it any way. A story forms in my mind and forms and forms and when it's ready to go, I strike it down - it takes just the time I sit at the typewriter. I never think about form at all. In fact, I would say that I've never been interested in anything about writing after having learned, I hope, to write. That is, I mastered my craft as well as I could. There is a technique, there is a craft, and you have to learn it. Well, I did as well as I could with that, but now all in the world I am interested in is telling a story. I have something to tell you that I, for some reason, think is worth telling, and so I want to tell it as clearly and purely and simply as I can. ...

INTERVIEWER: Did you find that the writing of *Ship of Fools* differed from the writing of shorter fiction?

PORTER: It's just a longer voyage, that's all. It was the question of keeping everything moving at once. There are about 45 main characters, all taking part in each others' lives, and then there was a steerage of sugar workers, deportees. It was all a matter of deciding which should come first, in order to keep the harmonious moving forward. A novel is really like a symphony, you know, where instrument after instrument has to come in at its own time, and no other. I tried to write it as a short novel, you know, but it just wouldn't confine itself. I wrote notes and sketches. And finally I gave in. "Oh, no, this is simply going to have to be a novel," I thought. That was a real horror. But it needed a book to contain its full movement: of the sea, and the ship on the sea, and the people going around the deck, and into the ship, and up from it. That whole movement, felt as one forward motion: I can feel it while I'm reading it. I didn't 'intend' it, but it took hold of me.

92. *WHIT & HALLIE BURNETT* —— 1964

aus "Introduction" zu *The Modern Short Story in the Making*, hrsg. von Whit and Hallie Burnett (New York & London, 1964), 10-12.

HYPOTHESIS - It is a theory of the editors that a short story generally demontrates, by the way it is written, a period in the author's career and that, with few exceptions, the growth of the author analogously parallels the historical growth of the short story.

TRADITIONAL STORY - The short story, being short and easily undertaken, like the narrative and lyric poem, is usually the first form of fiction which attracts the young when they begin to test their talents in writing. The first short stories of a beginning author (whether published then or later) are often written, as the first short stories historically and traditionally were written, out of a desire to tell a story - usually a simple, albeit absorbing one, its structure as uncomplicated as an incident or episode - a little moral tale, a parable, or an anecdote. First short stories, which may be based on such unsophisticated origins, are often derivative of something the author has read or been told, whether he is conscious of this or not. He encounters something in his own background or picks up something he has heard, and because it strikes him as something fitting into story form, he decides to set it down.

SUBJECTIVE STORY - The next state in the development of a short-story writer is usually his discovery that he himself is a personality, perhaps even his own best character, that there are depths in himself he should reveal because he alone can best reveal them, and that he, in his own way, is as much entitled to be a protagonist as Marcel Proust or J. D. Salinger. While it is in this second developmental stage that many short-story writers first find publication, this fact does not invalidate the theory that earlier than this important subjective writing stage there were many stories (still perhaps in the author's trunk) which he wrote before he discovered his own particular soul. ...

OBJECTIVE STORY - The third stage may be that in which the author makes a conscious attempt to suppress his own feeling and view of things for the sake of a more objective presentation of his story and characters.

EXPERIMENTAL AND SYMBOLIC STORY - The fourth stage is often the author's preoccupation with the story form itself. Here he begins to experiment with different approaches and treatments of his subject matter and his manner of presenting it and to search, perhaps, for less obvious, more symbolic, ways to evoke his meaning.

COMPLEX STORY - By the fifth stage, the author has written many stories such as those he has read by others; he has searched his own soul for insights and drama and put his soul into the story so often that either he or his reader has grown a little tired of that aspect of his art; he has written straight "objective" stories about people just as he found them; he has tried experiments with Joycean, Lawrentian, Proustian, and Hemingwayian styles and treatments; and now he finds himself writing on many levels to express the whole of his art and comprehensions.

UNIVERSAL STORY - From now on, if he has not wholly abandoned the art of the short story for the art of the novel, he looks around for stories which he hopes and believes will be so deeply felt and so widely applicable that he can achieve something of universality; he can even create, if he is lucky, a story or two that is nearly "great" - one, in short, that has everything.

EXCEPTIONS - ... [W]ile the editors believe that they have an interesting theory of the parallel growth of the short story and the short-story writer, given the nature of the people with which it deals, the theory does not always work out perfectly in practice. But in general short stories and their authors do seem to have come along in much the above order, together.

Fortunately, the short story is such a fluid form that it can accommodate almost anything, providing that somehow the impression of completeness is achieved, that something of a singleness has been attained in all the multiple possibilities inherent in creation.

LONGER FORMS - To writers who have worked in the short-story form, there is always a period when what they have to say will simply not confine itself to the few thousand words of the short story in its typical length. For them the mysteries and delights of longer forms, the novella, which has all the unity of the short story, and the short novel are still other stages of writing. These forms are also a bridge, and having worked up to them, the short-story writer now may be well on the way to crossing over to the realm of the full-length novel, where the unity of the short story loses itself in complexities and multiplicities, in greater length and further development; or, by now, he may start writing plays, which make use of all the short-story writer knows of dramatic elements, plus whatever he has learned of portraying character by speech, scene, and situation.

93. *FLANNERY O'CONNOR* —— *1964* ,1969

aus "Writing Short Stories" in *Mystery and Manners: Occasional Prose,* ausgew. & hrsg. von Sally und Robert Fitzgerald (New York, 1969), 87-106. - Ein nach dem Tode der Autorin (1925-1964) aus verschiedenen nachgelassenen, nach 1955 entstandenen Vortragsmanuskripten zusammengestellter Text. Den Kern bildet ein Vortrag, der auf einer Schriftstellertagung gehalten wurde, deren Ort und Datum nicht ermittelt werden konnte.

A story is a complete dramatic action - and in good stories, the characters are shown through the action and the action is controlled through the characters, and the result of this is meaning that derives from the whole presented experience. I myself prefer to say that a story is a dramatic event that involves a person because he is a person, and a particular person - that is, because he shares in the general human condition and in some specific human situation. A story always involves, in a dramatic way, the mystery of personality. ...

Your beliefs will be the light by which you see, but they will not be what you see and they will not be a substitute for seeing. For the writer of fiction, everything has its testing point in the eye, and the eye is an organ that eventually involves the whole personality, and as much of the world as can be got into it. It involves judgment. Judgment is something that begins in the act of vision, and when it does not, or when it becomes separated from vision, then a confusion exists in the mind which transfers itself to the story. ...

The first and most obvious characteristic of fiction is that it deals with reality through what can be seen, heard, smelt, tasted, and touched. ...

Fiction writing is very seldom a matter of saying things; it is a matter of showing things.

However, to say that fiction proceeds by the use of detail does not mean the simple, mechanical piling-up of detail. Detail has to be controlled by some overall purpose, and every detail has to be put to work for you. Art is selective. What is there is essential and creates movement.

Now all this requires time. A good short story should not have less meaning than a novel, nor should its action be less complete. Nothing essential to the main experience can be left out of a short story. All the action has to be satisfactorily accounted for in terms of motivation, and there has to be a beginning, a middle, and an end, though not necessarily in that order. ...

Perhaps the central question to be considered in any discussion of the short story is what do we mean by short. Being short does not mean being slight. A short story should be long in depth and should give us an experience of meaning. I have an aunt who thinks that nothing happens in a story unless somebody gets married or shot at the end of it. I wrote a story about a tramp who marries an old woman's idiot daughter in order to acquire the old woman's automobile. After the marriage, he takes the daughter off on a wedding trip in the automobile and abandons her in an eating place and drives on by himself. Now that is a complete story. There is nothing more relating to the mystery of that man's personality that could be shown through that particular dramatization. But I've never been able to convince my aunt that it's a complete story. She wants to know what happened to the idiot daughter after that. ...

Meaning is what keeps the short story from being short. I prefer to talk about the meaning in a story rather than the theme of a story. People talk about the theme of a story as if the theme were like the string that a sack of chicken feed is tied with. They think that if you can pick out the theme, the way you pick the right thread in the chicken-feed sack, you can rip the story open and feed the chickens. But this is not the way meaning works in fiction. ...

The meaning of a story has to be embodied in it, has to be made concrete in it. A story is a way to say something that can't be said any other way, and it takes every word in the story to say what the meaning is. You tell a story because a statement would be inadequate. ...

The peculiar problem of the short-story writer is how to make the action he describes reveal as much of the mystery of existence as possible. He has only a short space to do it in and he can't do it by statement. He has to do it by showing, not by saying, and by showing the concrete - so that his problem is really how to make the concrete work double time for him.

In good fiction, certain of the details will tend to accumulate meaning from the action of the story itself, and when this happens they become symbolic in the way they work. ...

You want to know how you can actually write a good story, and further, how you can tell when you've done it; and so you want to know what the form of a short story is, as if the form were something that existed outside of each story and could be applied or imposed on the material. Of course, the more you write, the more you will realize that the form is organic, that it is something that grows out of the material, that the form of each story is unique.

94. VICTOR S. PRITCHETT ——— 1966

"The Short story", *London Magazine,* N. S., VI (Sept., 1966), 6-9.

The short story is one of the inextinguishable lost causes. It has always dismayed publishers. It is treated perfunctorily by the over-worked novel-reviewers - chiefly because it is very hard to make anything of an assortment. The financial rewards are disgracefully low in England, even for the well known, the top price for anything good which has taken weeks, perhaps months of work being about £60. It is difficult to get a story longer than 7,000 words published at all; after 10,000 words, impossible. The periodicals on which the writer can rely have almost all vanished, driven out by expensive printing, by television and the hundred and one new diversions of an extravert and leisured society. Yet the annual number of volumes published is said to have increased and if the public is painfully small, it is addicted. The fact is that the short story is above all the memorable form of writing. Readers forget novels; stories stay in their minds. And it is not because there is less to remember; the short story is perfectly fitted to the glancing, allusive, nervously decisive and summary moods of contemporary life. Much in little - when short-story writers fail to give us that, they go flat and they fail.

What the reader responds to is concentration and intensity of form and experience; also an exercise in sudden truth telling; novelists find this hard to keep up. He also responds to the implicit intelligence test; how to know all from seeing only part. A few minutes, an hour, a day, a few days, are often given their indwelling value - which is rare in the novel. It is this intensity and the difficulty in achieving it that has also attracted the writer. A portion of life has been isolated; it has not been lost in some larger continuity. It is not the missing chapter of a novel but a thing standing on its own. It has the sustained, undispersed energy of the writer at the time. For this reason D. H. Lawrence's stories seem to me superior to his novels and will remain immune to fashion and to dating. The great novels are, almost all, imperfect; indeed the 'perfect' ones become tedious; the very shortness of the short story is a protection here, but the real advantages are its varying mixture of the poetic, the reported and what is, essentially, the wit of the closed form; also its closeness (in some writers) to the perpetual, unconscious story-telling of people in real life. In writing of this kind one cannot hide one's failure to make up one's mind by simply rambling on or ruminating at large. One cannot afford to make a mistake, for this is not an expansive art, but one which cuts down, telescopes and rejects; the reader is baffled if the necessary sentences, images and speeches do not appear in the right order.

This view of the short story - that it is a craft or, at its best, an art - has often been criticized; it leads (the critics say) to the sacrifice of a possibly rich content, to a form so rigid or trite, that the short story now tends to triviality or merely to showing how sensitive about small things a writer is. Kipling, our great master, is said to have gone dead in his later work, through excessive preoccupation with craftsmanship; other writers, especially the clever ones, sacrifice everything to formula and the sting in the tail and so on; the later Maupassant. Chekhov was abused because of his 'mood'. The truth is that there is fidgeting, mechanical or repetitious writing in any form, especially in the novel, and perhaps the short-story writer - who is a short-breath man, always obliged to begin again - is more exposed than others. The main attack, however, is on attention to detail; yet in fact one of the finest living short-story writers, Mary Lavin, who seems at first sight to have the freedom and power which has escaped formal restriction and to resemble the Russians in this, is in fact a formal artist: the form is scrupulously determined by the clouded emotional conflicts of her characters. On a second reading one sees how much construction has contributed to stories that seem loose. She writes from the outside, yet she makes us most aware of the minds of her people and their stunned relation to their environment. It is foolish to suppose that an 'outside' writer is not writing about the 'inside'. It is also foolish to think that a story which depends on the unfolding of a character has no 'plot', design or force - the Maugham fallacy.

Chekhov was a great master because he did not write one kind of story. He wrote stories of all kinds from skits, farces, jokes; he wrote neat stories and loose-seeming stories, poetic evocations of mood, tales of indignation, statements of social problems, melancholy stories of introspection. His insistence on form, whether directed from within or imposed from without, is obvious even if we did not have the evidence of his letters. Like all considerable writers he used many different attitudes to experience. Above all he insinuates environment - Russian life - as a silent character. So do the best American writers; English writers tend to miss the environmental presence. Chekhov did not regard the short story as a form of abstention or artistic holiness; he wrote continuously. He knew, in his early days, how to write to order; it was dangerous, but not bad training, for - and this is the crux - he had a distinctive personal voice.

Since the opportunities of publication are so few nowadays, short-story writers tend to become abstentionists, to wait for their moment. And the general weakness of short stories now is the lack of a distinctive, personal voice. Lacking that voice, the writer should become a novelist, however unusual his material. The great trap for the contemporary short-story writer is naturalism: to rely on that without the other ingredients of intensity and wit - meaning by wit trenchancy of mind, not witticism - simply means flat writing, the slice of life.

The economics of short-story writing are grim but eccentric. For twenty-five years I myself was paid ludicrous sums for all my stories: three pounds for *The Sailor*, working up to ten pounds. All my stories were rejected by the magazines that paid respectably in England and America. The prices in England are still miserable, but I rely on the occasional handsome stroke of luck in America. The short story is unquestionably more acceptable in America, perhaps because, as Frank O'Connor once said, the form is natural to anarchic societies; not to closely-knit ones like our own. But our society is also now going in the direction of the highway civilization and perhaps we shall start to value intensity and the singularity of voice. But the short-story writer has one secret economic advantage over the novelist:

he is continually re-printed, broadcast and re-broadcast. He has, like the playwright, established a minor income. And if television producers would forget what they were taught in the television training schools and study, for example, the very fine productions of D. H. Lawrence's stories early this year, the short-story writer would be in a thriving condition once more and would be encouraged, not to write for 'the medium' - always a mistake - but for himself. In fact, the cultivation of intensity is an excellent training for the drama: Chekhov showed this. A little less brashness and mechanical cocksureness in television circles; an intelligent reconsideration of what - unknown to many producers - is a basically literary medium, for the screen is really a crowded page, and our situation would greatly improve. As one can see by the 'discoveries' of early writers by television, the drama takes a long time to catch up with the printed word.

95. WILLIAM SANSOM —— 1966

aus "The Short Story", *London Magazine*, N. S., VI (Sept., 1966), 9-11.

The pleasure and motive, for me, is that here is something I can do and get off my chest and mind at one concentrated go, without devious planning, without the involved trial and rejection which must go to the making of a novel or a play. Here, the episode from the very start erects itself like a visible film, all clicked together and ready in front of the mind. Uncut, of course: there will be additions, colourings, alterations of all kinds during the writing, and it may have to be re-written altogether - but it starts from a solid whole, which a longer work never does. It can also be written at a shortish stretch, one, two, three weeks, with a degree of concentration unlikely in a long work.

The process is nearer to the poem than the novel; or at a simpler level to the desire of anyone to recount some significant happening that has occurred to him that day. Though the writer, hopefully, will have a visionary mind and will have been aware of that happening not on one plane but many, with a thousand inferences of behaviour and of the play of the world, so that the finished product should show that this is not just a happening in life but a major part of life itself. It should echo. It should spread beyond its economy: short, it should be enormous.

Conceived thus at some inspirational heat, it may often be over-written. Cutting and chiselling are a large part of the job: it must be made to billow out and furl in like a flag, giving a moving impression that it is larger than it is - which in fact, in theme, it is.

As to the recipient, the reader - short stories in book form, like pictures in galleries, create bad habits: read or seen one after the other, they cancel themselves out. It is best for a short story to be found in a magazine, as a picture is best isolated on a wall of its own.

Short stories will, I think, always be written, as that mixed-up longer affair called 'the novel' will. The first impulse is a pretty simple though a very strong one - the wish to tell. The art follows, according to the teller. It is a relic of the saga, the necessity of singing of stirring events. The technology changes - just as the saga has lost the bard's music, as type-setting and paper are replacing the moving lips of the Arab story-teller in the market. So stories may one day be written as fodder for ready-bugged ear-plugs or micro-discs, or whatever portends. But the stories will still be there with all their heart and art. Synopses will not do, synopses are nothing.

96. *WILLIAM SAROYAN* — 1969

aus "The International Symposium on the Short Story: Part Two", *The Kenyon Review*, XXXI (Jan., 1969), 58-62.

Writing is the man, and for some reason this is especially noticeable when the writing is in the form of the short story. The speed of it has something to do with the man's being simultaneously liberated and exposed in the short story. There isn't time for excessive concealment or clever revelation. ...

William Sydney Porter's short stories are tricky, like the achievements of a magician on a vaudeville stage. The trick happens right before our eyes and we marvel at it, but we don't quite know how to understand why so much skill should be employed to make a trick instead of something better. And his life and work are short because he began to repeat himself pretty much in the second short story he wrote - but this is not a criticism of the stories. It isn't necessary for O. Henry to be Henry James. ... He wrote folklore in the form of jokes, an astonished, sad, lonely, and earnest man pretending to be above astonishment, and so on.

How would it have gone with O. Henry had there not been the market there did in fact happen to be in his time for short stories - of any kind? Who knows? He might not have written at all, for he was certainly interested in other "easy" ways of getting money and fame; or he might have been driven to another and possibly superior form of story-writing. He was too much of the street for the novel form, and one gathers that boredom was a daily fight. He had no characters. His stories are about people. He himself was the only major character of his stories. ...

[T]he man who writes the writing, of whatever form, *is* the writing, cut it up or kick it around any way you like. There has got to be somebody there bugged and bothered, able, willing, compelled. That man is the form. He is the law. If theories and rules somewhat apply to his work, all well and good; if they don't, there are always plenty more where they came from.

Go back to the matter of the market for a moment. It figures. All of a sudden (taking about two decades) the bottom has dropped out of the short-story market in America. The magazines that still run them at all run fewer and fewer as time goes by: one story to anywhere from ten to twenty pieces of miscellaneous journalism, and/or the factual essay. ...

Can the story make a comeback? Yes, it can. Will it? Yes, it will. The market won't do it, editors of magazines won't do it, publishers won't do it, writers will do it. As matters stand, more good stories of all kinds are being written by American writers of all kinds than ever before, some of the stories swelling out very nearly into the form of the novel, not in length but in essence. That's just fine, but it isn't going to do anything for the short story as its own special self. The likening of the novel to whale and the short story to sardine is absurd. A bad novel is tediousness extended to the unbearable. A bad short story is much less rude, if only for its brevity.

The short story needs no excuse or apology. When it's great, it's great. If it were never great, it would be a useless form. Out of the hundreds of good short stories published every year, nobody in his right mind expects more than one or two to be great. ...

Bearded kids have been making a literary revolution in mimeographed magazines for about ten years, and, while nothing much has come of it so far, it is probably here, in these wild and frequently funny publications, that the short story will find its new life. The big new story-writers may start in the messy and frequently blurred pages of these publications, after which of course they'll wisely move along to a larger neighborhood. If you're willing to accept success of any kind, you pay the price, which is never excessive, and comes mainly to a little less kidding around and a little more respect - for the writer himself, the reader, the form, and the material whence stories must come: people in general, who still don't read at all, even after leaving college, for instance.

Well, now, what about the whole business of paper and print, writing and reading, in relation to the competing, time-taking communication forms: television, radio, long-play phonograph records, and their usages in new teaching techniques? What about the Canadian's hot theory that straight print and straight reading are *already* obsolescent, unnecessary, perhaps even undesirable? Well, of course the theory is just fine. Print and reading at best never engaged more than a very small percentage of the people. There's plenty of room in the world for *any* theory and any fact. What about the fun of Be-ins, sit-ins, marches, meetings, protests, and listening to the talkers, who are invariably in a state of high excitation? Well, it's all very nice, if boring.

But if what's happening is *Happenings,* what is likely to happen to the writing, printing, publishing, and reading of short stories? Well, to begin with, let's none of us worry too much, it'll be all right. Short-story writers certainly aren't going to organize and picket novel readers, for instance, or readers of newspapers, or people who take LSD trips, or go to Be-ins, or march, or only watch TV, or read only labels on bottles, or don't find it desirable to read anything at all. They will write short stories for the hell of it. They always have. ...

Now, finally, what can we think, what can we notice, what can we understand about short stories *away from print?* Well, to begin with, they *happen* daily to everydoby. They are told, with form and style, by the people one to another. This is what happened, this is how it happened, this is why it happened, and so on.

In short, the short story *is,* of itself, central to the human experience; so are the poem, the novel, and the play, but most naturally the short story.

The stand-up comedians of nightclubs and television tell short stories almost without exception: they don't tell essays or history, they tell short stories about themselves which are written for them by skilled experts, out of the character and style of the comedian: Jackie Gleason, Bill Cosby, Jackie Vernon, Flip Wilson, to name only four out of surely forty with national reputations. Are these told stories any good? Well, they're funny, and that's *always* good.

Is all this something like the return of the troubador, the bard, the singer of the tribal saga? The fact is, he never disappeared. Consider the poetry and prose readings of the past twenty years. There must be in the English-speaking world a thousand poets who have taken to the public platform, and at least that number of writers of special material (essentially short stories) for comedians.

To sum up: the short story is lived daily by everybody; recited unprofessionally daily by everybody, professionally by comedians; written for reading by hundreds of good writers; only occasionally chosen by magazine editors; and virtually by-passed by book publishers. The situation is as healthy as it has ever been, perhaps healthier.

97. JOHN WAIN ———————————————— 1969

aus "The International Symposium on the Short Story: Part Two" *The Kenyon Review*, XXXI (Jan., 1969), 82-85.

All literary forms have to some extent to be defined by negatives: drama is a way of telling a story that is not narrative, etc. This seems to me particularly so in the case of the short story, which did not come into its full power until after the rise of the novel. Such a judgment may seem odd in view of the presence in our tradition of so many masterpieces in short narrative form, down through the ages from the Old Testament through mediaeval literature to a master of the anecdote like Boccaccio. But to be a story and to be short does not quite make a "short story" in our modern sense; it really is a new *genre*, born in the nineteenth century and very quickly growing to maturity well before that century ended, and it defines itself against the novel; within the area of modern fiction, the short-story writer does those things that the novelist does not do. It sounds like a paradox, but is in fact the most sober statement of the matter that I can arrive at, to say that the shortness of a short story, its positive characteristic, is not particularly important; what is important is its negative characteristic, the fact that though it tells an imagined story it is not a novel. It has broken itself away from the novel so determinedly that since the appearance of the short story we have had to recognize the existence of an intermediate form to which we give the name of *conte* or *nouvelle* or *novella*. All these terms mean a story which can be short, almost as short as a long short story, and yet is not a short story but a kind of novel. (Characteristically, English has no word for this intermediate form, because the Anglo-Saxon mind, in its enthusiasm for empiricism, does not like making formal divisions within a subject, lest the forms should turn against it. We have, it is true, invented the word "novelette," but that is something else; it implies a moral judgment; Miss X and Mr. Y write novelettes, not because they exploit the possibilities of this third form but because they do not go deeply enough into their subjects.)

So the short story, if I am right, had to wait, before attaining the franchise, until the novel had explored its main possibilities. And what does the novel do? The novel is the most compendious of all literary forms; it has room for everything; D. H. Lawrence rightly remarked that if *Hamlet* had been a novel there would have been no mystery about it. (But, then, neither would it have been *Hamlet*.) The novel works by extracting all the meaning from the situation it deals with. Having put human beings into a certain situation, the novelist prods and prompts them until they move forward within that situation, exploring its dimensions, treading all the juice out of the grapes beneath their feet. If Jack and Connie love each other and Connie is unhappy with Mark, but on the other hand Jack respects Mark enormously and thinks of that respect as part of his own character, what will they *do*? And what will come of what they do? And what will they think and say about what comes of it? And so it goes on, like taking the mystery out of *Hamlet*. At each stage, alternatives appear and a choice is made, so that writing a novel (like living, perhaps?) is a matter of closing off possibilities; each time we have a choice between two possibilities and we choose one, the other ceases to be a possibility, it dies, and our lives, as we look at them, are marked by the gravestones of these possibilities we killed off, just as much as by the springing green life within those we assented to. A novelist, to try another metaphor, is like a man hollowing out a cave from the solid rock, and finding that the more he works, and the better he works, the smaller the cave becomes; in the end, he must break into the sunlight, on the other side of the mountain, through a space just big enough for one human being. This is because he must, as he works, close off one alternative after another, bringing his characters step by step to the only possible conclusion their story could have. If he has read their natures wrongly, if he has failed in his assessment of the situation he has put them in, the novel will go wrong and will strike the perceptive reader as false to experience. But in any case the author has to work like that, by a development of the situation which is always narrowing down, always tending to bring the characters to rest at a certain conclusion. Think of the immense range of possibilities in the opening chapters of *Dr. Zhivago*, and think how inescapably those possibilities are narrowed until we cannot but reach the brief doomed happiness at Varykino, and beyond it the agony of parting, the acceptance of suffering and inward collapse, and the heart attack on the crowded tramcar.

The novelist has to exhaust his action, while keeping enough sense of touch to halt it before it metamorphoses completely into a new action. And this is why we define the short-story writer by negatives. He is not under this obligation. He begins, as the novelist begins, by imagining people in a certain situation. But he need not go on until the situation is completely explored. It is enough for him to present the people and the situation vividly, to indicate, deftly, some of the possible ways in which they might react to it, and the reader is left with a new experience, a fresh sense of the variety and interest of life, which would be lost if he had to sit down and follow, page by page, as the writer took up all the slack in the situation.

If that last sentence made short-story writing sound easy, I must draw attention to the words "vividly" and "deftly." A short story needs to be better written than a novel. It cannot afford inert passages, descriptions and episodes which *almost* say what they mean, impressions that can be rounded out later. It is like a drawing, where the novel is like a painting. It is either entirely successful or entirely non-successful. A few poets can write good short stories; so can a few novelists; but being a poet or a novelist is not in itself a passport to the art of the short story, which is really a matter of having been born with the right knack. Because the possibilities are to be left undeveloped, because the characters are to be hit off rather than shown in depth, drawn rather than painted, the right economy and lucidity, the detail that reverberates with exactly the required suggestion and no other, *must* be forthcoming. If not, the result is nothing. I have never read a short story that struck me as *fairly* good. I have read very good ones, and very bad ones.

Once we have cheerfully faced this injustice, and admitted that many good and worthy writers simply can't write short stories and shouldn't try, we can see it for what it is - a marvelously cheerful form. Both for reader and for writer, it is eloquent of possibilities that are always opening out, never closing in. To leave the ends open, to position the characters so that their choices are still before them and they reveal themselves in the way they contemplate those choices rather than follow them through - this is almost to recapture the happiest moments of a writer's life. I say "almost" because, of course, a writer's happiest moments come not when he is working but when he is entering in his notebook that shining new idea on which he intends, at some future opportunity, to start work. The new idea, still untarnished, not yet familiar and stale, not yet mulishly refusing to obey the shaping hand, not yet assailed by doubt or fatigue, brings bliss that makes the whole struggle worth-while; which is why writers' notebooks make such buoyant and cheerful reading. To write short stories, or at any rate to write good ones, is to live almost in the warmth and confidence of one's notebook, almost within the circle of that pale, mysterious light.

98. *JAMES T. FARRELL* —————————————————————— 1970

aus "The International Symposium on the Short Story: Part Four", *The Kenyon Review*, XXXII (Jan., 1970), 84-89.

Chaucer's *Canterbury Tales* are stories. And, of course, Boccaccio's *Decameron* is a book of short stories. What is written comes out of what was spoken. The epic, the song, the tale are primitive forms of literature. And poetry, not prose, was the first form of communication that attained the level of art.

The Bible, from *Genesis* on, is full of stories, Job's life in *The Book of Job* is a story, a great one. The parables of Christ in the New Testament are stories. The account of Mary Magdalene is a story. The story of Christ at Golgatha is a great story, also. The *Arabian Nights*, *Aesop's Fables* are stories. The *Bhagavad-Gita* contains stories. "Al-Ghazzali: Confessions of a Troubled Believer" is a story.

There are many anthologies of short stories and tales from various countries and different epochs. We can note from even a few of these that short stories and tales have a continuity in culture as a whole, and within various cultures.

At this point, I should like partially to alter a classification of prose fiction - the novella. Many novels classified as novellas can be termed stories.

"The Devil Takes a Wife" by Niccolo Machiavelli, author of *The Prince* and *A History of Florence*, can be considered a short story. The father of the modern novel, author of one of the greatest of all novels, Cervantes, creator of *Don Quixote*, also wrote some novellas which are truly stories. The short story is integrally a part of the history of literature, the history of culture, and the history of man. It is psychologically rooted in the long and varied lives of the generations. It can even be found in stone in the remains of Sumerian civilizations in the Near East.

There is no need to defend the short story.

There are known and unknown, discovered and undiscovered continuities in culture. Known continuities indicate influences at play through long centuries of change and across the barriers of language. ...

Values by which we live in the present have grown out of the past. This is one of the reasons why we should see history, ideas, and art as we see science. That is, in terms of general conceptions of continuity and of change. We measure change by contrasts.

From our standpoint, all of history, all of science, and all that we do must be related to man. Science, ideas, and art embody what we know, what we can do, what we can make, the instrumentation by which we can do and make and communicate what we can remember, what life was like, what life is like, and what life might be like. ...

Science makes the universe recognizable, controllable, and relevant to human life. Ideas make the world more cognizant, intelligent, and intelligible. Art makes man more human to himself. It makes men more human to one another.

Art is, as John Dewey reminded us in *Art as Experience*, the most direct form of communication. Literature is vital in communicating to the future. The memory of mankind is preserved by art.

Because it deals with words, literature is crucial to mankind. This "direct form of communication" affords an imaginative realization and an intensified consciousness of thought, feelings, and destinies of human beings. It can enlarge experience; and to enlarge experience is to enlarge the self. This is part of the process of liberating the self.

The short story is one of the forms of literature, one of the forms of creative writing in prose fiction - although there have been many stories written in poetry.

Short stories are of major significance in all developed literature. Let us look to French literature of the nineteenth century. In Balzac's *Comédie Humaine* there are many stories. Some of these are among the high achievements of Balzac's great work...

Far different as a writer was Gêrard de Nêrval. His "Sylvie" is a story, a long one, but a story. It is as beautiful as the countryside in France where it is placed. This is the story of a dream, with some anticipation of Freud. It is one of the high points of writing of a classifiably Romantic character in the period of Romanticism.

Zola, Baudelaire, Flaubert, Gide, Anatole France, Villiers de l'Isle-Adam - all wrote short stories in addition to their other works. This is an incomplete list, but it is sufficient to reinforce my regard for the short story as valid and warranted.

Then, there was Guy de Maupassant. Maupassant, along with Chekhov and, perhaps, Edgar Allan Poe, endowed the short story with a respect and a stronger position among the forms of literary creation. These three were primarily short-story writers. (In the case of Chekhov, I refer to the time before the writing of his truly great plays.) Their stories added up to substantial bodies of work which gave to the short story greater separateness from the novel. Their work did much to make clear the value and worth of short stories. ...

A short story is a short piece of fiction. It is differentiated from a longer story, which might be called a novelette or a novella, and which in turn is differentiated from a novel. But the story often shades into the novella; and the novella into the novel.

However, length is not the most distinguishing and significant feature of a short story. Length is merely the most obviously marked feature. The short story differs *conceptually* from the novel, though a story can achieve effects similar to those of a novel. There can be tragic impact. (There is something of this in Theodore Dreiser's "The Last Phoebe.") However, there is a difference in scale. Details, characters, the manner in which meanings are concretely conceived are significant. It might be said that a short story is a flash of life, and that a novel is a floodlight that illuminates a segment of life for more than a flash. But this is an analogical metaphor that suggests the obvious. I present it here in order to emphasize that this differentiation is simple. Less simple is the matter of conceiving something happening, some kind of change, some movement - psychological or physical or social - some conflict within a relatively limited space.

There often is a functional relationship between short stories and novels. Short stories can prepare the way for novels, a function performed by George Ade in American literature with his *Fables in Slang,* and his other stories. Certainly this is true of Sherwood Anderson's *Winesburg, Ohio*.

Short stories can help create an audience, or a larger audience, for novels. This happened again and again.

But there is a different kind of functional relationship. All of life cannot be captured, known, or imagined in terms of the length and patterns and structures of the novel. There are incidents, impressions, events, happenings, fancies that are better developed in stories. As readers, we need only to catch truth, gain in awareness, and acquire an intensified consciousness of human worth. We gain from stories that we regard as true and good; and also from novels.

Although there is some difference in length and in conception, they serve the same purpose. We can become better people for having read them - stories and novels.

99. EDWARD HYAMS —— 1970

aus "The International Symposium on the Short Story: Part Four", *The Kenyon Review,* XXXII (Jan., 1970), 89-95.

Nobody writes sonnets now; or, if they do, nobody reads them. Tomorrow, nobody will write short stories.

Not that I have ever favored the view that the short story is a very special form: the best short-story writers are novelists and always have been. There are exceptions; Katherine Mansfield is a case in point. But is the short-story writer anything more than a novelist in little, a novelist short of staying-power? It is true that he or she has to be very good at writing economically, at making each word do a lot of work and at assembling the words in patterns which themselves do a lot of work. But ... well, the sprinter who runs 100 yards very fast is hardly as considerable a man as the long-distance runner. Like the poet, the short-story writer does more manipulation, more correction and polishing, than invention; that is the least taxing part of writing, and the form does not call for sustained endurance, for the ordeal of living with a passion and an idea for many months or even years.

Since the war the best short stories written in Britain have been Angus Wilson's social satires and a few brilliant works by S. F. writers. For the conventional story, the "psychological" (God help us) story of love or ambition or hate, there is still a market in the women's magazines; there is even a market for good yarns. It would be silly to denigrate either form, but such writings are not, I suppose, the subject of this essay. It is notable that the suppliers of these stories are almost all men and women of a certain age - raised, professionally speaking, in the Somerset Maugham tradition. There are few young writers in the field, and understandably so; for the young simply cannot, in 1970, feel that the little intimacies, the exquisite feelings of individual for individual living in a kind of politico-social vacuum (which is what, from a writer's point of view, a very stable society can be made to amount to) are important enough to be written about. I think I can emphasize this point by a demonstration; sit down and read, if you can stand the tedium, a collection of *New Yorker* stories; allow for the fact that they are seriously marred by being overworked, and you will still have to agree that their smallnesses are, or appear as, trivialities. They should not. But the miseries and tribulations of our time and the threats hanging over us have reduced the importance of men by comparison with Man. Our proper themes are big and coarse. It is witty and elegant to fiddle while Rome burns, but it is also trifling. The younger writers cannot trifle; they have been taught a bitter lesson by the political and social events of the past half century: it is that man is absurd and that if he is to be presented still in a heroic or tragic role, and not as merely ridiculous and pathetic (*vide* Angus Wilson's stories), he must be shown opposed to the gigantic and evil forces of great political or industrial or social institutions; or to the terrifying forces of the universe, which has suddenly been brought within our knowledge and is no longer bounded by the earth. You just cannot do this, or not very often, within the compass of a short story. Everything to be said about the intimate relations of men with other men, or with women, has been most wonderfully and variously said. *Our* themes are the relationship between men and mobs, crowds, nations; even time and space and the stars.

Writing short stories is like painting conventional water colors: it calls for as much skill as ever and it can convey considerable pleasure, but it has nothing to do with the age we live in and cannot say much about our predicament.

But let us suppose there are - as indeed there are - writers, even young ones, who wish still to say something about personal relations in a brief art form, even if, say, they are sufficiently influenced by the times and their nature to do so in the context of a social or political strife situation. They will not, nowadays, use the short story; and they will be right. Art imparts insights; it does so through the senses. In man, the master-sense is sight. In the short television play the writer has the means to convey his insights to the understanding and sensibility of his audience through both eyes and ears. (And to be very well paid for it.) And that is what the ambitious young writer will, rightly, try to do. Not too long ago I watched a play in point, by James Mitchell: in it the great stresses between Trade Union bosses, responsible to their members who are workers in a shipyard building tankers, and oil company managements trying to buy a cheap tanker and responsible to their shareholders, and the shipbuilder caught between the two of them, were vividly conveyed: this 50-minute play dealt with ambition in conflict with duty; with common sense in conflict with class loyalties and passions; with love in conflict with social and political convictions and loyalties; with the drama of economics as it effects the lives of ordinary, decent people; with the strife between the young and the old; with the tragedy of unemployment; with the comedy of man's inadequacy in the face of his destiny. Twenty years ago, such a story could only have been told in a novel or perhaps a film; yet here it all is at virtually short-story length. It is inevitable that young writers should be attracted to this medium, which offers an audience of millions, and should neglect the short story which deals in the small, the exquisite, the very intimate, in short with what is not really of our time at all; and which offers an audience of thousands.

It may be argued that a writer is an artist who wants to create works of literature as art; and that such plays as I have described are not art. Perhaps they are not, yet; but they obviously could be; talent can make literature out of them. The greatest literature is dramatic - the Greek dramatists, Shakespeare, Racine, Molière - and it could be so again, a new small-screen dramatic poetry. Here, indeed, is a field for the "born" short-story writer; for, since he has few words to do his work in, the short-story writer has to make them do the same kind of work as the poet's words, make them convey not only sense but color and texture. All right, so there are commercial problems: stupid and dull advertisers and sponsors dictating to cowardly producers their own base judgment of public taste. But the problems are no worse than in magazine publishing, producers no baser than editors; and not all of them are as base as all that, for much good work is being done by them.

In the '50s I wrote a lot of short stories to read aloud myself on the BBC's Third Programme; and a quite different series for publication in *The New Statesman*. In the course of reading my own stories I learned about language things that made me write the later stories in a new manner, using more spoken then literary English, or rather a mixture which slowly developed from story to story; the edge I could put on this language was so much sharper that I soon found myself writing the other stories, those for printing, in much the same language. In short, I was moving away from narrative and toward drama, a dramatic presentation of the incidents and predicaments of ordinary lives. Needless to say, I was far from being the only one. This kind of thing can go very far: something like this has led Alain Robbe-Grillet, significantly a Frenchman - that is, one living in a culture from which the short story as an art form has already vanished - from the novel to the film. We have become so accustomed to this kind of presentation that if, today, you read even the stories of W. Somerset Maugham, and God knows he was no highbrow, you find them literary to a degree which makes them tedious. Once again, then, it is not a great step from the spoken-word type of story to the short play of the kind for which, at last, we have the perfect medium.

I am aware that there are a few writers who are specifically short-story writers and *not* novelists. I have dared to wonder whether, in preferring that form, they have not shown that they prefer refining to inventing, exquisiteness of form to weight of matter, the short effort to the long haul; that is perhaps tantamount to calling them lazy. It may be that sometimes 1000 words can better convey a true insight than 100,000. The Chinese sages reckoned one picture worth 1000 words; so how about a motion picture?

But all that is about why not to write short stories and will not prevent me or anyone else from writing them; it is an attempt to explain the decline of this art form without cries of woe! woe! The fact remains that the form does survive and writers will go on using it, so I have tried to find out just what their chances are of finding publishers; that is, how much practical encouragement they can expect.

Experiment 1

I telephoned five leading London publishers and spoke with directors whom I knew. All of them are very experienced professionals of good will who have worked in one or more firms for many years and are prepared to lose money on good work from time to time. The imaginary answerer of the following questions is a syncretism of them all, or, more correctly, of their answers:

Q. 1: You have on your list a novelist whose books sell 7500 copies each. He offers you a book of short stories. They are very good indeed. How many copies of the volume would you print?

A. Probably 2000.

Q. 2: Would you sell them out?

A. I'd hope to. I'd expect to sell between 1000 and 1500.

Q. 3: How much would the author make?

A. Between £100 and £150.

Q. 4: And your firm?

A. A loss of several hundred pounds.

Q. 5: Thank you. Now take the case of the novelist of distinction, who is also a best seller, with sales of say 50,000 of each new book. What would you sell of a volume of his short stories?

A. Not more than 5000 at most.

Q. 6: A young writer comes to you with a volume of short stories. He has published nothing yet. The stories are brilliantly good. What would you do?

A. Ask him if he had a novel in mind.

Q. 7: All right, suppose he says yes.

A. I'd publish his book, sell about 1000 copies and lose about £500. I'd be investing in the future novelist.

Q. 8: Investing?

A. Call it gambling.

Q. 9: Suppose he says no, he's a short-story man, not a novelist.

A. It would be a serious deterrent. I might publish him if I felt we could afford to lose money on doing good works. Not otherwise. Short stories simply lose money.

Q. 10: Any exceptions?

A. Yes, at very long intervals. Far too rare to affect one's judgment.

Experiment 2

I telephoned two well-known literary agents and asked:

Q. 1: A young and clearly very gifted short-story writer, whose work is serious and has the quality of art, comes to you for help. What are the outlets which you could exploit on his behalf?

A. In Britain there are, say, three magazines which might buy his work. And the BBC Third Programme.

Q. 2: He asks you to tell him frankly what income he can expect from his work. What do you answer?

A. That he cannot count on making any income. I should say that with luck he might make a couple of hundred a year, but he would have to be lucky.

Q. 3: What about selling his work in America?

A. I should try. But it would be criminal to let him think it likely that I should succeed. Three or four English writers have succeeded in that quarter, but they all had names before they started in America.

Q. 4: Do you think the position will get better? Or worse?

A. Worse. The modern patron of periodical literature is the advertiser. The advertiser has moved, is moving, and will increasingly move away from magazines toward television. The writer must go where the money is if he wants to live by writing.

From all of which I draw these conclusions: that, like the miniaturist, the short-story writer will become a still rarer and finally extinct animal; that the social and literary work done by the short story in society will increasingly be done by the short television play; that good short stories will still be written from time to time; but that writers of the kind of short story which aspires to do more than entertain for ten minutes will be even less able than at present to make a living by their art, and more obliged than ever to practice their art for its own sake.

aus "The International Symposium on the Short Story: Part Four", *The Kenyon Review,* XXXII (Jan., 1970), 104-108.

The history of the short story, both past and present, is beset with odd myths, some of them plain silly, and a considerable number of contradictions, some of them difficult to explain. The notion that people do not read short stories in volume form, whereas they read them avidly in magazines, is itself a good example of both myth and contradiction and was already an old chestnut when I first began writing short stories more than thirty-five years ago. There was in fact little truth in it then, as the publishers of Hemingway, Maugham, Katherine Mansfield, Erskine Caldwell, Thurber, Lawrence, and many others could testify. There is even less today.

Another myth, which I shall proceed to demolish in more detail in a moment or two, is that the demise of so many so-called literary magazines in the twenty-odd years since the beginning of the war has been a source of serious discouragement to short-story writers, with the result that the contemporary scene is illuminated with nothing like the luster that burned so brightly, on both sides of the Atlantic, in the '20s and '30s.

This odd notion takes no notice of the fact that there has been a revolution in the magazine world in England since the war; or that the general level in interest in the short story, thanks to that revolution and the vast influence of radio, television, and paperbacks, has risen; or that really purposeful short-story writers simply do not succumb to suppression just because magazines like *The London Mercury, Life and Letters, The Criterion,* and *Horizon*, excellent as they may have been, eventually fade away. In fact, discouragement might well be said to spur on writers of the short story. In America it used to be claimed, before the war, that there were something like 20,000 short-story writers struggling for recognition, and I should be greatly surprised if the figures were not many times larger today.

That the situation in England is much the same is proved pretty clearly by two astonishing sets of figures: namely the number of entries in two short-story competitions run by two English Sunday newspapers some four or five years ago. To one newspaper no less than 10,000 stories came rolling in; to the other a mere 6000. But this is not all. These figures, remarkable enough in themselves, are capped by others even more remarkable.

The staggering fact is that out of 10,000 stories submitted to one journal not a dozen were worth printing, whereas the other journal could claim to have been just a little more fortunate; it, at least, managed to gather together a small, though undistinguished, anthology of winning entries. I find these figures a source of endless wonder and speculation. The readers of these newspapers were, presumably, a cut above those specializing in scandal, rape, and blood-and-thunder. It is even possible to assume, I suppose, that they were literary-minded. Behind them, also, lay an incomparable mountain of inspiration built in the '20s and '30s by a body of modern masters, both male and female, on both sides of the Atlantic, who gave to the short story a greater distinction than it had ever known before.

All, apparently, in vain. Prophecy, like lending money to friends, is a mug's game, but when I prophesied in *The Modern Short Story*, in 1941, that the inevitable distrust and dislocation of war's aftermath would surely lead new writers to find in the short story the essential medium for what they had to say, I felt certain I was right. Time has proved me wrong. It is true that a certain number of new short-story writers, notably Angus Wilson, Alan Sillitoe, John Wain, Roald Dahl, Elizabeth Taylor, and others have appeared, but the results have, on the whole, been thinnish and disappointing. There has not even been what Elizabeth Bowen once so aptly called "a minority-fervor."

The reasons, I confess, largely elude me. It would be possible, I suppose, to lay some blame at the door of publishers, who are all too ready to take the short story's unpopularity for granted and in consequence to publish volumes of it in apologetic despondency, not to say reluctant pain. Nor has their eternal opening question to young short-story writers, "When are you going to write a novel?" been of very great help. To my mind this is rather as if you signed on a soccer genius and then promptly asked him when he was going to play baseball. Similarly, it seems to me, literary editors are not entirely blameless. Like some innocent watcher at the night sky, hoping to detect an unknown comet, I still hopefully look forward to the day when volumes of short stories, expressions of prose's most exacting and difficult form, will *not* be strung together for review like links of chippolata sausages or relegated to the bottom of the book page, there to derive such comfort as they can from the chill company of those awful "shorter notices." Mr. Robert Shaw, who is both actor and writer, recently remarked with some pungency that he had come to the conclusion that literary editors as a whole didn't care much for novels; there are times when I think they don't care much for short stories either. ...

I have long maintained, and shall always maintain, that the short story is a poetic form; it is very much an affair of balance and distillation. At its best it has qualities both lyrical and pastoral. To a sour and abrasive younger generation these qualities, of course, are a little out of fashion. Something more than an angry sepsis has eaten into the bone of some of our younger writers, and I cannot think that poetry flourishes on the smell of gangrene. I am also unfashionable enough to think that the object of a story is to divert; it is no vehicle for messages, sermons, or self-dramatization.

There may, of course, be other reasons. Perhaps the age's chief distraction, television, the goggle-box, is in part to blame. Perhaps it is also a mug's game to bother to go through the tough mill of mastering the difficult art of the short story for the prospect of modest checks, when you can write television scripts for fat ones. Or perhaps it's just safer to take a job.

101. VICTOR S. PRITCHETT —— 1971

aus *Midnight Oil* (London, 1971), 214; 217-219.

I have rarely been interested in what are called "characters" i.e. eccentrics; reviewers are mistaken in saying I am. They misread me. I am interested in the revelations of a nature and (rather in Ibsen's fashion), of exposing the illusions or received ideas by which they live or protect their dignity. On the other hand, in the preoccupation with common speech which I suppose I owe to my story-telling mother and to listening closely to Spaniards and others abroad, I did not follow more than I could help the documentary realism that was fashionable in the thirties. The storyteller either digests or contemplates life for his own purposes. The story is a flash that suddenly illumines, then passes. ...

Because of its natural intensity the short story is a memorable if minor literary genre. There is the fascination of packing a great deal into very little space. The fact that form is decisive concentrates an impulse that is essentially poetic. The masters of the short story have rarely been good novelists: indeed the short story is a protest against the discursive. Tolstoy and Turgenev are exceptions, but Maupassant wrote only one novel of any account: *Une Vie*. Chekhov wrote no novels. D. H. Lawrence seems to me more penetrating as a short story writer than as a novelist. An original contemporary, Jorge Luis Borges, finds the great novels too loose. He is attracted to Poe's wish for the work of art one can see shaping instantly to the eye: the form attracts experiment. It is one for those who like difficulty, who like to write 150 pages in order to squeeze out twenty. At the time of the Spanish war when I had to go to a protest meeting in an industrial town, one of the speakers interested me. I wrote two pages about her and gave up. From year to year I used to look at this aborted piece. No difficulty: no progress. Suddenly, after twenty years I saw my chance. When one is making a speech one is standing with one's body and life exposed to the audience: the sensation is frightening. Write a story in which a woman making a speech in her public voice is silently telling by the private voice her own life story *while* she declaims something else. To do this was extremely difficult. One learns one's craft and craftsmanship is not much admired nowadays, for the writer is felt to be too much in control; but, in fact, the writer has always, even if secretively, to be in control. And there is the supreme pleasure of putting oneself in by leaving oneself out.

I have written six volumes of short stories and many others that have never appeared in book form. I am surrounded, as writers are, by the wreckage of stories that are half done or badly done. I believe in the habit of writing. In one dead period when I thought I had forgotten how to write, I set myself a well-known exercise which Maupassant, Henry James, Maugham and Chekhov were not too grand to try their hands at. It is the theme of the real, false or missing pearls. I was so desperate that I had to say to myself "I will write about the first person I see passing the window." It happened by ill luck (for I thought I knew little about the trade) to be a window cleaner. Whatever may be thought of this story - I myself do not like the end, which should have been far more open - it revealed to me as I wrote two things of importance in the creative imagination. The first: there is scarcely a glint of invented detail in this tale; it is a mosaic that can be broken down into fragments taken from things seen, heard or experienced from my whole life, though I never cleaned a window or stole a pearl. The second thing - and this is where the impulse to write was *felt* and not willed - is the link with childhood. To write well one must never lose touch with that fertilizing time. And, in this story, some words of my mother's about her father came back to me. He was a working gardener and coachman. It was part of the legend of her childhood that one morning his employer's wife called "Lock the drawers: the window cleaner is coming." I did not write about my grandfather but the universal myth relating to theft came brimming into my mind.

The Irish, the Italians, the Russians and the Americans have an instinctive gift for the short story. Alberto Moravia once told me that the Italian successes in this form and their relative failure in the novel is due to the fact that the Italian is so conceited that he dare not look long and steadily at his face in the mirror. I would have thought that the gift is due to the Italian's delight in the impromptu. Frank O'Connor used to say that the form is natural to societies where the element of anarchy is strong and the pressure of regard for society is weak. In English literature we indeed had to wait for the foreign rootlessness and rawness of Kipling before we had a master. Once discovered, this quickly appeared in Saki, in D. H. Lawrence, in the pastorals of A. E. Coppard and T. F. Powys, in Walter de la Mare, Max Beerbohm, H. E. Bates, Elizabeth Taylor, Frank Tuohy, James Stern and Angus Wilson. Late starters, we have done well.

102. *EUDORA WELTY* — 1972

aus "The Art of Fiction, XLVII", *The Paris Review*, no. 55 (Fall, 1972), 73-97.

WELTY: My natural temperament is one of positive feelings, and I really do work for resolution in a story. I don't think we often see life resolving itself, not in any sort of perfect way, but I like the fiction writer's feeling of being able to confront an experience and resolve it as art, however imperfectly and briefly - to give it a form and try to embody it - to hold it and express it in a story's terms. You have more chance to try it in a novel. A short story is confined to one mood, to which everything in the story pertains. Characters, setting, time, events, are all subject to the mood. And you can try more ephemeral, more fleeting things in a story - you can work more by suggestion - than in a novel. Less is resolved, more is suggested, perhaps.

INTERVIEWER: You reserve the short story for the ephemeral and the novel for the resolution?

WELTY: I can only say such things after the fact. If I'd known I was going to finish *Losing Battles* as a long novel, I don't know that I'd have begun it. I'm a short-story writer who writes novels the hard way, and by accident. You see, all my work grows out of the work itself. It seems to set its form from the idea which is complete from the start, and a sense of the form is like a vase into which you pour something and fill it up. I have that completely in mind from the beginning and I don't realize how far I can wander and yet come back. The flexibility and freedom are exciting to me, not being used to them, and they are hard to come by. But no one could have enjoyed more learning those lessons than I did. There's no end to what can be tried, is there?

103. WILLIAM SANSOM —— 1972

aus *The Birth of a Story* (London, 1972), 3-6; 8; 12 f.; 15 f.

1. *Why*? In the first place, why write a story at all?

Broadly, because to tell a story is an impulse as old as the bards and whoever preceded them. The hairy men with harps recited their sagas thousands of years ago, the storytellers in today's Arab markets still command an audience, money, entrancement. We ourselves, in our daily lives, give and take the drama of the day - we are forever telling each other stories of what happened round the corner last Wednesday. The impulse is as plain as a pikestaff, whatever that is; but in daily use it is a muddy pikestaff, and it is the professional writer's task or pleasure to pan that mud for its gold dust.

From time to time there rises the howl: 'The Novel is dead!' 'The Short Story is dead!'. This is nonsense. The form is being constantly modulated, but the narrative essence continues strong. Today there is less chance of that essence dying than of the disappearance of today's material means of communicating it, word and page. The far future hints that books may be replaced by projected microfilms; or audio-books of words, or of an actor reading words, or even of the whole thing being treated in dramatic form on micro-television. If it happens, it will be regrettable. Gone will be the luxury of turning back to dwell on this or that passage. Gone also the shape and spelling of words, aesthetic pleasures in themselves. And with the third alternative, tele-drama, we will be faced with all the serious limitations of television drama as we know it today. Gone also will be the flow of imagination in the mind of the reader - home-*cinéaste* in the studio of his own skull.

Until all this happens stories will go on being written. Even if the first outlets, magazines and newspapers, serve them not so well, they will nevertheless be written because writers like to write them. As with poetry, much of which never sees the light of a reader's eye.

2. *How*? And how to write a story?

There are no set rules. Like the novel, the short story is elastic in form. Broadly, the novel relates the interplay of a number of characters, whereas the short story is concerned with one episode or tendency in the lives of one or two people. The short story is really nearer to a poem than its apparent prose-brother, the novel. It is usually about one thing, blown up big or refined beneath the microscope. It can take the form of a moody piece occurring in one person's mind, or a stream of consciousness in the author's mind, or a classic narrative with a beginning, a middle and an end: to adopt this latter technique, it does not follow that the story is old fashioned, it can taste as fresh as tomorrow.

Similarly the plot or narrative of a story can be made to seem as fresh as next Tuesday, though it will probably be as old as the hills: we have often heard that there are only so and so many plots in the world, and this is true, though it is equally true, that their possibilities of permutation are endless. The success of a story is never so much what it is about as how it is told: what persons and scenes are projected, with what subtlety or force they are handled, and how the words themselves are chosen. This choice of words and their composite cadence is naturally the test of a good or bad writer. Whatever the style chosen, as toughly economic as Hemingway's, as involuted as Henry James's, as intentionally loose as Radiguet's, there are assonances for the inner ear of the speaking mind which, among much else, make or break prose. ...

To tell a story implies plainly a narrative ability. How to intersperse description with action, and in what quantities? How much to dwell on the minor activities of a character, which will reveal that character, before continuing the major action of the drama itself? How much dialogue? How much straight statement, how much silent implication of the underlying theme? And so on. All these quantities will depend on nothing but the quality of the author's taste, and on his response to certain undeniable influences of life outside literature.

I mean technical influences, like, say, the cinema. Add now television and the increase of the photographed image in newspapers, magazines. In short, the new great currency of the Image. ...

This has had its effect on writing. The pace has increased. It would have increased in any case, through the cutting away of the worst verbiage of the past, when manners were slower and to our present perceptions tediously involved. We are, at least superficially, quicker in everything. But the film, I think, has had a deeper effect on fiction than anything else. Usually, the words 'film' and 'literary man' used in the same breath invite suspicion: this is because many writers, particularly novelists, have debased their work by writing 'with an eye to film' - a bad habit, usually disastrous, a thoroughly self-conscious money-grubbing, and not worth discussing. I am talking of something quite different: of the aesthetic effects of the cinema on the mind of an author. For instance, the all-seing god-like camera eye has whisked away the last need for the presence in a story of a narrator, of the eyes of one credible human being with whom you may identify your own, and through *only* which you may see the action of the story. The camera, popping about everywhere, has dispensed with the need for this. Brainwashed in the huge dark dreamlike cinema, the bookwriter follows suit. The presence of a narrator may still have a place; but he is no longer usually a necessity.

Similarly, the story-writer has been affected by the pace of action in the cinema. Unconsciously he has copied the restless camera and moved his prose at a faster pace: the visualizing element just behind the bone of his forehead is itself a kind of cinema screen, and easily infected. It is infected by the worst, but also by the best - that is his choice as an artist.

Again, dialogue will have altered. There will not necessarily be less of it, but what there is will line by line be foreshortened. The author will feel the greater presence of the image which shortens dialogue on the screen itself with the help of facial expressions, thinnings of lips, rollings of eyes - and expect his readers to feel it too. A reasonable assumption, since they have been to the cinema too and are themselves part of this faster pace.

From this it may be feared that certain subtleties will suffer. The story-writer's one great plus over the other arts has hitherto been an ability to enter a character's mind and describe what goes on there. On the screen this can only be implied, by expression or action. It may be that now the story-writer also feels he must imply rather than state. In small doses, this has, I think always been a virtue in a writer: it is the subtler way to guide the reader's feelings into subtlety. But it can be taken too far: the writer can be un-nerved, and cut everything of the unspoken inside in favour of the spoken appearance. ...

3. *For whom*? For whom do you write a story?

Two opposing camps here. One says, write entirely for yourself, with thoughts of publication secondary, a pleasant consequence. The other says, write for a large audience, with publication well in mind. (Publication in either case follows; what I mean is the motive behind the writing: what kind of reader have you in mind?)

I belong near to camp one. I write for myself and a projection of myself, a tyrannical oligarchy of a dozen or more editors, distant schoolmasters, and literate friends whose taste I respect. With these in mind, the words come out with mixed feelings of discretion and rebellion: I fear my masters a bit, and at the same time I want to cock a snook at them.

This imaginary readership of an elect few does not mean that the work shall be over-intellectualized, full of five-syllable words and arcane references, so oblique as to be obscure. I deplore obscurity, and, although suffering from the writer's purple disease, try hard - and it is hard - to be as sparing and taut with words as I can; yet without sounding 'tough', or talking rather than writing. In the last few decades there has been a growing disposition for writers to write in a talkative way. It is thought to be frank, intimate, unassuming. The result is too often simply cheap. In the hands of a really good writer, like Salinger in *The Catcher in the Rye*, it comes off splendidly: but, like Hemingway with his deceptive simplicity, it is not only talk but double and treble talk, a lot of work or intuition has gone into formalizing an apparently straight monologue. My firm belief is that one should not write as one talks, but write as one would wish to talk given the time, trouble and fearlessness to do so. Nothing overdone, but equally nothing underdone. (In all this, I refer of course to the prose outside actual dialogue. The story or novel written entirely in dialogue is its own excuse.) ...

4. *What*? Questions of how, of form, bring us to questions of content - what to write a story about?

Of course, pretty well anything.

But let it, I think, be within the scope of the writer's own experience. This is not to say about himself, but about something he has himself experienced, perhaps only in a slight way, but nevertheless in a manner memorable enough to be safely exaggerated into a credible major experience. Also, characters and places and words known in actual life are the more visible and securely audible in the mind's eye and ear: their very solidity can also bring a chain reaction of forgotten memories, ready-made atmospheres and details which can then be safely adapted to the fiction involved. I have repeated 'safely', 'securely'; this, because a known thing has real presence - all-important, unanalysable details such as a torn shoe-lace or a special hair-colouring insert themselves with a mythical intensity - and also because the writer avoids factual mistakes, like the placing of dark granite in a similarly dark Italian tufa region, or the excrescence of impossible vegetations, or the mention, say, of 'coppers' in a uniquely brass and silver coinage. Little matters, but trip-ropes all - like beef in shepherd's pie, a patent impossibility, or putting anything else but walnut oil in a salad in the Perigord region. It can be and has been done carefully and successfully from imagination; but rarely outside the sphere of historical romance. One's own secure experience, sensually perceived, is the safe way; and this applies also to the people in stories, not necessarily pictures of particular acquaintances - dangerous! - but the mixing of those acquaintances with others of their type to make a credible amalgam. ...

I wrote above that a story can be about anything. That goes. But whether it is acceptable by a large public is another matter. There is the sad truth that man is still largely nine-tenths animal. Thus, sex and violence can be the easiest ways into him. I have noticed, with stories of mine which have been more than usually reprinted, that these have contained elements of sex or violence, and have been read at a very different level to what I intended: the profounder underlying themes have been ignored for the superficially excitant veneer.

BIBLIOGRAPHIEN

Weitere englische und amerikanische Beiträge zur Theorie der Short Story

Diese Bibliographie erfaßt alle über die Quellensammlung hinausgehenden Texte, die von den Herausgebern ermittelt wurden und die für eine größere theoriegeschichtliche Untersuchung der Short Story von Bedeutung sind.

Hier werden nicht nur, wie in der Quellensammlung, theoretische Beiträge von Kurzgeschichtenautoren aufgeführt (und durch kurze Kommentare über Art und Inhalt ihrer Äußerungen besonders kenntlich gemacht), sondern auch Publikationen von Literaturkritikern und anderen Autoren, die sich in Definitionsversuchen sowie theoretischen Reflexionen und Feststellungen an der Diskussion über die Gattungsmerkmale und -probleme der Short Story beteiligt haben. Es mag sich hierbei um Leitfäden für das Schreiben von Short Stories, gattungsgeschichtliche Darstellungen, kritische und zeitbezogene Situationsbestimmungen der Kurzgeschichte oder um Einführungen in Anthologien handeln, die die Merkmale, die Untertypen oder die historische Entwicklung der Gattung dokumentieren sollen. Die Berücksichtigung von Publikationen dieser Art - neben den Äußerungen der Kurzgeschichten-Autoren - ist, wie in der Einführung dargelegt wird, für das Verständnis der amerikanischen Theoriegeschichte der Short Story von besonderer Bedeutung.

Die amerikanischen Titel werden von den englischen durch Kursivsetzung der Autorennamen unterschieden. Wo bei unbekannten Autoren ihre Nationalität nicht mit Sicherheit festgestellt werden konnte, erfolgte die Zuordnung aufgrund des Erscheinungsortes ihres Beitrags. Die Anordnung ist chronologisch, und die Titel werden - im Anschluß an die in der voraufgehenden Sammlung abgedruckten Quellen - fortlaufend durchnumeriert.

1761

104. DODSLEY, ROBERT, "An Essay on Fable", in *Select Fables of Aesop and Other Fabulists* (London, 1761); Neudruck des Essays nach der Birminghamer Ausgabe von 1764 durch die Augustan Reprint Society, Publication No. 112 (Los Angeles, 1965). - Basierend auf La Mottes' *Discours sur la Fable* (1719) und Addisons *Spectator*-Essays über die Fabel gibt Dodsley eine normative Deskription der Fabeldichtung "fable", die positiv von "tale" ("mere narrative of an event") abgesetzt wird. Betont werden vor allem wie im *Spectator*-Essay No. 512 (Oct. 17, 1712) die aktive Leserrezeption sowie Funktionalität der Teile und Umfang. Eine Fabel "must not be composed of separate and independent actions, but must tend in all its circumstances to the completion of one single event...the incidents should not only be few, but short". Als stilistische Vorbilder werden genannt "Mr. *Addison's* little tales in the Spectator".

1801

105. [ANONYMUS], "Dissertation on Fable", *The Port Folio,* I. 15 & 16 (April 14 & 18, 1801), 115 f., 124 f. - Der Aufsatz, in einer amerikanischen Zeitschrift erschienen, stammt offensichtlich aus einer englischen Quelle. Seine detaillierte und gattungshistorisch fundierte Schreibanweisung für die Fabel zeigt, daß die Theorie dieses zumeist poetischen Typs der Erzählung durchaus in Verbindung mit der Theorie der kurzen Erzählung und der Kurzgeschichte gesehen werden kann. Die Ausführungen darüber, wie eine gute Fabel geschrieben werden muß, lassen sich in ihrer Art und Intention im übrigen gut mit den späteren Short Story-Schreibschulen vergleichen.

1805

106. [*ANONYMUS*], "On Story-Telling", *The Literary Magazine and American Register,* IV. 22 (July, 1805), 17-19. - Es ist möglich, daß dieser Beitrag über die Erfordernisse einer guten, mündlich erzählten Geschichte von C. B. Brown, dem Herausgeber der Zeitschrift, stammt. Er trägt die Signatur "O." und beginnt folgendermaßen: "Much has been written to explain and to teach the art of story-telling; but no science is more difficult to attain, nor can it be taught by any settled rules. If the teller can but contrive to keep the attention of his audience awake to the end of his tale, he has certainly gained a great point, let the method he has taken be what it will; and if he can add to their attention some emotions of pleasure and surprise, he may justly be deemed a good story-teller."

1819

107. HUNT, LEIGH, "How to Write a Grim Story", *The Indicator* (Dec. 15, 1819). Abgedruckt in Leigh Hunt, *Selected Essays* (London, 1929; repr. 1947), 281-288. Titel hier: "A Tale for a Chimney-Corner". - Ironische Anmerkungen Hunts zur Mode der "grim stories".

1827

108. [*ANONYMUS*], "[On Novel Writing, being a review of] *Almanacks*. A Novel. 2 vols. ... New York, 1827 [and] *Vivian Grey*. Part I and Part II. 3 vols. ... Philadelphia, 1827", *North American Review,* XXV (1827), 183-203. - Die Besprechung, die möglicherweise von W. H. Prescott stammt, geht im Zusammenhang mit der Diskussion des Romans auf S. 186 f. auf die italienische "novella" ein, ohne zwischen beiden einen Gattungsunterschied zu sehen.

1831

109. [ANONYMUS], "Eastern Story-Tellers", *The New-York Mirror*, VIII. 35 (March 5, 1831), 273. Nachgedruckt aus dem *London Amulet*. - Dieser Aufsatz handelt über das mündliche Erzählen.

1832

110. MARTINEAU, HARRIET, "Preface" zu *Illustrations of Political Economy*, I (London, 1832). - Die Autorin nimmt eine Funktionsbestimmung von *short fiction* vor. Die *Illustrations* seien ein Versuch, wichtige Grundbegriffe der politischen Ökonomie mithilfe von kurzen Erzählungen zu erläutern. Die Grundbegriffe "will be exemplified in sketches of society, in narratives of those who labour and earn and spend. ... This method of teaching Political Economy has never yet been tried, except in the instance of a short story or separate passage here and there."

1836

111. *POE, EDGAR ALLAN*, "Magazine Writing - Peter Snook", *Southern Literary Messenger* (October, 1836) in *The Complete Works of Edgar Allan Poe*, hrsg. von James A. Harrison, Virginia Edition (New York, 1902), XIV, 73-89. - Eine Art Rezension der in einer englischen Zeitschrift erschienenen Geschichte "Peter Snook" von James Dalton, die den von Poe gerühmten "magazine spirit" aufweist. In den einführenden und abschließenden kritisch-essayistischen Teilen erscheinen deutlich Elemente von Poes Kurzgeschichtentheorie.

1838

112. *POE, EDGAR ALLAN*, "How to Write a Blackwood Article", [ursprüngl. Titel "Psyche Zenobia"], *American Museum of Science, Literature and the Arts*, I (November, 1838), 301-310, in *The Complete Works of Edgar Allan Poe*, hrsg. von James A. Harrison, Virginia Edition (New York, 1902), II, 269-282. - Zusammen mit der exemplarischen Erzählung "A Predicament" [ursprünglicher Titel "The Scythe of Time"] eine Parodie auf die im englischen *Blackwood Magazine* gängigen Kurzgeschichten und, in satirischer Form, eine Vorwegnahme der Kurzgeschichten-Schreibschulen des ausgehenden 19. Jahrhunderts.

1839

113. *HALE, SARAH JOSEPHA*, [Instructions to the contributors of] *Godey's Lady's Book* (Dec., 1839), in Fred Lewis Pattee, *The Development of the American Short Story: An Historical Survey* (New York & London, 1923), 71. - Für die Zeitschrift gebraucht werden kurze Geschichten, denn sie sind populär - "short, racy, spirited essays; stories and sketches that embody pages of narrative and sentiment in a single paragraph."

1842

114. *POE, EDGAR ALLAN*, "[Review of] Twice-Told Tales. By Nathaniel Hawthorne ...", *Graham's Magazine*, XX (April, 1842), 254, in *The Complete Works of Edgar Allan Poe*, hrsg. von James A. Harrison, Virginia Edition (New York, 1902), XI, 102-104. - Vorankündigung der eigentlichen Hawthorne-Besprechung Poes (Nr. 21) mit den folgenden einführenden Sätzen: "We have always regarded the *Tale* (using the word in its popular acceptation) as affording the best prose opportunity for display of the highest talent. It has peculiar advantages which the novel does not admit. It is, of course,

a far finer field than the essay. It has even points of superiority over the poem."

1843

115. *SMITH, SEBA*, "How to Tell a Story", *Graham's Magazine*, XXII (1843), 33-35. - Über die ideale Situation des mündlichen Geschichtenerzählens.

1844

116. [*ANONYMUS*], "Story-Tellers", *Littell's Living Age*, II (1844), 72-75. - Über die Anforderungen an einen modernen Geschichtenerzähler, dem Nachfahren der mittelalterlichen Barden und Troubadours, und die Bedingungen des gesellschaftlichen Erzählens.

117. *HAWTHORNE, NATHANIEL*, "From the Writings of Aubépine [introductory to 'Rappaccini's Daughter']", *The Democratic Review* (Dec., 1844), in *The Works of Nathaniel Hawthorne*, Standard Library Edition, hrsg. von G. P. Lathrop (Boston & New York, 1891), II, 170 f. - Eine selbstkritische Äußerung des Autors über seine Kurzgeschichten.

1845

118. *POE, EDGAR ALLAN*, "Marginalia IV", *Godey's Lady's Book* (Sept., 1845), in *The Complete Works of Edgar Allan Poe*, hrsg. von James A. Harrison, Virginia Edition (New York, 1902), XVI, 82. - Über Zeitschriftenliteratur der Zeit, die Kürze verlangt.

1847

119. *GRISWOLD, RUFUS WILMOT*, *The Prose Writers of America* (Philadelphia, 1847), 32 f.

120. *POE, EDGAR ALLAN*, "Tale Writing - Mr. Hawthorne", *Godey's Magazine and Lady's Book*, XXXV (Nov., 1847), 252-256, in *The Complete Works of Edgar Allan Poe*, hrsg. von James A. Harrison, Virginia Edition (New York, 1902), XIII, 141-155. - Eine überarbeitete und erweiterte Fassung von Poes Besprechung von Hawthornes *Twice-Told Tales* aus dem Jahre 1842 (Nr. 21).

1849

121. *POE, EDGAR ALLAN*, "Marginalia XIV", *Southern Literary Messenger* (July, 1849), in *The Complete Works of Edgar Allan Poe*, hrsg. von James A. Harrison, Virginia Edition (New York, 1902), XVI, 171 f. - Über "plot" und die Wichtigkeit der Konstruktion in der Erzählung gegenüber dem Roman.

1851

122. *HAWTHORNE, NATHANIEL*, "Preface" zu *Twice-Told Tales* [1851 ed.], in *The Works of Nathaniel Hawthorne*, hrsg. von G. P. Lathrop, Standard Library Edition (Boston & New York, 1891), I, 15-17. - Datiert "January 11, 1851". Eine kritische Selbstdarstellung der Art seiner Erzählungen; vgl. Poes Besprechung aus den Jahren 1842 und 1847 (Nr. 21 und 120).

1866

123. *HARTE, BRET*, "Railway Reading", *The Californian* (June 9, 1866), in *Sketches of the Sixties*, by Bret Harte and Mark Twain ... (San Francisco, 1926), 86-91. - Im Unterschied zu Neals Essay über das mündliche Geschichtenerzählen auf Reisen aus dem Jahre 1835 (Nr. 18) über die Kurzgeschichten der Periodica als Reiselektüre.

1867

124. *SIMMS, WILLIAM GILMORE,* [A Letter to Eugene Lemoine Didier, August 22, 1867] in *The Letters of William Gilmore Simms,* 5 Bde., hrsg. von Mary C. Simms, Alfred Taylor Odell & Duncan Eaves (Columbia, S. C., 1952-56), V, 77. - Über den Vorzug einer "*short story*" gegenüber einer längeren "Serial Story" in der Zeitschrift und über die Schwierigkeit, sie zu schreiben.

1884

125. ELIOT, GEORGE, "Story-Telling" in *Essays and Leaves from a Note-Book,* hrsg. von Charles Lee Lewes (Edinburgh and London, 1884). Als Teil der "Leaves from a Note-Book" [dieser Titel stammt vom Herausgeber] dort zum ersten Mal posthum veröffentlicht. Das Entstehungsjahr konnte nicht ermittelt werden. Neuausgabe in Thomas Pinney (Hrsg.), *Essays of George Eliot* (London, 1963), 444-446. - Reflexionen über verschiedenartige "modes of telling a story" und ihre "effectiveness". Besonders gelobt werden "the short tales in which the French have a mastery never reached by the English."

126. [*MATTHEWS, BRANDER,*] "Short Stories", *The* [*London*] *Saturday Review,* (July 5, 1884), 32-34. - Dieser anonym erschienene Beitrag ist, darauf weist Matthews selbst hin, die erste Fassung seiner "Philosophy of the Short-Story" (Siehe Nr. 28 und 39).

127. STEVENSON, ROBERT LOUIS, "A Humble Remonstrance", *Longman's Magazine* (Dec., 1884), in *The Works of Robert Louis Stevenson,* IX (London, 1907), 161-174. - Dieser polemische Beitrag zu der von Walter Besant und Henry James im selben Jahr geführten Debatte über die "art of fiction" basiert auf einer Gegenüberstellung von Kunst und Wirklichkeit: "Life is monstruous, infinite, illogical, abrupt and poignant; a work of art, in comparison, is neat, finite, self-contained, rational, flowing and emasculate." Dieser Gegensatz gilt jedoch nicht für das mündliche Erzählen: "The real art that dealt with life directly was that of the first men who told their stories round the savage camp-fire."

1887

128. [ANONYMUS], "Some American Short Stories", *The Spectator* (April 23, 1887), 565 f. Teilweise abgedruckt in Alexander Jessup (Hrsg.), *Representative American Short Stories* (Boston, 1923), xvi-xvii. - Der Autor - nach Jessups Information handelt es sich um James Ashcroft Noble - kommt nach einem Vergleich der Kurzgeschichtenproduktion in England und Amerika zu einer positiven Würdigung der Kunstgattung Short Story, so wie sie sich in Amerika entwickelt hat. "No English writer, for example, has produced a series of tales brief enough to be read in one short sitting".

1889

129. *CABLE, GEORGE WASHINGTON,* "How I Got Them. 1882-89", in *Strange True Stories of Louisiana* (New York, 1889, 1903), 1 f. - Über "true stories" aus dem Leben, die dem Autor in die Hände fallen.

1890

130. *MATTHEWS, BRANDER,* "The Prose Tales of M. François Coppée", in *Aspects of Fiction and Other Ventures in Criticism* (New York, 1896), 189, 195. - Dieser literaturkritische Beitrag aus dem Jahre 1890 befaßt sich am Rande mit dem Wesen und der Geschichte der französischen "conte".

1891

131. *JAMES, HENRY,* [On the genesis of "The Real Thing", Feb. 22, 1891] in *The Notebooks of Henry James,* hrsg. von F. O. Matthiessen & Kenneth B. Murdock (New York, 1947), 102-104. - Eine für James exemplarische Darstellung der Entstehungsgeschichte einer Short Story.

1892

132. [*ANONYMUS*], "The Short Story", *Atlantic Monthly,* LXIX (Feb., 1892), 261-270. - Die Kurzgeschichte, so wird in dieser Besprechung einiger Short Story-Bände amerikanischer Autoren behauptet, ist eine besondere Errungenschaft und zugleich der vitalste Teil der amerikanischen Literatur.

1894

133. [*CODY, SHERWIN*], *How to write Fiction, especially the art of short story writing.* A practical course of instruction, after the French method of Maupassant. In facsimile from original manuscript (New York, 1894). Diese Ausgabe, die wie die im folgenden genannten nicht eingesehen werden konnte, wird im "National Union Catalog Pre-1956 Imprints" und im Katalog der British Museum Library nachgewiesen. Walter Blackburn Harte, "The Art of Short-Story Writing", *Arena* (April, 1895), i-v, bespricht *The Art of Short Story Writing* (New York; Charles T. Dillingham & Co., 1895), offensichtlich eine neue Ausgabe desselben Buches. Eine englische Ausgabe dieses ersten amerikanischen Leitfadens für das Schreiben von Prosadichtung und besonders von Kurzgeschichten erschien unter dem leicht abgeänderten Titel *How to write Fiction, especially the art of short story writing. A practical study of technique* (London: Bellairs & Co., 1895); nachgewiesen ebenfalls in den beiden obengenannten Katalogen.

1895

134. *BUNNER, HENRY CUYLER,* "Cheating at Letters", *Century,* N. S. XXVII (March, 1895), 716-722. - Über die Kunst des Geschichtenerzählens, die bis zu den prähistorischen Höhlenbewohnern zurückreicht.

135. MILMAN, LENA, "A Few Notes Upon Mr. James", in *The Yellow Book,* VII (Oct., 1895), 71-83.

1896

136. *SMITH, F. HOPKINSON,* "How to Write Short Stories. An Interview with F. Hopkinson Smith in the Boston *Herald*", *Current Literature* (June, 1896). In einem Auszug zitiert von C. R. Barrett, *Short Story Writing* (siehe Nr. 144), auf S. 16. - Hier heißt es u. a.: "A short story ... must lead up to something. It should have for its structure a plot, a bit of life, an incident such as you would find in a brief newspaper paragraph. ...a story is something more than incidents and descriptions. It is a definite thing. It progresses constantly. It arrives somewhere. It must enforce some idea (no matter what). It must be such a reality that a man who read it would carry away a definite impression."

1897

137. *BIERCE, AMBROSE,* "The Novel", in *The Collected Works of Ambrose Bierce,* X: *The Opinionator* (New York & Washington, 1911), 17-24. - Der 1897 datierte Essay enthält, mit den Argumenten Poes (siehe Nr. 21), eine Abwertung der "novel" gegenüber der "romance" und bringt dabei am Rande die Short Story ins Spiel (vgl. Nr. 35).

138. *JAMES, HENRY,* "Hubert Crackanthorpe", in *Last Studies* by Hubert Crackanthorpe (London, 1897), xi-xxiii. - Dieser einführende Essay in das Werk des englischen Autors enthält eine Definition zwei Typen von "short tale" (vgl. Nr. 37).

139. SYMONS, ARTHUR, "Guy de Maupassant" in *Studies in Two Literatures* (1897). Abgedruckt in *The Collected Works of Arthur Symons,* VIII (London, 1924), 232-234. - Im Vergleich zu Kiplings Short Stories ("a tale by Kipling is merely an anecdote") preist Symons Maupassant "as a writer of the *nouvelle,* or short story.... With Maupassant, the moral idea is always there...every story is thus rounded, and becomes complete in itself by becoming the part of a great whole."

140. *BARR, ROBERT,* [Erster Beitrag zu] "How to Write a Short Story. A Symposium", *The Bookman* [American Edition], V. 1 (March, 1897), 42-44.

141. *FREDERICK, HAROLD,* [Zweiter Beitrag zu] "How to Write a Short Story. A Symposium", 44-45.

142. *BARLOW, JANE,* [Dritter Beitrag zu] "How to Write a Short Story. A Symposium", 46. - Alle drei Beiträge zu diesem Symposium befassen sich, mit unterschiedlichen Akzenten, mit den Anforderungen einer gut konstruierten Kurzgeschichte.

143. *HARLAND, HENRY,* "Concerning the Short Story", *The Academy. A Weekly Review of Literature, Science, and Art,* LI (June 5, 1897), "Fiction Supplement", 6 f. - Ein Versuch, die mangelhafte Popularität der Short Story in England zu ergründen. Für den literarischen Geschmack des englischen Lesers "the short story comes to a termination too early and too abrupt; its end shocks him as untimely."

1898

144. *BARRETT, CHARLES RAYMOND, Short Story Writing. A Practical Treatise on the Art of the Short Story* (New York, 1898, 1900, 1913), besonders Kap. I, "The Short Story".

1899

145. BULLOCK, SHAN F., "The British Short Story", *The Bookman,* XVI (Aug., 1899), 125-127. - Bullock polemisiert gegen die Hochschätzung der französischen Short Story in der englischen Kritik und die damit verbundene normative Definition der Gattung. Er setzt dagegen: "The artist who is master of his craft will achieve something that shall conform not so much to any preconceived theories of his art as simply to the nature of his subject."

146. *CHOPIN, KATE,* "On Certain Brisk, Bright Days", [ursprünglich ohne Titel erschienen im St. Louis] *Post-Dispatch* (Nov. 26, 1899). Abgedruckt in *The Complete Works of Kate Chopin,* hrsg. von Per Seyersted (Baton Rouge, La., 1969), II, 721-723. - Eine Reflexion über den eigenen schöpferischen Prozeß beim Geschichtenschreiben.

1900

147. *FOSDICK, ARTHUR,* "Short Story Writing", *Writer,* (Jan., 1900), 2-5. [Eine Rezension von C. R. Barrett, *Short Story Writing* (Nr. 144)].

148. BLACK, EBENEZER CHARLTON, "The Future of the Short Story", *The International Monthly* (Feb., 1900), 205-216.

1901

149. *CANBY, HENRY SEIDEL,* "On the Short Story", *The Dial,* XXXI (Oct. 16, 1901), 271-273. [Stellungnahme zu der Besprechung von Matthews' "Philosophy of the Short Story" (siehe Nr. 39) in der Londoner Zeitschrift *Academy* (siehe Nr. 40)].

1902

150. *CANBY, HENRY SEIDEL, The Short Story* (New York, 1902), 30 S. Yale Studies in English XII. Dieser Essay erschien erneut unter gleichem Titel als Einführung in Alexander Jessup & Henry Seidel Canby, *The Book of the Short Story* (New York & London, 1903), 3-28, von dem 1948 eine erweiterte Auflage herausgegeben wurde.

151. *PERRY, BLISS,* "The Short Story", in *A Study of Prose Fiction* (Boston & New York, 1902), 300-334. Eine überarbeitete Neuauflage erschien 1920 in Boston.

152. *SMITH, LEWIS WORTHINGTON, The Writing of the Short Story* (Boston, 1902).

153. *PERRY, BLISS,* "The Short Story", *Atlantic Monthly,* XC (August, 1902), 241-252.

1903

154. *ALDRICH, THOMAS BAILEY,* [Vorbemerkung zu] *Ponkapog Papers - A Sea Turn and Other Matters,* in *The Works of Thomas Bailey Aldrich* (Boston & New York, 1903), 30. - Gedanken über einen geplanten aber wieder aufgegebenen Essay "On the Art of Short-Story Writing".

1904

155. *BALDWIN, CHARLES SEARS, American Short Stories* (New York, 1904), bes. die Einleitung.

1905

156. *LOVETT, ROBERT MORSS,* "The Beginning of the Short Story in America", *The Reader. An Illustrated Monthly Magazine,* VI (Aug., 1905), 347-352.

1906

157. *LONDON, JACK,* [Letter of April 10, 1906, to S. S. McClure,] in *Letters from Jack London ...,* hrsg. von King Hendricks and Irving Shepard (New York, 1965), 201 f. - Über das weithin praktizierte Verfahren, Zeitungsreportagen zur Grundlage von Kurzgeschichten zu machen.

158. *LONDON, JACK,* "Local Color" & "Amateur Night", in *The Moonface and Other Stories* (New York, 1906, 1924), 40 f., 70. - In diesen zwei Kurzgeschichten erteilt jeweils ein erfahrener Zeitungsredakteur einem jungen Mitarbeiter seine professionellen Ratschläge für das Schreiben einer Reportage, einer "feature story". Fred Lewis Pattee, *The Development of the American Short Story: An Historical Survey* (New York & London, 1923), 340, zitiert, ohne Quellenangabe, diese Textstellen in einer veränderten Form und meint, daß sie die zeitgemäßen Forderungen an eine auf eigene Erfahrung gegründete, neue Form der Kurzgeschichte enthalte.

159. *TWAIN, MARK, Mark Twain's Autobiography,* [ed.] with an introduction by Albert B. Paine (New York & London, 1924), I, 237 f. - Diese Stelle der Autobiographie, die Paine von Twain ab 1906 diktiert

wurde, vergleicht das mündliche Erzählen mit einem Bach, das schriftliche Erzählen mit einem Kanal. Dieses Konzept des Erzählens, das kein Gesetz kennt, widerstrebt jeder Gattungstheorie.

1907

160. *ALBRIGHT, EVELYN MAY, The Short Story: Its Principles and Structure* (New York & London, 1907, 1922).

161. DOYLE, ARTHUR CONAN, *Through the Magic Door* (London, 1907), 113-127. - Essayistische Antwort auf die Frage "Which are the great short stories of the English language?", die auf eine Unterscheidung zwischen Roman und Short Story hinausläuft: "The champion sprinter is seldom a five-miler as well". (Zur Metaphorik vgl. Galsworthy, Nr. 55) Die Kriterien für eine gute Short Story sind in Anlehnung an Poe "strength, novelty, compactness, intensity of interest, a single vivid impression left upon the mind".

162. *MATTHEWS, BRANDER,* "Introduction" zu *The Short Story. Specimens Illustrating Its Development* (New York etc., 1907), 7-40. - Ein Abriß der Geschichte der "more carelessly composed tale which happens to be brief", die bis in die Frühzeit der Menschheit zurückgeht, und der "true short-story", jener von Poe erstmals definierten Gattung, deren Entwicklung in Frankreich und in den Vereinigten Staaten im zweiten Viertel des 19. Jahrhunderts begann.

1908

163. *ESENWEIN, J. BERG, Writing the Short-Story: A Practical Handbook on the Rise, Structure, Writing and Sale of the Modern Short Story,* rev. ed. (Springfield, Mass.: The Home Correspondence School, 1908, 1918).

164. *HAMILTON, CLAYTON, Materials and Methods of Fiction,* with an introduction by Brander Matthews (New York, 1908).

165. *MABIE, H. W.,* "A Comment on the Short Story", *Outlook,* LXXXIX (May 16, 1908), 118-120.

1909

166. BENNETT, ARNOLD, "Poe and the Short Story" in *Books and Persons: Being Comments on a Past Epoch 1908-1911* (London, 1917), 84-87. Zuerst erschienen in *New Age* (Jan. 28, 1909). - Bennett polemisiert aus Anlaß des "Poe Centenary Year" gegen "our customary national nonsense about the 'art of the short story' ...Another platitude is that the short story is mysteriously somehow more difficult than the long story - the novel. Whenever I meet that phrase, 'art of the short story,' in the press I feel as if I had drunk mustard and water. And I would like here to state that there are as good short stories in English as in any language, and that the whole theory of the unsuitability of English soil to that trifling plant the short story is ridiculous."

167. *CABLE, GEORGE WASHINGTON,* "Introduction" zu *'Posson Jone' and Père Raphael* (New York, 1909), 11. Datiert "July, 1909". - Diese Einführung enthält drei Sätze, die ihrer Naturmetaphorik wegen interessant sind: "A story-teller does not so much make a story as find it. He finds the stone, he cuts the gem. Stories, like wild flowers, are the product of the soil that favors them..."

168. *CANBY, HENRY SEIDEL, The Short Story in English* (New York, 1909).

169. *GERWIG, GEORGE W., The Art of the Short Story* (Akron, Ohio, 1909).

170. *JAMES, HENRY,* "Preface" zu *The Golden Bowl,* New York Edition of *The Novels and Tales of Henry James,* XXIII (New York, 1909), v-vi. Abgedruckt in *The Art of Fiction: Critical Prefaces,* hrsg. von Richard P. Blackmur (New York & London, 1934), 327 f. - Über die Neigung des Autors, besonders seine kürzeren Geschichten durch die Augen eines imaginierten Beobachters, eines Augenzeugen oder Reporters, zu sehen und sie in seiner Perspektive zu erzählen.

171. *DAWSON, W. J.,* "The Modern Short Story", *North American Review,* CXC (Dec., 1909), 799-810.

172. BUCHAN, JOHN, "Introduction" zu E. A. Poe, *Tales of Mystery and Imagination* (London, o.J.), 5-11. Die "Introduction" trägt das Datum 1909. Der Katalog der British Museum Library verzeichnet 1911 als Erscheinungsjahr des Buches. - Buchan beschreibt Poes Leistung: "In all his tales there is a clear sequence of cause and effect which gives them an imaginative coherence and verisimilitude."

1910

173. *CHESTER, GEORGE RANDOLPH, Art of Short Story Writing* (Cincinnati, 1910).

174. *DAWSON, WILLIAM J. & CONINGSBY W. DAWSON, The Great English Short-Story Writers,* 2 Bde. (New York, 1910). Die Einleitung: "The Evolution of the Short Story".

175. *SMITH, CHARLES ALPHONSO, The American Short Story* (Berlin, 1910), Sonderdruck der *Internationalen Wochenschrift für Wissenschaft, Kunst und Technik* (Dez., 1910). Unter gleichem Titel erschienen 1912 in Boston. Die deutsche Fassung "Die amerikanische Short Story" in *Die Amerikanische Literatur* (Berlin, 1912), 337-368, Bibliothek der Amerikanischen Kulturgeschichte, Bd. 2.

1911

176. *CODY, SHERWIN, A Selection from the World's Greatest Short Stories, illustrative of the history of short story writing with critical and historical comments* (Chicago, 1911).

1912

177. *PHILLIPS, HENRY ALBERT, The Plot of the Short Story* (Larchmont, N. Y., 1912).

178. *PITKIN, WALTER B., The Art and Business of Story Writing* (New York, 1912, 1923).

1913

179. *CANBY, HENRY SEIDEL, A Study of the Short Story* (New York, 1913), bes. S. 1-3. Eine spätere und von Alfred Dashiell revidierte Auflage erschien 1935.

180. *ESENWEIN, J. BERG & MARY DAVOREN CHAMBERS, The Art of Story-Writing* (Springfield, Mass.: The Home Correspondence School, 1913, 1919).

181. *GRABO, CARL H., The Art of the Short Story* (New York, Chicago & Boston, 1913).

182. *WELLS, CAROLYN, The Technique of the Mystery Story,* [with an] Introduction by J. Berg Esenwein (Springfield, Mass.: The Home Correspondence School, 1913), The Writer's Library. - In einer vorwiegend stofflich-thematischen Darstellung bietet vor allem das

Kap. XXIII, "Structure", 277-289, allgemeine Reflexionen über das Längekriterium, das Verhältnis von Short Story und Novel, über "the singleness of plot", die Rolle des Erzählers und des "setting".

1914

183. *CROSS, ETHAN ALLEN, The Short Story: A Technical and Literary Study* (Chicago, 1914).

184. *NEAL, ROBERT WILSON, Short Stories in the Making. A writer's and student's introduction to the technique & practical composition of Short Stories, incl. and adaptation of the principles of the stage plots to short story writing* (New York: Oxford University Press, 1914).

185. *NOTESTEIN, LUCY LILLIAN & WALDO HILARY DUNN, The Modern Short-Story. A Study of the Form: Its Plot, Structure, Development and Other Requirements* (New York, 1914).

186. *SHERMAN, STUART P., A Book of Short Stories* (New York, 1914), bes. "Introduction", S. vii-xxxii.

187. WALKER, HUGH, "The Short Story in English" in H. S. Milford (Hrsg.), *Selected English Short Stories: XIX Century* (First Series), The World's Classics No. 193 (London, 1914), v-xxv.

1915

188. *EATON, WALTER PRITCHARD,* [Ein Beitrag zu dem Symposium] "Does character drawing or plot count more in fiction?", *The New York Sun,* LXXXII. 229 (April 17, 1915), Spring Literary Section. - Der Autor wendet sich gegen die Übertragung aristotelischer Konzepte auf die moderne Short Story und dagegen, daß sie "mystery, plot, and surprise" aufweisen müsse, wie M. D. Post (siehe Nr. 51) fordert. Regeln für die Kurzgeschichte aufzustellen, ist unmöglich, und jede Definition, welche nicht ihre vielfältigen Erscheinungen erfaßt, ist zu eng. Kurzgeschichten "depend for their greatness primarily on their profoundly human truth to life combined with their perfection of style."

189. *CANBY, HENRY SEIDEL,* "Free Fiction", *Atlantic Monthly,* CXVI (July, 1915), 60-68.

1916

190. *ATKINSON, W. PATTERSON, The Short Story* (Boston, 1916, 1923).

191. *BAKER, HARRY TORSEY, The Contemporary Short Story: A Practical Manual* (Boston, New York etc., 1916).

192. *MATTHEWS, BRANDER,* "Introductory Note" zu *The Stories of H. C. Bunner. First Series* (New York, 1916), x-xi. - Datiert "March, 1916". Er erwähnt Bunners *vers de société*, die sich durch die für diese Form charakteristische "brevity ... brilliancy and buoyancy" auszeichnen (vgl. Nr. 28). Bunner war seiner Meinung nach auch ein Meister in der Kunst der Kurzgeschichte: "Even those of his longer tales which stretch out almost to the dimensions of the novel, were really only short-stories writ large; they had the unity, the swiftness, the singleness of purpose which is the distinguishing characteristic of this form of fiction."

1917

193. *WILLIAMS, BLANCHE COLTON, A Handbook on Story Writing* (New York, 1917, 1922), bes. Kap. I "Definitions and Characterizations," S. 1-17.

194. *LAWRENCE, JAMES COOPER,* "A Theory of the Short Story", *North American Review,* CCV (Feb., 1917), 274-286.

195. *FULLER, HENRY B.,* "New Forms of Short Fiction", *The Dial,* LXII (March 8, 1917), 167-169. - Über die Bedingungen, welche die Publikationsmedien Zeitung, Zeitschrift und sogar Film für die "short fiction" schaffen.

196. *COLUM, MARY M.,* "The American Short Story", *The Dial,* LXII (April 19, 1917), 345-347.

197. *CORY, HERBERT ELLSWORTH,* "The Senility of the Short-Story", *The Dial,* LXII (May 3, 1917), 379-381.

1918

198. *HAMILTON, CLAYTON, A Manual of the Art of Fiction,* Prepared for the Use of Schools and Colleges, with an Introduction by Brander Matthews (Garden City, N. Y., 1918, 1922, 1933), bes. Kap. X, "The Novel, the Novelletee, and the Short Story", S. 172-187. Eine revidierte und erweiterte Ausgabe von *Materials and Methods in Fiction* (1908).

1919

199. WOOLF, VIRGINIA, "Modern Novels", *The Times Literary Supplement* (April 10, 1919), 189 f. Revidierter Abdruck unter dem Titel "Modern Fiction" in *The Common Reader* [First Series] (London, 1925), 184-195. - Unter Hinweis auf Tschechows Short Story "Gusev" wird postuliert: "For the moderns...the point of interest lies very likely in the dark places of psychology." Daraus ergeben sich strukturelle Konsequenzen, die zu einer Auflösung der konventionellen Gattungsvorstellung ("short stories, we have been taught, should be brief and conclusive") führen müssen.

1922

200. MOULT, THOMAS, "The Renascence of the English Short Story", *Discovery,* III (Feb., April, 1922), 48-50, 105-107. - Der historisch-typologische Überblick über die englische Short Story führt zu einer Deskription der von den Autoren wieder entdeckten Kunstgattung Short Story. Ihre normative Definition lautet: "The short story is a single-themed narrative, artistically presenting characters in a struggle or complication which has a definite outcome."

1923

201. DAVIES, K. C. J., *The Art of Short Story Writing* (Vancouver, 1923).

202. *FAGIN, BRYLLION, Short Story-Writing: An Art or a Trade?* (New York, 1923).

203. *SMERTENKO, JOHAN J.,* "The American Short Story", *The Bookman,* LVI (Jan., 1923), 584-587.

1924

204. *ANDERSON, SHERWOOD,* "A Chicago Hamlet", in *Horses and Men* (London, 1924, 1927), 72. - Eine Stelle dieser Kurzgeschichte geht ein auf das Verhältnis zwischen mündlichem und schriftlichem Geschichtenerzählen.

205. *FREDERICK, JOHN T., A Handbook of Short Story Writing* (New York, 1924).

206. JAMES, MONTAGUE R., "Introduction" zu V. H. Collins (Hrsg.), *Ghosts and Marvels*. A Selection of Uncanny Tales from Daniel Defoe to Algernon Blackwood (London, 1924), v-xiii. - Für James ist die "ghost story...only a particular sort of short story, and is subject to the same broad rules as the whole mass of them." Spezifische Merkmale sind: "the atmosphere and the nicely managed crescendo."

207. *LARDNER, RING,* "Preface" zu *How to Write Short Stories (with Samples)* (New York, 1924), v-x. - Eine Art Parodie auf die Kurzgeschichten-Schreibschulen der Zeit.

208. WARD, ALFRED C., *Aspects of the Modern Short Story: English and American* (London, 1924), bes. "Author's Foreword" und Kap. I: "Introductory".

1925

209. *CATHER, WILLA,* "Preface" zu *The Best Stories of Sarah Orne Jewett* (New York, 1949), x-xii, xviii. - Datiert "February, 1925." Über die künstlerischen Anforderungen und Qualitäten einer "great story".

210. GALSWORTHY, JOHN, "Foreword" zu *Caravan: The Assembled Tales of John Galsworthy* (London, 1925), vii-viii. - Galsworthy formuliert seine Absage an die gängigen Muster der Short Story, die von ihr "pep" verlangen und eine Pointe am Schluß ("sting in the tail"). Er setzt dagegen: "If the writer of the short tale submit himself to the discipline demanded by the crisp and clear expression of his genuine fancies and his genuine moods, he has submitted to quite enough."

1926

211. *JOSEPH, MICHAEL, How to Write a Short Story* (New York, 1926).

1928

212. *ELLIS, AMANDA M., Representative Short Stories* (New York, 1928).

213. *ESENWEIN, J. BERG, Studying the Short Story* (New York, 1928), bes. "An Introduction to the Study of the Short Story," S. xiii-xxx.

214. *GALLISHAW, JOHN, The Only Two Ways to Write a Story* (New York & London, 1928).

215. LAWRENCE, D. H., "Introduction" zu seiner Übersetzung von Giovanni Verga, *Cavalleria Rusticana* (London, 1928). Abgedruckt in D. H. Lawrence, *Selected Literary Criticism,* hrsg. von Anthony Beal (London, 1956), 279-291. - Lawrence äußert sich zur Selektionstechnik der Short Story. Vergas Geschichten, die nach einem theoretischen Konzept ("self-effacement in art") verfaßt worden seien, wirkten durch übertriebene "concision" zu gekünstelt. Lawrence setzt dagegen: "We need more looseness. We need an apparent formlessness, definite form is mechanical. We need more easy transition from mood to mood and from deed to deed. A great deal of the meaning of life and of art lies in the apparently dull spaces, the pauses, the unimportant passages."

216. MAUGHAM, W. SOMERSET, "Preface" zu *Ashenden* (London, 1928), v-x. - Im Rahmen allgemeiner Erörterung des Wesens von "fiction" erteilt der Autor der Short Story-Konzeption der Tschechow-Nachfolge eine Absage - unter starker Betonung der "plot-story."

1929

217. *BEACH, STEWART, Short-Story Technique* (Boston, 1929).

218. *GALLISHAW, JOHN, Twenty Problems of the Fiction Writer: A Series of Lectures on the Craftmanship of the Modern Short Story* (New York & London, 1929).

219. *O'BRIEN, EDWARD J., The Dance of the Machines: The American Short Story and the Industrial Age* (New York, 1929), bes. Kap. IV, S. 115-173.

1930

220. [ANONYMUS], "Life and the Short Story", *The Times Literary Supplement* (Jan. 16, 1930), 33 f. - Ausgehend von einer einfachen Funktionsbestimmung der Short Story ("good entertainment") wird die "machine-made story built round a formula" abgelehnt. Zugleich wird ein grundlegender Wandel in Thematik und Form der zeitgenössischen Short Story registriert: "A new realism appealing against aestheticism."

1931

221. *BEMENT, DOUGLAS, Weaving the Short Story* (New York, 1931).

222. MELVILLE, LEWIS und REGINALD HARGREAVES, "Introduction" zu ihrer Anthologie *Great English Short Stories* (London, 1931), ix-xiv.

223. WARD, ALFRED C., "The Short Story" in *Foundations of English Prose* (London, 1931), 119-134.

1932

224. STRONG, L. A. G., "Concerning Short Stories", *The Bookman,* LXXV (Nov., 1932), 709-712.

1934

225. *CROSS, ETHAN ALLEN, A Book of the Short Story* (New York & Cincinnati, 1934).

1935

226. *O'BRIEN, EDWARD J., The Short Story Case Book* (New York, 1935).

227. *SAROYAN, WILLIAM,* "What is a Story", *Saturday Review of Literature,* XI (Jan. 5, 1935), 409. - Ein Dokument für die Ablehnung einer formalen Gattungsfixierung der Short Story: Wichtig ist nur ihre künstlerisch-schöpferische Integration, ihre "wholeness".

1936

228. *FAGIN, NATHAN BRYLLION,* Hrsg., *America Through the Short Story* (Boston, 1936), bes. "Introduction", S. 3-19.

229. *WARREN, ROBERT PENN,* zusammen mit *CLEANTH BROOKS* & *J. T. PURSER,* "Introduction" zu *An Approach to Literature,* 3rd ed. (New York, 1936, 1952), 28-30. - Über die bisherigen verschiedenen Klassifizierungsversuche der Short Story mit folgender abschließenden Aussage: "The short story, after all, may be what its name applies - a short piece of fiction. This means that it has all the qualities which fiction as fiction has, ... and that the special qualities which it, as opposed to the novel or novelette, possesses or lacks are to be understood as contingent upon the fact of the brevity of the form."

1938

230. *BAKER, HOWARD,* "The Contemporary Short Story," *Southern Review,* III (Winter, 1938), 576-596.

1939

231. HADFIELD, JOHN, "Introduction" zu seiner Anthologie *Modern Short Stories* (London, 1939), v-ix. Everyman's Library No. 954.

232. *HAMILTON, CLAYTON, The Art of Fiction* (New York, 1939). Eine neue Ausgabe von *A Manual of the Art of Fiction* (1922).

233. *MIRRIELEES, EDITH RONALD, Story Writer* (1939).

1940

234. *CAMPBELL, WALTER S., Writing Magazine Fiction* (New York, 1940).

1941

235. *PORTER, KATHERINE ANNE,* "Introduction" zu *A Curtain of Green* by Eudora Welty, (New York, 1941), xi-xxiii. - Die Bewältigung des Mediums der Kurzgeschichte, so sagt die Autorin in zwei kurzen Bemerkungen, "is part of a cellular growth in a most complex organism" - "it is a special and difficult medium, and contrary to a widely spread popular superstition it has no formula that can be taught by correspondence school."

236. PRITCHETT, V. S., [Rezensionsartikel über James Joyces *Dubliners* unter dem Titel] "Current Literature: Books in General", *The New Statesman and Nation* (Feb. 15, 1941), 162. Eine deutsche Übersetzung (von Rolf Dornbacher) dieses Artikels findet sich in Klaus Reichert et al. (Hrsg.), *Materialien zu James Joyces 'Dubliner',* edition suhrkamp 357 (Frankfurt am Main, 1969), 182-188. - Ausführungen zur Suggestionskraft der modernen Short Story (am Beispiel von Joyces *The Dead*), die sich nicht in "action" und "plot" erschöpft. Sie fordert also den aktiven Leser, denn "the subject of a story is not the events in the story, nor its dialogue nor its action, nor its people, but something which arises from and lives between all these."

237. *FERGUSON, OTIS,* "Story-Teller's Workshop", *Accent,* I. 3 (Spring, 1941), 170-173. - Dieser Beitrag über Erskine Caldwell beginnt mit einer allgemeinen Reflexion über das Schreiben der Short Story.

238. *SHAW, HARRY,* "Some Clinical Notes", *Saturday Review of Literature,* XXIV (Nov. 22, 1941), 3, 23-25.

239. *OVERSTREET, BONARO,* "Little Story, What Now?", *Saturday Review of Literature,* XXIV (Nov. 22, 1941), 3-5, 25 f.

1943

240. *BECK, WARREN,* "Art and Formula in the Short Story", *College English,* V (Nov., 1943), 55-62. - Eine kritische Auseinandersetzung zwischen zwei Typen der Short Story: der populären und kommerziellen und der literarischen und experimentellen Kurzgeschichte.

1944

241. *BYRNES, THOMAS E.,* "Essentials of the Short Story", in *The Writer's Handbook,* hrsg. von A. S. Burack (Boston, 1944).

1945

242. *BADER, A. L.,* "The Structure of the Modern Short Story", *College English,* VII (Nov., 1945), 86-92.

1946

243. *DERLETH, AUGUST, Writing Fiction* (Boston, 1946). - Ein Buch für die angehenden Berufsschriftsteller, über "stories" der verschiedensten Art, nicht speziell über Short Stories.

1947

244. *KEMPTON, KENNETH PAYSON, The Short Story* (Cambridge, Mass., 1947, 1967).

245. MAUGHAM, W. SOMERSET, "The Short Story" [Read Nov. 12th, 1947] in *Essays by Divers Hands; Being the Transactions of the Royal Society of Literature,* Third Series, XXV (1950), 120-134. - Maugham verknüpft seinen Überblick über die Entwicklung der Short Story mit der Diskussion wirkungsästhetischer Probleme. Abschließend gibt er eine simple Definition: "I should define a short story as a piece of fiction that has unity of impression and that can be read at a sitting. I should be inclined to say that the only test of its excellence is that it interests."

246. *MIRRIELEES, EDITH RONALD, Story Writing* (Boston, 1947). Revidierte und erweiterte Ausgabe von *Story Writer* (1939).

1948

247. O'FAOLAIN, SEAN, *The Short Story* (London, 1948; New York, 1951). - O'Faolain gründet seine Deskription der Gattung Short Story auf eine analytische Betrachtung der Geschichten von Daudet, Tschechov und Maupassant. Die Ausführungen zur Form konzentrieren sich auf die Aspekte "convention", "subject", "construction" und "language". Die ursprünglich angefügten Beispiele der Gattung aus verschiedenen Nationalliteraturen fehlen in der Neuausgabe, Mercier Paperback (Cork, 1972).

248. *SUMMERS, RICHARD ALDRICH, Craft of the Short Story* (New York & Toronto, 1948).

1949

249. *GILKES, LILLIAN B.,* "An Introduction to Short Story Writing", in *Short Story Craft,* [hrsg. von] Lillian Gilkes & Warren Bower (New York, 1949), 1-27.

250. *BRICKELL, HERSCHEL,* "The Contemporary Short Story", *University of Kansas City Review,* XV (Summer, 1949), 267-270.

1950

251. *SCHORER, MARK* (Hrsg.), *The Story. A Critical Anthology* (New York, 1950, 3rd ed. 1953).

1951

252. *BRICKELL, HERSCHEL,* "What Happened to the Short Story?", *Atlantic Monthly,* CLXXXVIII (Sept., 1951), 74-76.

1953

253. *BAKER, FALKON O.,* "Short Stories for the Millions", *Saturday Review,* XXXVI (Dec. 19, 1953), 7-9, 48 f.

1954

254. *CREELEY, ROBERT,* "Preface" zu *The Gold Diggers* (1954), in *New American Story,* hrsg. von Donald M. Allen und Robert Creeley (Harmondsworth: Penguin Books, 1965, 1971), 270. - Über die Gestalt und

Form einer Kurzgeschichte oder Erzählung, für die die alten Voraussetzungen von Anfang und Ende weggefallen sind.

255. MAUGHAM, W. SOMERSET, "The Art of Fiction" in *Ten Novels and Their Authors* (London, 1954), 1-20. - Enthält Ansätze für einen Vergleich zwischen "novel" und "short story".

256. *GORDON, CAROLINE* and *ALLEN TATE*, Hrsg., *The House of Fiction.* An Anthology of the Short Story with Commentary (New York, 1954), bes. "Preface", S. vii-viii, und "Appendices A & B": The Arts of Fiction; Faults of the Amateur", S. 621-637. - Die beiden Autoren gehen mehr auf allgemeine Probleme der Prosadichtung, der "fiction", ein und formulieren für die Short Story kein besonderes Gattungskonzept.

257. [ANONYMUS], "The Art of the Short Story: Principles and Practices in the United States", *The Times Literary Supplement* (Sept. 17, 1954), "Special Number Devoted to American Writing To-day: Its Independence and Vigour", xl, xlii. - Der Überblick über die bedeutendsten Verfasser von Short Stories in Amerika geht aus von einer Gattungsbestimmung, die sich an Elizabeth Bowens Aussagen zur Kunstform Short Story orientiert: "Its effects are gained through implication and suggestion, rather than through detailed description, or delineation of character. ... And if in some cases it is nearer to the drama than the novel, in others it is nearer to the poem."

1955

258. *FAULKNER, WILLIAM*, in "The Art of Fiction: An Interview with William Faulkner - September, 1955" by Cynthia Grenier, *Accent*, XVI (Summer, 1956), 168, 171. - Kurze Bemerkungen über seine schriftstellerischen Erfahrungen im Bereich (des Romans und) der Short Story "which is the most demanding form after poetry."

259. *WELTY, EUDORA*, "How I Write", *Virginia Quarterly Review*, XXXI. 2 (Spring, 1955), 240-251. - Eine auf ihre eigene Praxis bezogene Reflexion über das Schreiben von Geschichten.

1957

260. O'CONNOR, FRANK, "Introduction" zu seiner Anthologie *Modern Irish Short Stories*, (London, 1957), ix-xv, The World's Classics No. 560. - O'Connor postuliert die Eigenständigkeit der "Irish short story" als einer "distinct art form" im Gegensatz zur "English short story". Für sein eigenes Werk gilt: "I have preferred to keep to my own idea of the short story as an art form distinct from the tale, though I realize that the distinction may be more philosophical than critical. As I understand it, the short story derives from the novel, and like the novel has attempted suçcessfully to combine artistic and scientific truth."

261. *WEST, RAY B. JR.*, "The Modern Short Story and the Highest Forms of Art", *English Journal*, XLVI (Dec., 1957), 531-539.

1958

262. *FRIEDMAN, NORMAN*, "What Makes A Short Story Short?", *Modern Fiction Studies*, IV (1958), 103-117.

1961

263. O'FAOLAIN, SEAN, "Introduction" zu seiner kommentierten Anthologie *Short Stories: A Study in Pleasure* (Boston, 1961), 1-25. -

Versuch eines Zugangs zur Short Story über das "Pleasure Principle" das als Gegenpol definiert wird zum "fissurating effect" der analytischen Methode: "The Pleasure Principle analyzes not so much the story (poem, play, or picture) as our own possible pleasurable reactions, our own possible emotional satisfactions in the presence of the work of art." Diskutiert werden vor allem "the pleasures of Recognition, or Identification, or Moral Shock, or Extension of Sympathies."

1962

264. *FAGIN, NATHAN BRYLLION,* "Short Story", in Joseph T.Shipley (Hrsg.), *Dictionary of World Literature: Criticism, Forms, Technique* (Paterson, N. J., 1962), 373 f.

265. *JARRELL, RANDALL,* "Stories", in *A Sad Heart at the Supermarket* (New York, 1962), 20-27. - Reflexionen über "stories" in Prosa und Vers unabhängig von jedem Längekriterium, über Motive und Arten des Erzählens von Geschichten.

1963

266. BOWEN, ELIZABETH, "Introduction" zu *The Stories of William Sansom* (London, 1963), 7-12. - Die positive Würdigung Sansoms basiert auf einer Definition der Gattung Short Story: "This form needs the kind of imagination which is able to concentrate at high power. ... That need to gain an immediate hold on the reader (a hold which must also be a compulsive one) rules out the writer who is a slow starter. ... There is also the necessity to project, to make seen, and make seen with significance - the short story is for the eye (if the mind's eye). Also the short story, though it high-lights what appears to be reality, is not - cannot wish or afford to be - realistic: it relies on devices, foreshortenings, 'effects'. In the narration there must be an element of conjury."

267. *HEMINGWAY, ERNEST,* [Interview] in *Writers at Work. The Paris Review Interviews. Second Series,* [ed. &] introd. by Van Wyck Brooks (New York, 1963), 230, 233, 235 f. - Kurze, den theoretischen Fragen ausweichende Äußerungen über das Schreiben seiner Kurzgeschichten.

268. *SUMMERS, HOLLIS,* "Introduction" zu *Discussions of the Short Story,* hrsg. von H. Summers (Boston, 1963), vii-ix.

1964

269. BEACHCROFT, T. O., *The English Short Story,* 2 Bde. (London, 1964), Writers and Their Work Nos. 168/169. Eine rev. und erweiterte Fassung erschien unter dem Titel *The Modest Art: A Survey of the Short Story in English* (London, 1968). - Dieser historische Überblick über "short fiction" seit den Anfängen der englischen Literatur basiert auf der These, die kurze Geschichte müsse als "modest art" verstanden werden. Andererseits betont Beachcroft (als Short Story Writer) in seinen Würdigungen der Kurzgeschichten-Autoren spezifisch künstlerische Anforderungen der Gattung; so ist der Kurzgeschichtenautor "a strange mixture of poet, reporter and aphorist". V. S. Pritchett rezensiert Beachcroft (1968): vgl. hier Text Nr. 297.

270. *STUART, JESSE,* "The Tall Tale [Interview]", in *The Modern Short Story in the Making,* hrsg. von Whit & Hallie Burnett (New York & London, 1964), 42-44. - Eine Darstellung der eigenen schrift-

stellerischen Erfahrungen zusammen mit einer kurzen Definition der Short Story: "It is an exciting slice of life."

271. [*BURNETT, WHIT & HALLIE*], "The Anecdote Expanded", in *The Modern Short Story in the Making*, 63-65. - Über das Verhältnis von Short Story und Anekdote.

272. *SCHMITT, GLADYS*, "Myself, a Mood [Interview]", in *The Modern Short Story in the Making*, 122-124. - Äußerungen über die eigene schriftstellerische Praxis und eine kurze Definition der Short Story: "A full-rendered incident, of some moral significance, dealing with a well-defined problem and a limited cast (three or four characters)."

273. *McCLEARY, DOROTHY*, "One Character Close Up [Interview]", in *The Modern Short Story in the Making*, 166 f. - Einige Äußerungen zur eigenen schriftstellerischen Praxis ("Writing an objective story always presents the difficult problem of writing, in effect, a one-act play without a stage or actors.") und eine kurze Definition der Short Story: "A moment (long or short) during which something is shown to be very much at stake for a character or characters dramatically worth the watching."

274. *CALDWELL, ERSKINE*, "A Neighbor in Maine [Interview]", in *The Modern Short Story in the Making*, 183 f. - Kurze Definition einer Short Story: "The revelation of character in reaction to an unusual incident."

275. *BOYLE, KAY*, "Portraiture Understood [Interview]", in *The Modern Short Story in the Making*, 192-194. - Unter Hinweis auf die Definition Washington Irvings eine kurze eigene Definition der Short Story: "A statement of one's understanding of the predicament of other men."

276. *CAPOTE, TRUMAN*, "Objectivized Subjective [Interview]", in *The Modern Short Story in the Making*, 205 f. - U. a. eine kurze Definition der Short Story: "A work of fictional art that accommodates depth but excludes length."

277. *BURNETT, HALLIE*, "Reportage Carried Further [Interview]", in *The Modern Short Story in the Making*, 240 f. - Äußerungen über das eigene Schaffen und eine kurze Definition der Short Story: "A short, unified narrative in which an explosion takes place."

278. *HITCHCOCK, GEORGE*, "The Power of the Released Imagination [Interview]", in *The Modern Short Story in the Making*, 249 f. - Neben kurzen Bemerkungen über das eigene Schaffen eine Definition der Short Story: "a readable piece of fiction shorter than the novella."

279. *TAYLOR, KRESSMANN*, "The Conventional Letter Form Reconsidered [Interview]", in *The Modern Short Story in the Making*, 287-291. - Eine Darstellung der eigenen schriftstellerischen Erfahrungen und, unter Hinweis auf Eudora Welty (Nr. 74), eine kurze Definition der Short Story: "... a live experience caught within a slant of light uniquely its own, in which some genuine tension moves toward a peak of intensity or else moves through an imaginative exploration which will relax or resolve it."

280. *D'AGNOSTINO, GUIDO*, "A Dream Too Big For One Man [Interview]", in *The Modern Short Story in the Making*, 336-338. - Neben Bemerkungen über das eigene Schaffen eine kurze Definition der Short Story: "... the accomplishment in words of a single emotional or dramatic effect ..."

281. *GULLASON, THOMAS H.*, "The Short Story: An Underrated Art", *Studies in Short Fiction,* II (1964), 13-31.

1965

282. *KENNER, HUGH, Studies in Change.* (Englewood Cliffs, N. J., 1965).

283. *MILLER, JAMES A. & BERNICE SLOTE,* "Notes on the Short Story", in *The Dimensions of the Short Story: A Critical Anthology* (New York & Toronto, 1965), 509-516.

284. *ULANOV, BARRY,* "The Short Story", in *The Two Worlds of American Art, the Private and the Popular* (New York & London, 1965), 190-208.

285. *CASTRO-BENITEZ, JOSEFA,* "The Short Story - Art of Brevity", *Far Eastern University Faculty Journal,* X (3rd Quarter, 1965-66), 17-22.

286. *KOSTELANETZ, RICHARD,* "Notes on the American Short Story Today", *Minnesota Review,* V (August-October, 1965), 214-221.

287. *KOSTELANETZ, RICHARD,* "The Short Story in Search of Status", *Twentieth Century,* CLXXIV, no. 1027 (Autumn, 1965), 65-69.

1966

288. PRITCHETT, V. S., "Satan Comes to Georgia", *New Statesman* (April 1, 1966), 469, 472. - In diesem Rezensionsartikel zum Short Story-Band von Flannery O'Connor, *Everything That Rises Must Converge,* rekurriert Pritchett auf die These O'Connors (*The Lonely Voice,* 1963 [vgl. hier Text Nr. 90]), daß sich die Short Story vornehmlich mit dem vereinsamten Individuum beschäftige, um damit die besondere Qualität der amerikanischen Short Story zu erklären. Grundsätzlich gilt: "A short story ought to be faultless without being mechanical. The wrong word, a misplaced paragraph, an inadequate phrase or a convenient explanation, start fatal leaks in this kind of writing, which is formally very close to poetry. It must be totally sustained."

289. KING, FRANCIS, in "The Short Story", *London Magazine,* N. S. VI, No. 6 (Sept., 1966), 11 f. - Darstellung der Lage auf dem literarischen Markt für Short Story-Schreiber. King konstatiert eine Verwandtschaft der Short Story mit "poetry" "in the concentration they exact from both reader and writer...".

1968

290. *ASTOR, STUART L.* und *LEONARD R. N. ASHLEY,* "The Modern Short Story: A Reader's Introduction", in *British Short Stories. Classics and Criticism* (Englewood Cliffs, N. J., 1968), 1-12.

291. STEAD, CHRISTINA, [Beitrag zu] "The International Symposium on the Short Story. Part One", *Kenyon Review,* XXX (1968), 444-450. - Stead begreift das Erzählen als eine Grundqualität des Menschen; deshalb polemisiert sie gegen jede mechanistische Konzeption: "The short story can't wither and, living, can't be tied to a plan. It is only when the short story is written to a rigid plan, or done as an imitation, that it dies."

292. *GOLD, HERBERT,* [Beitrag zu] "The International Symposium on the Short Story. Part One", *Kenyon Review,* XXX (1968), 450-453. - Einige Bemerkungen über die moralischen Beziehungen des Geschichtenerzählers zu seiner Geschichte.

293. GORDIMER, NADINE, [Beitrag zu] "The International Symposium on the Short Story. Part One", *Kenyon Review,* XXX (1968), 457-463. -

Aus der Gegenüberstellung von Roman und Kurzgeschichte gewinnt die südafrikanische Autorin die besonderen Vorzüge der Short Story in der Darstellung modernen Lebens: "The short story as a form and as *a kind of creative vision* must be better equipped to attempt the capture of ultimate reality."

294. KIELY, BENEDICT, [Beitrag zu] "The International Symposium on the Short Story. Part One", *Kenyon Review*, XXX (1968), 463-469. - Ein impressionistischer Versuch des irischen Autors, Entstehungsbedingungen und Merkmale der irischen Short Story vor allem in Auseinandersetzung mit Frank O'Connors Short-Story-Konzeption zu beschreiben.

295. HOOD, HUGH, [Beitrag zu] "The International Symposium on the Short Story. Part One", *Kenyon Review*, XXX (1968), 469-477. - Nach einer positiven Würdigung der Marktlage für Kurzgeschichtenautoren gewinnt der Kanadier Hood seine Funktionsbestimmung von Literatur: "The chief *telos* of fiction in all its forms, whether in verse or prose, the long fiction or the short, epic, romance, myth, novel, tale, story, is located in the storyteller's function, which is that of giving assurance to his readers or hearers of the persistence of the inner values of their culture. Story is by nature 'realist' and the great story forms are realistic and historical, about the behaviour of men and women...in real observable human societies."

296. DRAKE-BROCKMAN, HENRIETTA, [Beitrag zu] "The International Symposium on the Short Story. Part One", *Kenyon Review*,XXX (1968), 478-485. - Wie Stevenson (vgl. Nr. 127) verweist auch die australische Autorin für den Ursprung der australischen Short Story auf die "Aborigines as they sat around their campfires...". In der Moderne "the short story aptly fills many small gaps in understanding and still fits the continent's pattern".

297. PRITCHETT, V. S., "The Anti-Soporific Art", *New Statesman* (Dec. 6, 1968), 793 f. - In diesem Rezensionsartikel zu T. O. Beachcrofts *The Modest Art: A Survey of the Short Story in English* kennzeichnet Pritchett die Besonderheit der Short Story gegenüber dem Roman: "Modest in length a short story is and as modest in its attraction for the gourmandising novel reader; but as a way of writing it is as excellent as the sonnet, the ballad or the play; as piercing as a piece of music or sculpture, as evocative as a water-colour. It is above all, the *memorable* art. We forget whole slabs of the famous novels - only a character or a scene or two stick in the mind - but the short story stays whole."

1969

298. SHADBOLT, MAURICE, [Beitrag zu] "The International Symposium on the Short Story. Part Two", *Kenyon Review*,XXXI (1969), 69-74. - Der neuseeländische Autor betont: "...a rewarding short story is inconceivable without some high degree of conscious or instinctive craftsmanship."Denn "the real challenge is...no less than the endeavor to pull as much of life as a story can bear into the fewest possible pages...".

299. *BROWN, JAMES OLIVER*, "An Agent's View", in "The International Symposium on the Short Story. Part Two", *Kenyon Review*,XXXI (1969), 92-94.

300. *GARRETT, GEORGE*, [Beitrag zu] "The International Symposium on the Short Story. Part Three", *Kenyon Review*, XXXI (1969), 461-468. - U. a. über die Marktlage der Short Story.

301. TAYLOR, ELIZABETH, [Beitrag zu] "The International Symposium on the Short Story. Part Three", *Kenyon Review*, XXXI (1969), 469-473. - "The short story is like a piece of music in that it can be experienced in one go - and not laid down and taken up, day after day, as novels usually must be - so that the reading of it may be a curiously intense experience; a destillation, a perfection."

302. MPHAHLELE, EZEKIEL, [Beitrag zu] "The International Symposium on the Short Story. Part Three", *Kenyon Review*, XXXI (1969), 473-479. - Der südafrikanische Autor gibt einen Überblick über die spezifische Entwicklung der Gattung Short Story in Afrika unter Hinweis auf die für ihn bedeutsamen Traditionen der "African folk tales", der "English and Scottish ballads" und des mündlichen Erzählens.

303. HARROWER, ELIZABETH, [Beitrag zu] "The International Symposium on the Short Story. Part Three", *Kenyon Review*, XXXI (1969), 479-485. - Anhand einer Marktanalyse gibt die australische Autorin eine Darstellung der spezifischen Entstehungsmöglichkeiten und Rezeptionsbedingungen für die Short Story in ihrem Heimatland.

1970

304. COPE, JACK, [Beitrag zu] "The International Symposium on the Short Story. Part Four", *Kenyon Review*, XXXII (1970), 78-84. - Der südafrikanische Autor stellt in typologischer Unterscheidung "folktale" ("the essence is in the telling, the magical process of communication, the electric spell a story-teller at once establishes over his audience" der modernen Short Story gegenüber: "It is essentially the literary form of the city - the prose-poem...in the industrial age..." Ihre Hauptmerkmale sind: "...an almost lyrical intensity and economy in the use of language...".

305. BALLANTYNE, DAVID, [Beitrag zu] "The International Symposium on the Short Story. Part Four", *Kenyon Review*, XXXII (1970), 97-104. - Darstellung der Produktions- und Rezeptionsbedingungen für die Short Story vom Standpunkt des neuseeländischen Autors u. a. im Vergleich zum Fernsehspiel.

306. STERN, JAMES, [Beitrag zu] "Some Notes on Writing Stories", *London Magazine*, N. S. IX (March, 1970), 6 f. - Als Wesensmerkmal der Short Story wird ihre poetische Qualität konstatiert.

307. GLANVILLE, BRIAN, [Beitrag zu] "Some Notes on Writing Stories", *London Magazine*, N. S. IX (March, 1970), 7 f. - Glanville definiert die Short Story als "a kind of halfway house between poetry and that hardy hybrid, the novel."Deshalb gilt: "The problem in the short story, still more than in the novel, is for experience to be distilled and refined, instead of being allowed to overwhelm aesthetic need."

308. TAYLOR, ELIZABETH, [Beitrag zu] "Some Notes on Writing Stories", *London Magazine*, N. S. IX (March, 1970), 8-10. - Hinweis auf die besondere Leistung der Short Story: "There may be something therein that may attain perfection, as novels never do, some magic distillation, almost certainly an intensity of experience."

309. TREVOR, WILLIAM, [Beitrag zu] "Some Notes on Writing Stories", *London Magazine*, N. S. IX (March, 1970), 10-12. - Am Beispiel einer eigenen Geschichte verweist Trevor auf den Unterschied in der Darstellungsweise zwischen Short Story und Roman.

310. FELD, MICHAEL, [Beitrag zu] "Some Notes on Writing Stories", *London Magazine*, N. S. IX (March, 1970), 13 f. - Hinweise auf seinen Werdegang und seine Arbeitsmethoden.

311. RABAN, JONATHAN, [Beitrag zu] "Some Notes on Writing Stories", *London Magazine*, N. S. IX (March, 1970), 14 f. - Für die Short Story hält Raban als Leistung fest: "To mediate between the familiar, contingent patterns of a society inhabited by the writer and his readers, and the new, intensified, often metaphoric shape of the fiction. Much more than the novel, the short story deals in pastiche, in metaphor, in mimetic social detail."

312. TUOHY, FRANK, [Beitrag zu] "Some Notes on Writing Stories", *London Magazine*, N. S. IX (March, 1970), 16. - Gegenüberstellung von "novel" und "short story" in Bezug auf "setting" und "subject".

1972

313. GREENE, GRAHAM, "Introduction" zu *Collected Stories*, Collected Edition, Bd. VIII (London, 1972), vii-xii. - Gedanken zu einer Wesensbestimmung der Short Story im Vergleich zum Roman: "...the short story for the novelist is often a form of escape - escape from having to live with another character for years on end...". "Simplicity of language" und "the sense of life as it is lived" werden als Qualitäten der Kurzgeschichte herausgestellt.

1973

314. SILLITOE, ALAN, aus "Author's Note" zu *Men, Women and Children* (London, 1973), 9-11. - Ausgehend vom genetischen Aspekt entwickelt Sillitoe formale und inhaltliche Konstituanten seiner Short Stories: "The problems I associate with short stories are essentially poetic problems.... style and language are all-important, though not so vital that they obscure the tale that is to be told....A story deals fundamentally with one person, one basic incident, one state of mind which fate is about to give a vicious twist to. However, the possibilities of extension within these limits can be wide enough."

315. SILLITOE, ALAN, "Alan Sillitoe: An Interview by M. Lefranc", *Etudes Anglaises*, XXVI (1973), 35-48. - Das Interview, das in der Hauptsache auf thematische Aspekte von Sillitoes Werk eingeht, enthält auch Aussagen über einzelne Short Stories, insbesondere aus der Sammlung *The Loneliness of the Long-distance Runner*. Sillitoe gibt seine persönliche Einschätzung der Short Story im Vergleich zum Gedicht: "Let me say that I am happiest when I write a poem. It is pure. There is nothing extraneous in it...I am happy when I write short stories...perhaps...because short stories too have to be worked over like gold, like poems almost."

Symposien und Textsammlungen zur Theorie der Short Story

Die bisher erschienenen Symposien und Textsammlungen zur Theorie der Short Story in England und Amerika werden hier gesondert erfaßt. Dabei werden die Autoren der hier publizierten theoretischen Beiträge einzeln aufgeführt und es wird (in Klammern hinter jedem Namen) jeweils auf die Nummer des Textes in der vorliegenden "Quellensammlung" bzw. in der Bibliographie der "Weiteren englischen und amerikanischen Beiträge zur Theorie der Short Story" verwiesen. Dieser Teil der Bibliographie ist ebenfalls chronologisch geordnet.

1897

"How to Write a Short Story. A Symposium", *The Bookman* [American Edition], V. 1 (March, 1897), 42-46. - Enthält Beiträge von Robert Barr (140), Harold Frederick (141), und Jane Barlow (142).

1915

"Does character drawing or plot count more in fiction", *The New York Sun*, LXXXII. 229 (April 17, 1915), Spring Literary Section, 1-3. - Eine Autorenkontroverse, in der nur von Melville Davisson Post (51) und Walter Pritchard Eaton (188) speziell auf die Short Story eingegangen wird.

1923

Hoffman, Arthur Sullivant (Hrsg.), *Fiction Writers on Fiction Writing. Advice, Opinions and a Statement of Their Own Working Methods by More Than One Hundred Authors* (Indianapolis, 1923). Diese Sammlung von Äußerungen von 115 heute zumeist unbekannten amerikanischen und englischen Romanciers und Kurzgeschichtenautoren über das Schreiben von Prosadichtung ist die Zusammenfassung von Antworten auf eine Reihe von Fragen, mit denen sich der Herausgeber an die einzelnen Autoren wandte - Fragen wie diese: "I. What is the genesis of a story with you ...? II. Do you map it out in advance, or do you start with, say, a character or situation, and let the story tell itself as you write? ... V. Have you had a class-room or correspondence course on writing fiction? ... VII. What is your general feeling on the value of technique? VIII. What is most interesting and important to you in your writing - plot, structure, style, material, setting, character, color etc.? ..." Ziel dieses Unternehmens eines langjährigen Zeitschriftenherausgebers ist es, Anfängern und Fortgeschrittenen eine Hilfe für das Schreiben von Geschichten an die Hand zu geben, die von den üblichen "general formulas and iron-clad rules" vergleichbarer Leitfäden Abstand nimmt und erfolgreiche Autoren selbst zu Worte kommen läßt, "each telling in detail his own processes of creation". Der theoretische Wert dieser Äußerungen ist gering, obwohl hier Autoren wie Samuel Hopkins Adams, Walter Pritchard Eaton (vgl. Nr. 188), Joseph Hergesheimer, Will Irwin, Sinclair Lewis, Rose Macaulay, Booth Tarkington und Ben Ames Williams (vgl. Nr. 54) erscheinen.

1941

"The Short Story: A Balance Sheet", *Saturday Review of Literature,* XXIV (Nov. 22, 1941), 3-7, 23-26. - Enthält Beiträge von Harry Shaw (238) und Bonaro Overstreet (239).

1946

Haycraft, Howard (Hrsg.), *The Art of the Mystery Story. A Collection of Critical Essays* (New York, 1946). - Im Vorwort auf S. v wird gesagt: "The purpose of this book is to bring together under one cover a representative selection of the best critical and informative writing about the modern mystery-crime-detective story, from Poe to the present time." Es soll hier als Beispiel für eine Textsammlung genannt werden, die eine Reihe allgemeiner Beschreibungen eines besonderen thematischen Bereichs der Kurzgeschichte enthält, aufgrund dieser Begrenzung für die Theoriegeschichte der Short Story aber nur am Rande von Interesse ist.

1961

Current-Garcia, Eugene & Walton R. Patrick (Hrsg.), *What is the Short Story? Case Studies in the Development of a Literary Form* (Glenview, Ill., 1961). - Der erste Teil unter dem Titel "Critical Theory" enthält Äußerungen über die Short Story von Washington Irving (14, 15), Edgar Allan Poe (21, 22, 120), Nathaniel Hawthorne (117, 122), Frederick B. Perkins (27), Henry James (131), Bret Harte (38), Brander Matthews (28, 39), [Anonymus,1901] (40), H. S. Canby (149, 189), J. Berg Esenwein (163), Herbert Ellsworth Cory (197), N. Bryllion Fagin (202), Sherwood Anderson (57), Ring Lardner (207), L. A. G. Strong (224), William Saroyan (227), Bonaro Overstreet (239), Harry Shaw (238), Eudora Welty (74), Herschell Brickell (252), V. S. Pritchett (80), Falcon O. Baker (253), Truman Capote (83), Frank O'Connor (84), W. Somerset Maugham (87).

1963

Summers, Hollis (Hrsg.), *Discussions of the Short Story* (Boston, 1963). - Enthält Äußerungen über die Short Story von Edgar Allan Poe (21), Bret Harte (38), Brander Matthews (28, 39), Randall Jarrell (265), Arnold Bader (242), Kenneth Payson Kempton (244), Frank O'Connor (84) u. a.

1964

Burnett, Whit & Hallie (Hrsg.), *The Modern Short Story in the Making* (New York & London, 1964). - Enthält Äußerungen über die Short Story von den Herausgebern, die sich selbst als Kurzgeschichtenautoren einen Namen gemacht haben (92, 271, 277) sowie von Jesse Stuart (270), Erskine Caldwell (274), Gladys Schmitt (272), Dorothy McCleary (273), Kay Boyle (275), Truman Capote (276), George Hitchcock (278), Kressmann Taylor (279) und Guido D'Agnostino (280).

1966

"The Short Story", in *London Magazine,* N. S. VI (Sept., 1966), 6-12. - Enthält die Beiträge von V. S. Pritchett (94), William Sansom (95) und Francis King (289).

1968-70

"The International Symposium on the Short Story", *Kenyon Review*, [in vier Teilen:]

"Part One", XXX (April, 1968), 443-490 - enthält u. a. Beiträge von Christina Stead (291), Herbert Gold (292), Nadine Gordimer (293), Benedict Kiely (294), Hugh Hood (295), Henrietta Drake-Brockman (296).

"Part Two", XXXI (Jan., 1969), 57-94 - enthält u. a. Beiträge von William Saroyan (96), Maurice Shadbolt (298), John Wain (97), James Oliver Brown (299).

"Part Three", XXXI (April, 1969), 449-503 - enthält u. a. Beiträge von George Garrett (300), Elizabeth Taylor (301), Ezekiel Mphahlele (302), Elizabeth Harrower (303).

"Part Four", XXXII (Jan., 1970), 77-108 - enthält u. a. Beiträge von Jack Cope (304), James T. Farrell (98), Edward Hyams (99), David Ballantyne (305), H. E. Bates (100).

1970

"Some Notes on Writing Stories", in *London Magazine*, N. S. IX (March, 1970), 6-16. - Enthält die Beiträge von James Stern (306), Brian Glanville (307), Elizabeth Taylor (308), William Trevor (309), Michael Feld (310), Jonathan Raban (311), Frank Tuohy (312).

1971

Weber, Alfred, "Eine Kleine Quellensammlung Amerikanischer Theorien der Kurzgeschichte," in *Studien und Materialien zur Short Story*, hrsg. von Paul Goetsch, 2. Auflage (Frankfurt/Main, Berlin, München, 1971, 1973), 115-133. - Enthält Äußerungen über die Short Story von Frank Norris (33), William Dean Howells (41), Henry James (42, 43, 44, 170), Sherwood Anderson (58, 52), Edith Wharton (60), James T. Farrell (66), Katherine Anne Porter (71) und William Carlos Williams (75).

1972

Bungert, Hans (Hrsg.), *Die Amerikanische Short Story. Theorie und Entwicklung* (Darmstadt: Wissenschaftliche Buchgesellschaft, 1972), Wege der Forschung, Bd. CCLVI. - Enthält die Beiträge von Edgar Allan Poe (21), Brander Matthews (28), Bret Harte (38), William Dean Howells (41), Henry Seidel Canby (149), Howard Baker (230), Bonaro Overstreet (239), H. E. Bates (69), Eudora Welty (74), Herschell Brickell (252), Arno L. Bader (242), [Anonymus,1954] (257), Norman Friedman (262), Richard Kostelanetz (286).

Zwei deutsche Sammlungen zur Theoriegeschichte der Novelle sind in diesem Zusammenhang erwähnenswert:

Kunz, Josef (Hrsg.),*Novelle* (Darmstadt: Wissenschaftliche Buchgesellschaft, 1968), Wege der Forschung, Bd. LV.

Polheim, Karl Konrad (Hrsg.),*Theorie und Kritik der deutschen Novelle von Wieland bis Musil* (Tübingen, 1970), Deutsche Texte 13.

Sekundärliteratur zur Theoriegeschichte und Entwicklung der Short Story

Die folgende Bibliographie bietet einmal einen Überblick über die nicht sehr zahlreichen Publikationen zur amerikanischen und englischen Theoriegeschichte der Short Story, zum anderen eine Auswahl von Quellen und Studien zur deutschen Theorie der Kurzgeschichte und der Novelle.

Aufgenommen wurden des weiteren eine Reihe ausgewählter Publikationen über die Entwicklung der Short-Story Praxis in England und in den Vereinigten Staaten, nicht zuletzt deshalb, weil sie gelegentlich auch auf theoretische Äußerungen einzelner Autoren und theoriegeschichtliche Aspekte eingehen. Die gattungshistorischen Publikationen, in denen die Autoren eigene theoretische Aussagen über die Short Story machen, sind in der Quellensammlung (Nr. 1-103) bzw. in der weiterführenden Bibliographie (Nr. 104-315) aufgeführt und werden hier nicht noch einmal genannt.

Alterton, Margaret, *Origins of Poe's Critical Principles*, University of Iowa Humanistic Studies, vol. II, no. 3 (Iowa City, 1925).

Baldeshwiler, Eileen, "Katherine Mansfield's Theory of Fiction", *Studies in Short Fiction*, VII (1970), 421-432.

Bender, Hans, "Ortsbestimmung der Kurzgeschichte", *Akzente*, IX (1962), 205-255.

——, [Beitrag zu] "The International Symposium on the Short Story", *Kenyon Review*, XXXI (Jan., 1969), 85-92.

Boyce, Benjamin, "English Short Fiction in the Eighteenth Century: A Preliminary View", *Studies in Short Fiction*, V (1967/68), 95-112.

Bungert, Hans, "Einleitung" zu: *Die Amerikanische Short Story. Theorie und Entwicklung*, hrsg. v. Hans Bungert, Wege der Forschung, Bd. CCLVI (Darmstadt, 1972), vii-xvii.

Cobb, Palmer, "Edgar Allan Poe and Friedrich Spielhagen. Their Theory of the Short Story", *Modern Language Notes*, XXV (1910), 67-72.

Conron, John Joseph, *Poe and the Theory of the Short Story* (Diss. University of Michigan, 1970).

Doderer, Klaus, "Die angelsächsische *short story* und die deutsche Kurzgeschichte", *Die Neueren Sprachen*, II (1953), 417-424.

——, *Die Kurzgeschichte in Deutschland. Ihre Form und ihre Entwicklung* (Wiesbaden, 1953). - Zweite, durchges. u. berichtigte Aufl. (Darmstadt, 1969).

Dollerup, Cay, "Concepts of 'Tension', 'Intensity', and 'Suspense' in Short Story Theory", *Orbis Litterarum*, XXV (1970), 314-337.

Domaniecki, Hildegard, *Zum Problem literarischer Ökonomie: Henry James' Erzählungen zwischen Markt und Kunst*, Amerikastudien, Bd. 38 (Stuttgart, 1974).

Duncan, Edgar Hill, "Short Fiction in Medieval English: A Survey", *Studies in Short Fiction*, IX (1972), 1-28.

——, "Short Fiction in Medieval English: II. The Middle English Period", *Studies in Short Fiction*, XI (1974), 227-241.

Evans, Oliver and Harry Finestone, *The World of the Short Story: Archetypes in Action* (New York, 1971).

Ejxenbaum, B. M., *O. Henry and the Theory of the Short Story*, transl. by I. R. Titunik (Ann Arbor, Mich., 1968).

Elliott, George P., "A Defense of Fiction", *Hudson Review*, XVI (1963), 9-48.

Foerster, Norman, "Quantity and Quality in Poe's Aesthetic", *Studies in Philology*, XX (1923), 310-335. - Siehe auch sein späteres Buch *American Criticism: Studies in Literary Theory from Poe to the Present* (Boston & New York, 1928).

Freese, Peter, Dietrich Jäger, Horst Kruse, *Die amerikanische Short Story: Ein Überblick* (Neumünster, 1971).

Gillespie, Gerald, "Novella, Nouvelle, Novelle, Short Novel? - A Review of Terms", *Neophilologus*, LI (1967), 117-127; 225-230.

Goetsch, Paul, "Probleme und Methoden der Short Story Interpretation"; "Arten der Situationsverknüpfung: Eine Studie zum *explosive principle* in der modernen Short Story"; "Aussagen über die Kürze" und "Arbeiten zur Short Story und Kurzgeschichte (1950-1968): Eine ausgewählte Bibliographie" in: *Studien und Materialien zur Short Story*, hrsg. v. Paul Goetsch, Schule und Forschung, 15 (Frankfurt/Main, 1971), 27-39; 40-63; 104-114 und 146-171.

——, "Die Begrenzung der Short Story" in: *Die Amerikanische Short Story. Theorie und Entwicklung*, hrsg. v. Hans Bungert, Wege der Forschung, Bd. CCLVI (Darmstadt, 1972), 368-387.

Göller, Karl Heinz und Gerhard Hoffmann (Hrsg.), *Die amerikanische Kurzgeschichte* (Düsseldorf, 1972).

——, und Gerhard Hoffmann (Hrsg.), *Die englische Kurzgeschichte* (Düsseldorf, 1973).

Gullason, Thomas, "The Short Story: An Underrated Art", *Studies in Short Fiction*, II (1964/65), 13-31.

——, "Revelation and Evolution: A Neglected Dimension of the Short Story", *Studies in Short Fiction*, X (1973), 347-356.

Haas, Rudolf, "Poe und die Entwicklung der amerikanischen Short Story" in: Rudolf Haas, *Amerikanische Literaturgeschichte*, Bd. 2 (Heidelberg, 1974), 7-44.

Harris, Wendell V., "English Short Fiction in the Nineteenth Century", *Studies in Short Fiction*, VI (1968/69), 1-93.

Hecht, Ilse (Hrsg.), *Englische Kurzgeschichten von Scott bis Stevenson* (Leipzig, 1947).

Heinrich, Erika, *Die englische Kurzgeschichte im 19. und 20. Jahrhundert* (Diss. Innsbruck, 1952).

Höllerer, Walter, "Die kurze Form der Prosa", *Akzente*, IX (1962), 226-245.

Kelly, George, "Poe's Theory of Unity", *Philological Quarterly*, XXXVII (1958), 34-44.

Kilchenmann, Ruth J., "Die amerikanische und die deutsche Kurzgeschichte: Beziehungen und Einflüsse", *Proceedings of the 4th Congress of the International Comparative Literature Association*, vol. II (The Hague, Paris, 1966), 1105-1112.

——, *Die Kurzgeschichte: Formen und Entwicklung* (Stuttgart, 1967).

Klein, Johannes, *Geschichte der deutschen Novelle von Goethe bis zur Gegenwart* (Wiesbaden, 1954).

——, "Kurzgeschichte" in: *Reallexikon der Deutschen Literaturgeschichte*, hrsg. v. Werner Kohlschmidt u. Wolfgang Mohr, 2. Aufl., Bd. I (Berlin, 1958), 912-915.

Krauss, Werner, "Novela - Novella - Roman", *Zeitschrift für Romanische Philologie*, LX (1940), 16-28.

Kunz, Josef (Hrsg.), *Novelle*, Wege der Forschung, Bd. LV (Darmstadt, 1968).

Lang, Wolfgang, *Themen und Motive und ihre formale Durchführung in der literarischen Kurzprosa früher amerikanischer Zeitschriften: Ein Beitrag zur Theorie der amerikanischen Short Story zur Zeit Hawthornes und Poes* (Diss. Tübingen, 1968).

Link, Franz H., "'Tale', 'Sketch', 'Essay' und 'Short Story'", *Die Neueren Sprachen*, VI (1957), 345-352.

Malmede, Hans Hermann, *Wege zur Novelle. Theorie und Interpretation der Gattung Novelle in der deutschen Literaturwissenschaft* (Stuttgart, 1966).

Marler, Robert F., "From Tale to Short Story: The Emergence of a New Genre in the 1850's", *American Literature*, XLVI (1974), 153-169.

Marks, Emerson R., "Poe as a Literary Theorist: A Reappraisal", *American Literature*, XXXIII (1961), 296-306.

Mertner, Edgar, "Zur Theorie der Short Story in England und Amerika", *Anglia*, LXV (1941), 188-205.

Mish, Charles C., "English Short Fiction in the Seventeenth Century", *Studies in Short Fiction*, VI (1968/69), 233-330.

Mitchell, McBurney, "Poe and Spielhagen: *Novelle* and *Short Story*", *Modern Language Notes*, XXIX (1914), 36-41.

Newman, Frances, *The Short Story's Mutations: From Petronius to Paul Morand* (New York, 1924).

O'Brien, E. J., *The Advance of the American Short Story*, rev. ed. (New York, 1931).

Pattee, Fred Lewis, *The Development of the American Short Story. An Historical Survey* (New York, 1924; repr. 1966).

Paulson, Ronald (Hrsg.), *The Novelette Before 1900* (Englewood Cliffs, N.J., 1965).

Peden, William, *The American Short Story: Front Line in the National Defense of Literature* (Boston, 1964).

Polheim, Karl Konrad, *Novellentheorie und Novellenforschung. Ein Forschungsbericht 1945-64* (Stuttgart, 1964).

Rohner, Ludwig, *Theorie der Kurzgeschichte* (Frankfurt, 1973).

Rohrberger, Mary, *Hawthorne und the Modern Short Story: A Study in Genre* (The Hague, Paris, 1966).

Ross, Danforth R., *The American Short Story*, University of Minneapolis Pamphlets on American Literature, 14 (Minneapolis, 1961).

Schlauch, Margaret, "English Short Fiction in the Fifteenth and Sixteenth Centuries", *Studies in Short Fiction*, III (1965/66), 393-434.

Schumann, Kuno, *Die erzählende Prosa Edgar Allan Poes: Ein Beitrag zu einer Gattungsgeschichte der "Short Story"*, Frankfurter Arbeiten auf dem Gebiete der Anglistik und der Amerikastudien, 5 (Heidelberg, 1958).

Sengle, Friedrich, "Der Umfang als ein Problem der Dichtungswissenschaft" in: *Gestaltprobleme der Dichtung*, hrsg. v. Richard Alewyn, H. E. Hass, C. Heselhaus (Bonn, 1957), 299-306.

Smith, H. E., "Poe's Extension of His Theory of the Tale", *Modern Philology*, XVI (1918), 195-203.

Träbing, Gerhard, "Ansätze zu einer Theorie der deutschen 'Geschichte'", *DVjS*, 41 (1967), 468-498.

Voss, Arthur, *The American Short Story: A Critical Survey* (Norman, Okl., 1973).

Waidson, H. M., "The German Short Story as a Literary Form", *Modern Languages*, XL (1959), 121-127.

Weber, Alfred, "Amerikanische Theorien der Kurzgeschichte: Vorbemerkungen zu einer historischen Poetik der Short Story" in: *Studien und Materialien zur Short Story*, hrsg. von Paul Goetsch (Frankfurt/Main, 1971), 5-26.

West, Ray B., *The Short Story in America, 1900-1950* (Chicago, 1952; repr. Freeport, N.Y., 1968).

Wiese, Benno von, *Novelle*, 2. Aufl. (Stuttgart, 1964).

Wilt, Napier, "Poe's Attitude toward His Tales", *Modern Philology*, XXV (1927), 101-105.

Wolpers, Theodor, "Kürze im Erzählen. Überlegungen zu einer Poetik und Geschichte kurzen Erzählens und zur angloamerikanischen 'short story' im 19. und 20. Jahrhundert", *Anglia*, 89 (1971), 48-86. - Abdruck einer erweiterten Fassung in: Hans Bungert (Hrsg.), *Die amerikanische Short Story. Theorie und Entwicklung* (Darmstadt, 1972), 388-426.

Wright, Austin McGiffert, *The American Short Story in the Twenties* (Chicago, 1961).

INDEX

Namens- und Titelverzeichnis für die Quellensammlung

In diesem Verzeichnis sind alle Namen und Titel aufgeführt, die in den Texten der Quellensammlung genannt werden. Die Hinweise erfolgen hier durch Angabe der Textnummer (nicht durch Seitenangabe). Die Titel aller literarischen Werke und Publikationen sind kursiv gedruckt.

Das Verzeichnis erschließt einen Teil der Literatur, auf die sich die theoretischen Äußerungen beziehen bzw. die zur Illustration der theoretischen Aussagen herangezogen wird. Dies könnte zu weiterführenden Untersuchungen anregen, in denen auch die durch Kürzungen entfallenen Teile der Texte dieser Sammlung sowie die in der weiterführenden Bibliographie englischer und amerikanischer Theoriebeiträge (Nr. 104 bis 315) aufgeführten Titel mit einbezogen werden.

SCHLAGWORTVERZEICHNIS FÜR DIE QUELLENSAMMLUNG

In diesem Schlagwortverzeichnis sind die in der Theoriegeschichte der Short Story wichtigen Begriffe und Aspekte aufgeführt, die in den Texten der Quellensammlung (Nr. 1 bis 103) erscheinen. Bei der Ausarbeitung dieses Verzeichnisses war das Orientierungsmodell von Einfluß, das M. H. Abrams 1953 in *The Mirror and the Lamp* für seine Darstellung der englischen Geschichte der Literaturtheorie und -kritik entwickelt hat. Er legt dar, daß jede literarische Theorie, die in ihren Aussagen Vollständigkeit erstrebt, immer auf vier wesentliche Aspekte eingeht: 1. auf das WERK (hier auf die Kurzgeschichte bzw. die kurze schriftliche oder mündliche Erzählung) - 2. auf den AUTOR, von dem dieses Werk stammt - 3. auf den Stoff, den Gegenstand oder INHALT, den das Werk vermittelt und gestaltet - und 4. auf das PUBLIKUM der Hörer und Leser, an die sich das Werk wendet und von dem es aufgenommen wird.

Bei dem Versuch, die hier gesammelten theoriebezogenen Aussagen zu erschließen, wurde - auf induktivem Wege, aber doch aufbauend auf dem System von Abrams - die folgende Systematik ausgearbeitet:

A. AUTORENBEZOGENE ASPEKTE

1. *Autor und Erzähler*
2. *Fähigkeiten und Qualifikationen des Autors*
3. *Schöpferischer Prozeß des Schreibens und mündlichen Erzählens*
4. *Motivation und Intention des Autors*
5. *Erzähltechnik*
6. *Konzentration, Komprimierung und Kondensierung*
7. *Kürze und räumlich-zeitliche Begrenzung*

B. WERKBEZOGENE ASPEKTE

1. *Kunstcharakter*
2. *Ganzheit, Geschlossenheit und Einheit*
3. *Konzentration, Komprimierung und Kondensierung*
4. *Kürze und räumlich-zeitliche Begrenzung*
5. *Begrenzung auf ein einziges und besonderes Phänomen*
6. *Strukturelle Elemente*
7. *Geschehensdarstellung*
8. *Menschen- und Charakterdarstellung*
9. *Sprachliche Mittel*
10. *Qualitäten der Short Story*
11. *Zeitliche Aspekte*

C. INHALTLICHE ASPEKTE

1. *Thematik, Gegenstand und Material*
2. *Geschehensdarstellung*
3. *Menschen- und Charakterdarstellung*
4. *Ort und Umwelt*
5. *Wirklichkeitsbezug*
6. *Gedanken und Ideen*
7. *Bedeutung*

D. PUBLIKUMSBEZOGENE ASPEKTE

1. *Publikum*
2. *Rezeption (Lesen und Hören)*
3. *Wirkung und Funktion*
4. *Markt*

E. WEITERE ASPEKTE

1. *Gattungs- und Formvorstellungen von der Short Story*
2. *Vergleiche mit anderen literarischen Gattungen und Formen*
3. *Wertungsaussagen zur Short Story*
4. *Zeitbezüge und Entwicklung der Short Story*
5. *Medienbezug der Short Story*
6. *Erzählende Prosa, Formen und Bezeichnungen*
7. *Lyrik, Formen und Bezeichnungen*
8. *Drama, Formen und Bezeichnungen*
9. *Hinweise auf andere Short-Story-Theorien und Probleme der Theoriebildung*
10. *Vergleiche mit den nicht-literarischen Künsten*

Alle diese Aspekte finden sich - mit Verweisen zu den ihnen untergeordneten Begriffen - im folgenden alphabetischen Verzeichnis aufgeführt. Dabei ist zu beachten, daß viele Begriffe mehrdeutig sind, je nach dem Kontext, in dem sie bei verschiedenen Autoren erscheinen. Sie haben demnach ihren Platz an verschiedenen Stellen der Systematik.

Die englischen Begriffe werden so, wie sie sich in den Texten finden, in kleinen Buchstaben gedruckt (von Substantiven nur die Form des Singular, bei Adjektiven und Adverbien nur die adjektivische Form). Für die Ideen und Aspekte jedoch, die sich mit keinem im Text befindlichen englischen Begriff verbinden lassen oder die nicht auf einen im Text vorhandenen spezifischen englischen Begriff zu bringen sind, wurde ein Sammelbegriff oder eine Aspektbezeichnung auf Deutsch formuliert. Diese deutschen Begriffe und Bezeichnungen werden ebenfalls in das alphabetische Verzeichnis aufgenommen und erscheinen kursiv. Verweise in die Texte erfolgen durch Angabe der Textnummer (nicht durch Seitenangabe).

Gesamtverzeichnis
der Autoren
theoretischer Äusserungen zur Short Story

Hier sind die Autoren aller Beiträge aufgeführt, die in der "Quellensammlung" zitiert und in der Bibliographie der "Weiteren englischen und amerikanischen Beiträge zur Theorie der Short Story" genannt wurden. Bei amerikanischen Beiträgen und Publikationen werden die Autorennamen kursiv gesetzt. Hinter dem Namen des Autors wird von jedem erfaßten Beitrag das Erscheinungs- bzw. Entstehungsjahr (in Klammern) und danach die Textnummer angegeben: In die "Quellensammlung" aufgenommene Beiträge haben die Nummern 1 bis 103 - in der Bibliographie genannte und zum Teil kommentierte Beiträge haben die Nummern 104-315.